LITERARY CRITICISM IN THE RENAISSANCE

A HISTORY

OF

LITERARY CRITICISM
IN THE RENAISSANCE

BY

J. E. SPINGARN

SECOND EDITION

GREENWOOD PRESS, PUBLISHERS
WESTPORT, CONNECTICUT

Library of Congress Cataloging in Publication Data

Spingarn, Joel Elias, 1875-1939.
　A history of literary criticism in the
Renaissance.

　　Reprint of the 1924 ed. published by Columbia
University Press, New York, in series: Columbia
University studies in comparative literature.
　　Bibliography: p.
　　Includes index.
　　1.　Criticism--History.　I.　Title.　II.　Series:
Columbia University studies in English and
comparative literature.
PN88.S6　1976　　　801'.95'09024　　　76-27737
ISBN 0-8371-9025-8

COPYRIGHT 1899 BY THE MACMILLAN COMPANY

COPYRIGHT 1924 BY COLUMBIA UNIVERSITY PRESS

FIRST EDITION 1899
SECOND EDITION 1908

This edition originally published in 1924 by Columbia University Pres

Reprinted in 1976 by Greenwood Press,
a division of Williamhouse-Regency Inc.

Library of Congress Catalog Card Number　76-27737

ISBN 0-8371-9025-8

Printed in the United States of America

PREFACE

It is twenty-five years since this book was originally published, and sixteen years since the appearance of the second edition, which merely reproduced the first except for a few trifling corrections and the addition of a new "Conclusion." At that time the Italian critics of the sixteenth century, with whom this book is chiefly concerned, were quite unknown to English scholars, and little attention had been paid to them by the scholars of the continent, even in Italy. I still remember the youthful pride with which I received a letter from the poet Carducci thanking me "in the name of Italian literature" for having brought to the attention of Italian scholars an important body of their own literature which they themselves had neglected. It is now generally recognized, I think, that these sixteenth century theorists and commentators were the founders of modern criticism, indeed the first of all critics, ancient or modern, to develop a complete literary theory, and that the critical system of "neo-classicism" is due to them rather than to their French followers in the seventeenth century. Since 1899, much of interest and importance has been written concerning them, not only in general works like Saintsbury's *History of*

iii

Criticism and Trabalza's history of Italian criticism, but in an ever growing body of monographs, of which it suffices to mention Toffanin's *La Fine dell' Umanesimo* and Charlton's *Castelvetro's Theory of Poetry*. None of these later investigations has materially affected the main conclusions at which I arrived when I first wrote this book, and so this new impression reproduces the second edition without change except for the addition of two footnotes.

It is only fair to state, however, that the Italian translation of this book,[1] which appeared in 1905, contains much important material which for one reason or another I have not included in any of the editions in English. In fact, I virtually rewrote the book from beginning to end for the benefit of my translator, and his version is so much fuller and maturer than the original that the latter is completely superseded by it; and every serious student of the subject is advised to consult the Italian edition.

J. E. S.

TROUTBECK,
November, 1924.

[1] *La Critica letteraria nel Rinascimento*, Italian translation by Antonio Fusco, with corrections and additions by the author and a preface by Benedetto Croce (Bari, 1905). Fusco, the translator, was killed shortly afterwards in the Messina earthquake, and a charming sketch of his life by Croce will be found in *La Critica*, 1909.

PREFACE TO THE FIRST EDITION

THIS essay undertakes to treat the history of
literary criticism in the Renaissance. The three
sections into which the essay is divided are devoted, respectively, to Italian criticism from Dante
to Tasso, to French criticism from Du Bellay to
Boileau, and to English criticism from Ascham to
Milton; but the critical activity of the sixteenth
century has been the main theme, and the earlier
or later literature has received treatment only in
so far as it serves to explain the causes or consequences of the critical development of this central
period. It was at this epoch that modern criticism
began, and that the ancient ideals of art seemed
once more to sway the minds of men; so that
the history of sixteenth-century criticism must of
necessity include a study of the beginnings of
critical activity in modern Europe and of the gradual introduction of the Aristotelian canons into
modern literature.

This study has been made subservient, more particularly, to two specific purposes. While the
critical activity of the period is important and
even interesting in itself, it has been here studied
primarily for the purpose of tracing the origin and

causes of the classic spirit in modern letters and of discovering the sources of the rules and theories embodied in the neo-classic literature of the seventeenth and eighteenth centuries. How did the classic spirit arise? Whence did it come, and how did it develop? What was the origin of the principles and precepts of neo-classicism? These are some of the questions I have attempted to answer in this essay; and, in answering them, I have tried to remember that this is a history, not of critical literature, but of literary criticism. For this reason I have given to individual books and authors less prominence than some of them perhaps deserved, and have confined myself almost exclusively to the origin of principles, theories, and rules, and to the general temper of classicism. For a similar reason I have been obliged to say little or nothing of the methods and results of applied, or concrete, criticism.

This, then, has been the main design of the essay; but furthermore, as is indicated in the title, I have attempted to point out the part played by Italy in the growth of this neo-classic spirit and in the formulation of these neo-classic principles. The influence of the Italian Renaissance in the development of modern science, philosophy, art, and creative literature has been for a long time the subject of much study. It has been my more modest task to trace the indebtedness of the modern world to Italy in the domain of literary criticism; and I trust that I have shown the Renaissance influence to be as great in this as in the other realms of study. The

birth of modern criticism was due to the critical
activity of Italian humanism; and it is in sixteenth-
century Italy that we shall find, more or less
matured, the general spirit and even the specific
principles of French classicism. The second half
of the design, then, is the history of the Italian
influence in literary criticism; and with Milton, the
last of the humanists in England, the essay naturally closes. But we shall find, I think, that the
influence of the Italian Renaissance in the domain
of literary criticism was not even then all de-
cayed, and that Lessing and Shelley, to mention no
others, were the legitimate inheritors of the Italian
tradition.

The bibliography at the end of the essay indicates sufficiently my obligations to preceding
writers. It has been prepared chiefly for the
purpose of facilitating reference to works cited in
the text and in the foot-notes, and should be consulted for the full titles of books therein mentioned; it makes no pretence of being a complete
bibliography of the subject. It will be seen that
the history of Italian criticism in the sixteenth
century has received scarcely any attention from
modern scholars. The most complete lists of the
critical works of the Renaissance are to be found
in Crescimbeni's *Istoria della Volgar Poesia* (Rome,
1698) and in Blankenburg's *Litterarische Zusätze
zu Sulzer's Allgemeiner Theorie der schönen Künste*
(Leipzig, 1796–98). In regard to Aristotle's *Poetics*,
I have used the text, and in general followed the
interpretation, given in Professor S. H. Butcher's

Aristotle's Theory of Poetry and Fine Art, a noble monument of scholarship vivified by literary feeling. I desire also to express my obligations to Professor Butcher for an abstract of Zabarella, to Mr. P. O. Skinner of Harvard for an analysis of Capriano, to my friend, Mr. F. W. Chandler, for summaries of several early English rhetorical treatises, and to Professor Cavalier Speranza for a few corrections; also to my friends, Mr. J. G. Underhill, Mr. Lewis Einstein, and Mr. H. A. Uterhart, and to my brother, Mr. A. B. Spingarn, for incidental assistance of some importance.

But, above all, I desire to acknowledge my indebtedness to Professor George E. Woodberry. This book is the fruit of his instruction; and in writing it, also, I have had recourse to him for assistance and criticism. Without the aid so kindly accorded by him, the book could hardly have been written, and certainly would never have assumed its present form. But my obligations to him are not limited to the subject or contents of the present essay. Through a period of five years the inspiration derived from his instruction and encouragement has been so great as to preclude the possibility of its expression in a preface. *Quare habe tibi quidquid hoc libelli.*

NEW YORK,
  March, 1899.

CONTENTS

PART FIRST

LITERARY CRITICISM IN ITALY

ix

PART SECOND

LITERARY CRITICISM IN FRANCE

PART THIRD

LITERARY CRITICISM IN ENGLAND

PART FIRST

LITERARY CRITICISM IN ITALY

LITERARY CRITICISM IN ITALY

CHAPTER I

THE FUNDAMENTAL PROBLEM OF RENAISSANCE CRITICISM

THE first problem of Renaissance criticism was the justification of imaginative literature. The existence and continuity of the æsthetic consciousness, and perhaps, in a less degree, of the critical faculty, throughout the Middle Ages, can hardly be denied; yet distrust of literature was keenest among the very class of men in whom the critical faculty might be presupposed, and it was as the handmaid of philosophy, and most of all as the vassal of theology, that poetry was chiefly valued. In other words, the criteria by which imaginative literature was judged during the Middle Ages were not literary criteria. Poetry was disregarded or contemned, or was valued if at all for virtues that least belong to it. The Renaissance was thus confronted with the necessity of justifying its appreciation of the vast body of literature which the Revival of Learning had recovered for the modern world; and the function of Renaissance criticism was to reëstablish the æsthetic foundations of literature, to reaffirm the eternal lesson of Hellenic culture, and to restore once and for all the element of beauty to its rightful place in human life and in the world of art.

I. *Mediæval Conceptions of Poetry*

The mediæval distrust of literature was the result of several coöperating causes. Popular literature had fallen into decay, and in its contemporary form was beneath serious consideration. Classical literature was unfortunately pagan, and was moreover but imperfectly known. The mediæval Church from its earliest stages had regarded pagan culture with suspicion, and had come to look upon the development of popular literature as antagonistic to its own supremacy. But beyond this, the distrust of literature went deeper, and was grounded upon certain theoretical and fundamental objections to all the works of the imagination.

These theoretical objections were in nowise new to the Middle Ages. They had been stated in antiquity with much more directness and philosophical efficacy than was possible in the mediæval period. Plato had tried imaginative literature by the criteria of reality and morality, both of which are unæsthetic criteria, although fundamentally applicable to poetry. In respect to reality, he had shown that poetry is three removes from the truth, being but the imitation, by the artist, of the imitation, in life, of an idea in the mind of God. In respect to morality, he had discovered in Homer, the greatest

of poets, deviations from truth, blasphemy against
the gods, and obscenity of various sorts. Furthermore, he had found that creative literature excites
the emotions more than does actual life, and stirs
up ignoble passions which were better restrained.

These ideas ran throughout the Middle Ages,
and indeed persisted even beyond the Renaissance.
Poetry was judged by these same criteria, but it
was natural that mediæval writers should substitute
more practical reasons for the metaphysical arguments of Plato. According to the criterion of
reality, it was urged that poetry in its very essence
is untrue, that at bottom it is fiction, and therefore
false. Thus Tertullian said that "the Author of
truth hates all the false; He regards as adultery all
that is unreal. . . . He never will approve pre-
tended loves, and wraths, and groans, and tears;"[1]
and he affirmed that in place of these pagan works
there was in the Bible and the Fathers, a vast
body of Christian literature and that this is "not
fabulous, but true, not tricks of art, but plain realities."[2] According to the criterion of morality, it
was urged that as few works of the imagination
were entirely free from obscenity and blasphemy,
such blemishes are inseparable from the poetic
art; and accordingly, Isidore of Seville says that
a Christian is forbidden to read the figments of the
poets, "quia per oblectamenta inanium fabularum
mentem excitant ad incentiva libidinum."[3]

The third, or psychological objection, made by
Plato, was similarly emphasized. Thus Tertullian

---

[1] *De Spectac.* xxiii.   [2] *Ibid.* xxii.   [3] *Differentiæ,* iii. 13, 1.

pointed out that while God has enjoined us to deal
calmly and gently and quietly with the Holy Spirit,
literature, and especially dramatic literature, leads
to spiritual agitation.[1] This point seemed to the
mediæval mind fundamental, for in real beauty,
as Thomas Aquinas insisted, desire is quieted.[2]
Furthermore, it was shown that the only body of
literary work worthy of serious study dealt with
pagan divinities and with religious practices which
were in direct antagonism to Christianity. Other
objections, also, were incidentally alluded to by
mediæval writers. For example, it was said, the
supreme question in all matters of life is the question of conduct, and it was not apparent in what
manner poetry conduces to action. Poetry has no
practical use; it rather enervates men than urges
them to the call of duty; and above all, there are
more profitable occupations in which the righteous
man may be engaged.

These objections to literature are not character-
istically mediæval. They have sprung up in every
period of the world's history, and especially recur
in all ages in which ascetic or theological conceptions
of life are dominant. They were stock questions
of the Greek schools, and there are extant treatises
by Maximus of Tyre and others on the problem
whether or not Plato was justified in expelling
Homer from his ideal commonwealth. The same
objections prevailed beyond the Renaissance; and
they were urged in Italy by Savonarola, in Ger-

[1] *De Spectac.* xv.   *Cf.* Cyprian, *Epist. ad Donat.* viii.
[2] *Cf.* Bosanquet. *Hist. of Æsthetic,* p. 148.

many by Cornelius Agrippa, in England by Gosson
and Prynne, and in France by Bossuet and other
ecclesiastics.

II. *The Moral Justification of Poetry*

The allegorical method of interpreting literature
was the result of the mediæval attempt to answer
the objections just stated. This method owed its
origin to the mode of interpreting the popular
mythology first employed by the Sophists and
more thoroughly by the later Stoics. Such heroes
as Hercules and Theseus, instead of being mere
brute conquerors of monsters and giants, were regarded by the Stoic philosophers as symbols of the
early sages who had combated the vices and passions of mankind, and they became in the course of
time types of pagan saints. The same mode of interpretation was later applied to the stories of the
Old Testament by Philo Judæus, and was first
introduced into Occidental Europe by Hilary of
Poitiers and Ambrose, Bishop of Milan.[1] Abra-
ham, Adam, Eve, Jacob, became types of various
virtues, and the biblical stories were considered as
symbolical of the various moral struggles in the
soul of man. The first instance of the systematic
application of the method to the pagan myths
occurs in the *Mythologicon* of Fulgentius, who probably flourished in the first half of the sixth century;
and in his *Virgiliana Continentia*, the *Æneid* is

---

[1] *Cf.* St. Augustine, *Confess.* v. 14, vi. 4; Clemens Alex.
Stromata, v. 8.

treated as an image of life, and the travels of
Æneas as the symbol of the progress of the
human soul, from nature, through wisdom, to final
happiness.

From this period, the allegorical method became the recognized mode of interpreting literature, whether sacred or profane. Petrarch, in his
letter, *De quibusdam fictionibus Virgilij*,[1] treats the
Æneid after the manner of Fulgentius; and even
at the very end of the Renaissance Tasso inter-
preted his own romantic epics in the same way.
After the acceptance of the method, its application was further complicated. Gregory the Great
ascribes three meanings to the Bible, — the literal,
the typical or allegorical, and the moral.   Still
later, a fourth meaning was added; and Dante
distinctly claims all four, the literal, the allegorical, the moral or philosophical, and the anagogical
or mystical, for his *Divine Comedy*.[2]

This method, while perhaps justifying poetry
from the standpoint of ethics and divinity, gives it
no place as an independent art; thus considered,
poetry becomes merely a popularized form of theology. Both Petrarch and Boccaccio regarded allegory as the warp and woof of poetry; but they
modified the mediæval point of view by arguing
conversely that theology itself is a form of poetry,
— the poetry of God. Both of them insist that the
Bible is essentially poetical, and that Christ himself spoke largely in poetical images. This point

[1] *Opera*, p. 867.
[2] *Cf*. Dante, *Epist.* xi. 7; *Convito*, ii. **1, 1.**

was so emphasized by Renaissance critics that
Berni, in his *Dialogo contra i Poeti* (1537), condemns the poets for speaking of God as Jupiter
and of the saints as Mercury, Hercules, Bacchus,
and for even having the audacity to call the
prophets and the writers of the Scriptures poets
and makers of verses.[1]

The fourteenth and fifteenth books of Boccaccio's
treatise, *De Genealogia Deorum*, have been called
"the first defence of poesy in honor of his own art
by a poet of the modern world;" but Boccaccio's
justification of imaginative literature is still primarily based on the usual mediæval grounds. The
reality of poetry is dependent on its allegorical
foundations; its moral teachings are to be sought
in the hidden meanings discoverable beneath the
literal expression; pagan poetry is defended for
Christianity on the ground that the references to
Greek and Roman gods and rituals are to be regarded only as symbolical truths. The poet's function, for Boccaccio, as for Dante and Petrarch, was
to hide and obscure the actual truth behind a veil
of beautiful fictions — *veritatem rerum pulchris vela-
minibus adornare.*[2]

The humanistic point of view, in regard to poetry, was of a more practical and far-reaching nature
than that of the Middle Ages. The allegorical
interpretation did indeed continue throughout the
Renaissance, and Mantuan, for example, can only

[1] Berni, p. 226 *sq*.
[2] Petrarch, *Opera*, p. 1205; *cf*. Boccaccio, *Gen. degli Dei,*
p. 250, v.

define a poem as a literary form which is bound by
the stricter laws of metre, and which has its fundamental truths hidden under the literal expressions
of the fable. For still later writers, this mode of
regarding literature seemed to present the only
loophole of escape from the moral objections to
poetry. But in employing the old method, the
humanists carried it far beyond its original application. Thus, Lionardo Bruni, in his *De Studiis et
Literis* (c. 1405), after dwelling on the allegorical
interpretation of the pagan myths, argues that
when one reads the story of Æneas and Dido, he
pays his tribute of admiration to the genius of the
poet, but the matter itself is known to be fiction,
and so leaves no moral impression.[1] By this Bruni
means that fiction as such, when known to be fiction, can leave no moral impression, and secondly,
that poetry is to be judged by the success of the
artist, and not by the efficacy of the moralist.
Similarly, Battista Guarino, in his *De Ordine Do-
cendi et Studendi* (1459), says that we are not disturbed by the impieties, cruelties, horrors, which we
find in poetry; we judge these things simply by
their congruity with the characters and incidents
described. In other words, " we criticise the artist,
not the moralist." [2] This is a distinct attempt at
the æsthetic appreciation of literature, but while
such ideas are not uncommon about this time, they
express isolated sentiments, rather than a doctrine
strictly coördinated with an æsthetic theory of
poetry.

[1] Woodward, *Vittorino da Feltre*, p. 132.   [2] *Ibid.* p. 175.

The more strict defence of poetry was attempted
for the most part on the grounds set forth by
Horace in his *Ars Poetica*. At no period from the
Augustan Age to the Renaissance does the *Ars
Poetica* seem to have been entirely lost. It is
mentioned or quoted, for example, by Isidore of
Seville[1] in the sixth century, by John of Salis-
bury[2] in the twelfth century, and by Dante[3] in the
fourteenth. Horace insists on the mingled instruc-
tiveness and pleasurableness of poetry; and beyond
this, he points out the value of poetry as a civilizing factor in history, regarding the early poets as
sages and prophets, and the inventors of arts and
sciences: —

> "Orpheus, inspired by more than human power,
> Did not, as poets feigned, tame savage beasts,
> But men as lawless and as wild as they,
> And first dissuaded them from rage and blood.
> Thus when Amphion built the Theban wall,
> They feigned the stones obeyed his magic lute;
> Poets, the first instructors of mankind,
> Brought all things to their proper native use;
> Some they appropriated to the gods,
> And some to public, some to private ends:
> Promiscuous love by marriage was restrained,
> Cities were built, and useful laws were made;
> So ancient is the pedigree of verse,
> And so divine the poet's function."[4]

This conception of the early poet's function was
an old one. It is to be found in Aristophanes;[5] it

---

[1] *Etymologiæ*, viii. 7, 5.   [2] *Policraticus*, i. 8.
[3] Moore, *Dante and his Early Biographers*, London, 1890,
pp. 173, 174.
[4] *Ars Poet.* 391 (Roscommon).   [5] *Frogs*, 1030 *sq.*

runs through Renaissance criticism; and even in this very century, Shelley [1] speaks of poets as "the authors of language, and of music, of the dance, and architecture, and statuary, and painting," as "the institutors of laws, and the founders of civil society, and the inventors of the arts of life." To-day the idealist takes refuge in the same faith: "The tree of knowledge is of equal date with the tree of life; nor were even the tamer of horses, the worker in metals, or the sower, elder than those twin guardians of the soul, — the poet and the priest. Conscience and imagination were the pioneers who made earth habitable for the human spirit." [2]

It was this ethical and civilizing function of poetry which was first in the minds of the humanists. Action being the test of all studies,[3] poetry must stand or fall in proportion as it conduces to righteous action. Thus, Lionardo Bruni [4] speaks of poetry as "so valuable an aid to knowledge, and so ennobling a source of pleasure"; and Æneas Sylvius Piccolomini, in his treatise *De Liberorum Educatione* (1450), declares that the crucial question is not, Is poetry to be contemned? but, How are the poets to be used? and he solves his own question by asserting that we are to welcome all that poets can render in praise of integrity and in condemnation of vice, and that all else is to be left unheeded.[5] Beyond this, the humanists urged in

[1] *Defence of Poetry*, ed. Cook, p. 5.

[2] Woodberry, " A New Defence of Poetry," in *Heart of Man*, New York, 1899, p. 76.

[3] Woodward, p. 182 *sq.*   [4] *Ibid.* p. 131.   [5] *Ibid.* p. 150.

favor of poetry the fact of its antiquity and divine origin, and the further fact that it had been praised by great men of all professions, and its creators patronized by kings and emperors from time immemorial.

There were then at the end of the Middle Ages, and the beginning of the Renaissance, two opposing tendencies in regard to the poetic art, one representing the humanistic reverence for ancient culture, and for poetry as one of the phases of that culture, and the other representing not only the mediæval tradition, but a purism allied to that of early Christianity, and akin to the ascetic conceptions of life found in almost every period. These two tendencies are expressed specifically in their noblest forms by the great humanist Poliziano, and the great moral reformer Savonarola. In the *Sylvæ*, written toward the close of the fifteenth century, Poliziano dwells on the divine origin of poetry, as Boccaccio had done in his *Vita di Dante ;* and then, after the manner of Horace, he describes its ennobling influence on man, and its general influence on the progress of civilization.[1] He then proceeds to survey the progress of poetry from the most ancient times, and in so doing may be said to have written the first modern history of literature. The second section of the *Sylvæ* discusses the bucolic poets; the third contains that glorification of Virgil which began during the Middle Ages, and, continued by Vida and others, became in

---

[1] Pope, *Selecta Poemata*, ii. 108; *cf. Ars Poet.* 398.

Scaliger literary deification; and the last section
is devoted to Homer, who is considered as the great
teacher of wisdom, and the wisest of the ancients.
Nowhere does Poliziano exhibit any appreciation
of the æsthetic value of poetry, but his enthusiasm
for the great poets, and indeed for all forms of
ancient culture, is unmistakable, and combined
with his immense erudition marks him as a representative poet of humanism.[1]

On the other hand, the puristic conception of art
is elaborated at great length by Savonarola in an
apology for poetry contained in his tractate, *De
Divisione ac Utilitate Omnium Scientarum*,[2] written
about 1492. After classifying the sciences in true
scholastic fashion, and arranging them according
to their relative importance and their respective
utility for Christianity, he attacks all learning as
superfluous and dangerous, unless restricted to a
chosen few. Poetry, according to the scholastic
arrangement, is grouped with logic and grammar;
and this mediæval classification fixes Savonarola's
conception of the theory of poetic art. He expressly
says that he attacks the abuse of poetry and not
poetry itself, but there can be no doubt that, at
bottom, he was intolerant of creative literature.
Like Plato, like moral reformers of all ages, he
feared the free play of the imaginative faculty ;
and in connecting poetry with logic he was tending
toward the elimination of the imagination in art.
The basis of his æsthetic system, such as it is,

---

[1] *Cf.* Gaspary, ii. 220.
[2] Villari, p. 501 *sq.*, and Perrens, ii. 328 *sq.*

rests wholly on that of Thomas Aquinas; [1] but he
is in closer accord with Aristotle when he points out
that versification, a merely conventional accompaniment of poetry, is not to be confounded with
the essence of poetry itself. This distinction is
urged to defend the Scriptures, which he regards
as the highest and holiest form of poetry. For
him poetry is coördinate with philosophy and with
thought; but in his intolerance of poetry in its
lower forms, he would follow Plato in banishing
poets from an ideal state. The imitation of the
ancient poets especially falls under his suspicion,
and in an age given up to their worship he denies
both their supremacy and their utility. In fine,
as a reformer, he represents for us the religious
reaction against the paganization of culture by the
humanists. But the forces against him were too
strong. Even the Christianization of culture effected during the next century by the Council of
Trent was hardly more than temporary. Humanism, which represents the revival of ancient pagan culture, and rationalism, which represents the
growth of the modern spirit in science and art,
were currents too powerful to be impeded by any
reformer, however great, and, when combined in
classicism, were to reign supreme in literature
for centuries to come. But Savonarola and Poliziano serve to indicate that modern literary criticism had not yet begun. For until some rational
answer to the objections urged against poetry in

---

[1] *Cf*. Cartier, *L'Esthétique de Savonarole*, in Didron's *An-
nales Archéologiques*, 1847, vii. 255 *sq*.

antiquity and in the Middle Ages was forthcoming, literary criticism in any true sense was fundamentally impossible; and that answer came only with the recovery of Aristotle's *Poetics*.

III.   *The Final Justification of Poetry*

The influence of Aristotle's *Poetics* in classical antiquity, so far as it is possible to judge, was very slight; there is no apparent reference to the *Poetics* in Horace, Cicero, or Quintilian,[1] and it was entirely lost sight of during the Middle Ages. Its modern transmission was due almost exclusively to Orientals.[2] The first Oriental version of Aristotle's treatise appears to have been that made by Abu-Baschar, a Nestorian Christian, from the Syriac into Arabic, about the year 935. Two centuries later, the Moslem philosopher Averroës made an abridged version of the *Poetics*, which was translated into Latin in the thirteenth century, by a certain German, named Hermann, and again, by Mantinus of Tortosa in Spain, in the fourteenth century. Hermann's version seems to have circulated considerably in the Middle Ages, but it had no traceable influence on critical literature whatsoever. It is mentioned and censured by Roger Bacon, but the *Poetics* in any form was probably unknown to Dante, to Boccaccio, and beyond a single obscure reference, to Petrarch. Some of the humanists, such as Benvenuto da Imola in his commentary on Dante, cite the

[1] Egger, 209 *sq*.   [2] *Ibid*. 555 *sq*.

version of Averroës; but the critical ideas of
the period show slight indication of Aristotelian
influence, and during the sixteenth century
itself there seems to have been a well-defined
impression that the *Poetics* had been recovered
only after centuries of oblivion. Thus, Bernardo
Segni, who translated the *Poetics* into Italian in
1549, speaks of it as "abandoned and neglected
for a long time";[1] and Bernardo Tasso, some
ten years later, refers to it as "buried for so
long a time in the obscure shadows of ignorance."[2]

It was then as a new work of Aristotle that the
Latin translation by Giorgio Valla, published at
Venice in 1498, must have appeared to Valla's contemporaries. Though hardly successful as a work
of scholarship, this translation, and the Greek text
of the *Poetics* published in the Aldine *Rhetores
Græci* in 1508, had considerable influence on dramatic literature, but scarcely any immediate influence on literary criticism. Somewhat later, in
1536, Alessandro de' Pazzi published a revised
Latin version, accompanied by the original; and
from this time, the influence of the Aristotelian
canons becomes manifest in critical literature. In
1548, Robertelli produced the first critical edition
of the *Poetics*, with a Latin translation and a
learned commentary, and in the very next year the
first Italian translation was given to the world

---

[1] Segni, p. 160.
[2] B. Tasso, *Lettere*, ii. 525. So also, Robortelli, 1548, "Jacuit
liber hic neglectus, ad nostra fere haec usque tempora."

c

by Bernardo Segni. From that day to this the editions and translations of the *Poetics* have increased
beyond number, and there is hardly a single passage in Aristotle's treatise which has not been discussed by innumerable commentators and critics.

It was in Aristotle's *Poetics* that the Renaissance
was to find, if not a complete, at least a rational
justification of poetry, and an answer to every one
of the Platonic and mediæval objections to imaginative literature. As to the assertion that poetry
diverges from actual reality, Aristotle[1] contended
that there is to be found in poetry a higher reality
than that of mere commonplace fact, that poetry
deals not with particulars, but with universals, and
that it aims at describing not what has been, but
what might have been or ought to be. In other
words, poetry has little regard for the actuality of
the specific event, but aims at the reality of an eternal probability. It matters not whether Achilles
or Æneas did this thing, or that thing, which
Homer or Virgil ascribes to either, but if Achilles
or Æneas was such a man as the poet describes, he
must necessarily act as Homer or Virgil has made
him do. It is needless to say that Aristotle is here
simply distinguishing between ideal truth and
actual fact, and in asserting that it is the function
of poetry to imitate only ideal truth he laid the
foundations, not only of an answer to mediæval
objections, but also of modern æsthetic criticism.

Beyond this, poetry is justified on the grounds of
morality, for while not having a distinctly moral

[1] *Poet.* ix.

aim, it is essentially moral, because it is this ideal
representation of life, and an idealized version of
human life must necessarily present it in its moral
aspects. Aristotle distinctly combats the traditional
Greek conception of the didactic function of poetry,
but it is evident that he insists fundamentally that
literature must be moral, for he sternly rebukes
Euripides several times on grounds that are moral,
rather than purely æsthetic. In answer to the objection that poetry, instead of calming, stirs and
excites our meanest passions, that it "waters and
cherishes those emotions which ought to wither
with drought, and constitutes them our rulers,
when they ought to be our subjects,"[1] Aristotle
taught those in the Renaissance who were able to
understand him, that poetry, and especially dramatic poetry, does not indeed starve the emotions,
but excites them only to allay and to regulate them,
and in this æsthetic process purifies and ennobles
them.[2] In pointing out these things he has justified
the utility of poetry, regarding it as more serious and
philosophic than history, because it universalizes
mere fact, and imitates life in its noblest aspects.

These arguments were incorporated into Renaissance criticism; they were emphasized, as we shall
see, over and over again, and they formed the basis
of the justification of poetry in modern critical
literature. At the same time, this purely æsthetic
conception of art did not prevail by itself in the
sixteenth century, even in those for whom Aristotle
meant most, and who best understood his meaning;

---

[1] Plato, *Rep.* x. 600. [2] *Poet.* vi. 2; *Pol.* viii. 7.

the Horatian elements, also, as found in the early humanists, were elaborated and discussed. In the *Poetica* of Daniello (1536), these Horatian elements form the basis for a defence of poetry [1] that has many marked resemblances to various passages in Sir Philip Sidney's *Defence of Poesy*. After referring to the antiquity and nobility of poetry, and affirming that no other art is nobler or more ancient, Daniello shows that all things known to man, all the secrets of God and nature, are described by the poets in musical numbers and with exquisite ornament. He furthermore asserts, in the manner of Horace, that the poets were the inventors of the arts of life; and in answer to the objection that it was the philosophers who in reality did these things, he shows that while instruction is more proper to the philosopher than to the poet, poets teach too, in many more ways, and far more pleasantly, than any philosopher can. They hide their useful teachings under various fictions and fabulous veils, as the physician covers bitter medicine with a sweet coating. The style of the philosopher is dry and obscure, without any force or beauty by itself; and the delightful instruction of poetry is far more effective than the abstract and harsh teachings of philosophy. Poetry, indeed, was the only form of philosophy that primitive men had, and Plato, while regarding himself as an enemy of poets, was really a great poet himself, for he expresses all his ideas in a wondrously harmonious rhythm, and with great splendor of words and images. This defence of

[1] Daniello, p. 10 *sq*.

Daniello's is interesting, as anticipating the general form of such apologies throughout the sixteenth century.

Similarly, Minturno in his *De Poeta* (1559), elaborates the Horatian suggestions for a defence of poetry. He begins by pointing out the broad inclusiveness of poetry, which may be said to comprehend in itself every form of human learning, and by showing that no form of learning can be found before the first poets, and that no nation, however barbarous, has ever been averse to poetry. The Hebrews praised God in verse; the Greeks, Italians, Germans, and British have all honored poetry; the Persians have had their Magi and the Gauls their bards. Verse, while not essential to poetry, gives the latter much of its delightful effectiveness, and if the gods ever speak, they certainly speak in verse; indeed, in primitive times it was in verse that all sciences, history, and philosophy were written.[1]

To answer the traditional objections against imaginative literature which had survived beyond the Middle Ages seemed to the Renaissance a simpler task, however, than to answer the more philosophical objections urged in the Platonic dialogues. The authority of Plato during the Renaissance made it impossible to slight the arguments stated by him in the *Republic*, and elsewhere. The writers of this period were particularly anxious to refute, or at least to explain away, the reasons for which Plato had banished poets from his ideal commonwealth.

[1] *De Poeta*, p. 13 *sq.*

Some critics, like Bernardo Tasso[1] and Daniello,[2] asserted that Plato had not argued against poetry itself, but only against the abuse of poetry. Thus, according to Tasso, only impure and effeminate poets were to be excluded from the ideal state, and according to Daniello, only the more immoral tragic poets, and especially the authors of obscene and lampooning comedies. Other Renaissance writers, like Minturno[3] and Fracastoro,[4] answered the Platonic objections on more philosophical grounds. Thus Fracastoro answers Plato's charge that, since poetry is three removes from ideal truth, poets are fundamentally ignorant of the realities they attempt to imitate, by pointing out that the poet is indeed ignorant of what he is speaking of, in so far as he is a versifier and skilled in language, just as the philosopher or historian is ignorant of natural or historical facts in so far as he, too, is merely skilled in language, but knows these facts in so far as he is learned, and has thought out the problems of nature and history. The poet, as well as the philosopher and the historian, must possess knowledge, if he is to teach anything; he, too, must learn the things he is going to write about, and must solve the problems of life and thought; he, too, must have a philosophical and an historical training. Plato's objection, indeed, applies to the philosopher, to the orator, to the historian, quite as much as to the poet. As to Plato's second charge, that imagination naturally tends toward the worst things,

[1] *Lettere*, ii. 526.   [3] *De Poeta*, p. 30 *sq.*
[2] *Poetica*, p. 14 *sq.*   [4] *Opera*, i. 361 *sq.*

and accordingly that poets write obscenely and blasphemously, Fracastoro points out that this is not the fault of the art, but of those who abuse it; there are, indeed, immoral and enervating poets, and they ought to be excluded, not only from Plato's, but from every commonwealth. Thus various Aristotelian and Horatian elements were combined to form a definite body of Renaissance criticism.

CHAPTER II

In the first book of his *Geography* Strabo defines
poetry as " a kind of elementary philosophy, which
introduces us early to life, and gives us pleasurable instruction in reference to character, emotion,
action." This passage sounds the keynote of the
Renaissance theory of poetry. Poetry is therein
stated to be a form of philosophy, and, moreover, a
philosophy whose subject is life, and its object is
said to be pleasurable instruction.

I. *Poetry as a Form of Scholastic Philosophy*

In the first place, poetry is a form of philosophy.
Savonarola had classed poetry with logic and
grammar, and had asserted that a knowledge of
logic is essential to the composing of poetry. The
division of the sciences and the relative importance
of each were a source of infinite scholastic discussion during the Middle Ages. Aristotle had first
placed dialectic or logic, rhetoric, and poetics in
the same category of efficient philosophy. But
Averroës was probably the first to confuse the
function of poetics with that of logic, and to make

24

the former a subdivision, or form, of the latter; and this classification appears to have been accepted by the scholastic philosophers of the Middle Ages.

This conception of the position of poetry in the body of human knowledge may be found, however, throughout the Renaissance. Thus, Robortelli, in his commentary on Aristotle's *Poetics* (1548), gives the usual scholastic distinctions between the various forms of the written or spoken word (*oratio*): the demonstrative, which deals with the true; the dialectic, which deals with the probable; the rhetorical, with the persuasive; and the poetic, with the false or fabulous.[1] By the term "false" or "fabulous" is meant merely that the subject of poetry is not actual fact, but that it deals with things as they ought to be, rather than as they are. Varchi, in his public lectures on poetry (1553), divides philosophy into two forms, real and rational. Real philosophy deals with things, and includes metaphysics, ethics, physics, geometry, and the like; while rational philosophy, which includes logic, dialectic, rhetoric, history, poetry, and grammar, deals not with things, but with words, and is not philosophy proper, but the instrument of philosophy. Poetry is therefore, strictly speaking, neither an art nor a science, but an instrument or faculty; and it is only an art in the sense that it has been reduced to rules and precepts. It is, in fact, a form of logic, and no man, according to Varchi, can be a poet unless he is a logician; the better logician he is,

---

[1] Robortelli, p. 1 *sq.*

the better poet he will be. Logic and poetry differ, however, in their matter and their instruments ;
for the subject of logic is truth, arrived at by means
of the demonstrative syllogism, while the subject of
poetry is fiction or invention, arrived at by means
of that form of the syllogism known as the example.
Here the enthymeme, or example, which Aristotle
has made the instrument of rhetoric, becomes the
instrument of poetry.

This classification survived in the Aristotelian
schools at Padua and elsewhere as late as Zabarella
and Campanella. Zabarella, a professor of logic
and later of philosophy at Padua from 1564 to
1589, explains at length Averroës's theory that
poetics is a form of logic, in a treatise on the
nature of logic, published in 1578.[1] He concludes
that the two faculties, logic and poetics, are not
instruments of philosophy in general, but only of a
part of it, for they refer rather to action than to
knowledge; that is, they come under Aristotle's
category of efficient philosophy. They are not the
instruments of useful art or of moral philosophy,
the end of which is to make one's self good; but of
civil philosophy, the end of which is to make others
good. If it be objected that they are $\tau\hat{\omega}\nu$ $\epsilon\hat{\upsilon}\alpha\nu\tau\acute{\iota}\omega\nu$,
that is, of both good and evil, it may be answered
that their proper end is good. Thus, in the *Sympo-*

---

[1] This analysis of Zabarella, *Opera Logica, De Natura
Logicæ*, ii. 13–23 I owe to the kindness of Professor Butcher
of Edinburgh. Zabarella probably derived his knowledge of
Aristotle's *Poetics* from Robortelli, under whom he studied
Greek. *Cf*. Bayle, *Dict.* **s. v.** Zabarella.

sium, the true poet is praised; while in the *Republic*
the poets who aim at pleasure and who corrupt their
audiences are censured; and Aristotle in his definition of tragedy says that the end of tragedy is to
purge the passions and to correct the morals of men
(*affectiones animi purgare et mores corrigere*).

Even later than Zabarella, we find in the *Poetica*
of Campanella a division of the sciences very similar to that of Savonarola and Varchi. Theology is
there placed at the head of all knowledge, in
accordance with the mediæval tradition, while
poetics, with dialectic, grammar, and rhetoric, is
placed among the logical sciences. Considering
poetica as a form of philosophy, another commentator on Aristotle, Maggi (1550), takes great pains
to distinguish its various manifestations. *Poetica*
is the art of composing poetry, *poesis*, the poetry
composed according to this art, *poeta*, the composer
of poetry, and *poema*, a single specimen of poetry.[1]
This distinction is a commonplace of classical
criticism, and appears in Varro, Plutarch, Hermogenes, and Aphthonius.

II. *Poetry as an Imitation of Life*

In the second place, according to the passage
from Strabo cited at the beginning of this chapter,
poetry introduces us early to life, or, in other words,
its subject is human action, and it is what Aristotle
calls it, an imitation of human life. This raises

[1] Maggi, p. 28 *sq.* *Cf.* B. Tasso, *Lettere*, ii. 514; Scaliger,
Poet. i. 2; Castelvetro, *Poetica*, p. 7; Salviati, Cod. Magliabech.
ii. ii. 11, fol. 384 v.; B. Jonson, *Timber*, p 74.

two distinct problems.   First, what is the meaning of imitation ? and what in life is the subject-matter of this imitation ?

The conception of imitation held by the critics of the Renaissance was that expressed by Aristotle in the ninth chapter of the *Poetics*.   The passage is as follows : —

" It is evident from what has been said that it is not the function of the poet to relate what has happened, but what may happen, — what is possible according to the law of probability or necessity. The poet and the historian differ not by writing in verse or in prose.   The work of Herodotus might be put into verse, and it would still be a species of history, with metre no less than without it.   The true difference is that one relates what has happened, the other what may happen.   Poetry, therefore, is a more philosophical and a higher thing than history ; for poetry tends to express the universal, history the particular.   The universal tells us how a person of given character will on occasion speak or act, according to the law of probability or necessity ; and it is this universality at which poetry aims in giving expressive names to the characters."

In this passage Aristotle has briefly formulated a conception of ideal imitation which may be regarded as universally valid, and which, repeated over and over again, became the basis of Renaissance criticism.

In the *Poetica* of Daniello (1536), occurs the first allusion in modern literary criticism to the Aristotelian notion of ideal imitation.   According to Daniello, the poet, unlike the historian, can mingle fictions with facts, because he is not obliged, as is the historian, to describe things as they actually are or have been, but rather as they ought to be; and it is in this that the poet most differs from the historian, and not in the writing of verses; for even if Livy's works were versified, they would still be histories as before.[1] This is of course almost a paraphrase of the passage in Aristotle; but that Daniello did not completely understand the ideal element in Aristotle's conception is shown by the further distinction which he draws between the historian and the poet. For he adds that the poet and the historian have much in common; in both there are descriptions of places, peoples, laws; both contain the representation of vices and virtues; in both, amplification, variety, and digressions are proper; and both teach, delight, and profit at the same time. They differ, however, in that the historian, in telling his story, recounts it exactly as it happened, and adds nothing; whereas the poet is permitted to add whatever he desires, so long as the fictitious events have all the appearance of truth.

Somewhat later, Robortelli treats the question of æsthetic imitation from another point of view. The poet deals with things as they ought to be, but he can either appropriate actual fact, or he can invent his material. If he does the former, he narrates the truth not as it really happened, but as it might or ought to happen; while if he invents his material, he must do so in accordance with the law of possibility, or necessity, or probability and veri-

[1] Daniello, p. 41 *sq.*

similitude.[1] Thus Xenophon, in describing Cyrus,
does not depict him as he actually was, but as the
best and noblest king can be and ought to be; and
Cicero, in describing the orator, follows the same
method. From this it is evident that the poet can
invent things transcending the order of nature;
but if he does so, he should describe what might or
ought to have been.

Here Robortelli answers a possible objection to
Aristotle's statement that poets deal only with
what is possible and verisimilar. Is it possible
and verisimilar that the gods should eat ambrosia
and drink nectar, as Homer describes, and that
such a being as Cerberus should have several
heads, as we find in Virgil, not to mention various
improbable things that occur in many other poets?
The answer to such an objection is that poets can
invent in two ways. They can invent either things
according to nature or things transcending nature.
In the former case, these things must be in keeping with the laws of probability and necessity; but
in the latter case, the things are treated according
to a process described by Aristotle himself, and
called paralogism, which means, not necessarily
false reasoning, but the natural, if quite inconclu-
sive, logical inference that the things we know not
of are subject to the same laws as the things we
know. The poets accept the existence of the gods
from the common notion of men, and then treat all
that relates to these deities in accordance with this
system of paralogism. In tragedy and comedy

[1] Robortelli, p. 86 *sq.*

men are described as acting in accordance with the
ordinary occurrences of nature; but in epic poetry
this is not entirely the case, and the marvellous is
therefore admitted. Accordingly, this marvellous
element has the widest scope in epic poetry; while
in comedy, which treats of things nearest to our
own time, it ought not to be admitted at all.

But there is another problem suggested by the
passage from the *Poetics* which has been cited.
Aristotle says that imitation, and not metre, is the
test of poetry; that even if a history were versified, it would still remain history. The question
then arises whether a writer who imitates in prose,
that is, without verse, would be worthy of the title
of poet. Robortelli answers this question by pointing out that metre does not constitute the nature,
force, or essence of poetry, which depends entirely
on the fact of imitation; but at the same time,
while one who imitates without verse is a poet, in
the best and truest poetry imitation and metre are
combined.[1]

In Fracastoro's *Naugerius, sive de Poetica Dia-
logus* (1555), there is the completest explanation
of the ideal element in the Aristotelian conception
of imitation. The poet, according to Aristotle, differs from other writers in that the latter consider
merely the particular, while the poet aims at the
universal. He is, in other words, attempting to
describe the simple and essential truth of things,
not by depicting the nude thing as it is, but the
idea of things clothed in all their beauties.[2] Here

[1] Robortelli, p. 90 *sq*.   [2] Fracastoro, i. 340.

Fracastoro attempts to explain the Aristotelian conception of the type with the aid of the Platonic
notion of beauty.   There were, in fact, in the
Renaissance, three conceptions of beauty in general vogue.   First, the purely objective conception
that beauty is fixed or formal, that it consists in
approximating to a certain mechanical or geometri-
cal form, such as roundness, squareness, or straight-
ness; secondly, the Platonic conception, ethical
rather than æsthetic, connecting the beautiful with
the good, and regarding both as the manifestation
of divine power; and, thirdly, a more purely æsthetic conception of beauty, connecting it either
with grace or conformity, or in a higher sense with
whatever is proper or fitting to an object.   This
last idea, which at times approaches the modern
conception that beauty consists in the realization
of the objective character of any particular thing
and in the fulfilment of the law of its own being,
seems to have been derived from the *Idea* of the
Greek rhetorician Hermogenes, whose influence
during the sixteenth century was considerable,
even as early as the time of Filelfo.   It was the
celebrated rhetorician Giulio Cammillo, however,
who appears to have popularized Hermogenes in
the sixteenth century, by translating the *Idea* into
Italian, and by expounding it in a discourse published posthumously in 1544.

As will be seen, Fracastoro's conception of beauty
approximates both to the Platonic and to the more
purely æsthetic doctrines which we have mentioned; and he expounds and elaborates this

æsthetic notion in the following manner. Each
art has its own rules of proper expression. The
historian or the philosopher does not aim at all the
beauties or elegancies of expression, but only such
as are proper to history or philosophy. But to the
poet no grace, no embellishment, no ornament, is
ever alien; he does not consider the particular
beauty of any one field, — that is, the singular, or
particular, of Aristotle, — but all that pertains to
the simple idea of beauty and of beautiful speech.
Yet this universalized beauty is no extraneous
thing; it cannot be added to objects in which it
has no place, as a golden coat on a rustic; all the
essential beauty of each species is to be the es-
pecial regard of the poet. For in imitating persons and things, he neglects no beauty or elegance
which he can attribute to them; he strives only
after the most beautiful and most excellent, and
in this way affects the minds of men in the direction of excellence and beauty.

This suggests a problem which is at the very
root of Aristotle's conception of ideal imitation;
and it is Fracastoro's high merit that he was one
of the first writers of the Renaissance to explain
away the objection, and to formulate in the most
perfect manner what Aristotle really meant. For,
even granting that the poet teaches more than
others, may it not be urged that it is not what pertains to the thing itself, but the beauties which he
adds to them, — that it is ornament, extraneous to
the thing itself (*extra rem*), and not the thing
itself, — which seems to be the chief regard of the

D

poet? But after all, what is *extra rem* ? Are beautiful columns, domes, peristyles *extra rem*, because a thatched roof will protect us from rain and frost; or is noble raiment *extra rem*, because a rustic garment would suffice? The poet, so far from adding anything extraneous to the things he imitates, depicts them in their very essence; and it is because he alone finds the true beauty in things, because he attributes to them their true nobility and perfection, that he is more useful than any other writer. The poet does not, as some think, deal with the false and the unreal.[1] He assumes nothing openly alien to truth, though he may permit himself to treat of old and obscure legends which cannot be verified, or of things which are regarded as true on account of their appearance, their allegorical signification (such as the ancient myths and fables), or their common acceptance by men. So we may conclude that not every one who uses verse is a poet, but only he who is moved by the true beauty of things — by their simple and essential beauties, not merely apparent ones. This is Fracastoro's conclusion, and it contains that mingling of Platonism and Aristotelianism which may be found somewhat later in Tasso and Sir Philip Sidney. It is the chief merit of Fracastoro's dialogue, that even while emphasizing this Platonic element, he clearly distinguishes and defines the ideal element in æsthetic imitation.

About the same time, in the public lectures of Varchi (1553), there was an attempt to formulate

[1] Fracastoro, i. 357 *sq.*

a more explicit definition of poetry on the basis of Aristotle's definition[1] of tragedy. Poetry, according to Varchi, is an imitation of certain actions, passions, habits of mind, with song, diction, and harmony, together or separately, for the purpose of removing the vices of men and inciting them to virtue, in order that they may attain their true happiness and beatitude.[2] In the first place, poetry is an imitation. Every poet imitates, and any one who does not imitate cannot be called a poet. Accordingly, Varchi follows Maggi in distinguishing three classes of poets, — the poets *par excellence*, who imitate in verse; the poets who imitate without using verse, such as Lucian, Boccaccio in the *Decameron*, and Sannazaro in the *Arcadia;* and the poets, commonly but less properly so called, who use verse, but who do not imitate. Verse, while not an essential attribute of poetry, is generally required; for men's innate love of harmony, according to Aristotle, was one of the causes that gave rise to poetic composition. Certain forms of poetry however, such as tragedy, cannot be written without verse; for "embellished language," that is, verse, is included in the very definition of tragedy as given by Aristotle.

The question whether poetry could be written in prose was a source of much discussion in the Renaissance; but the consensus of opinion was overwhelmingly against the prose drama. Comedy in prose was the usual Italian practice of this period, and various scholars[3] even sanction the

[1] *Poet.* vi. 2.   [2] Varchi, p. 578.   [3] *E.g.* Piccolomini, p. 27 *sq.*

practice on theoretical grounds. But the controversy was not brought to a head until the publication of Agostino Michele's *Discorso in cui si dimos-
tra come si possono scrivere le Commedie e le Tragedie
in Prosa* in 1592; and eight years later, in 1600,
Paolo Beni published his Latin dissertation, *Dis-
putatio in qua ostenditur præstare Comœdiam atque
Tragœdiam metrorum vinculis solvere.*[1] The language of Beni's treatise was strong — its very title
speaks of liberating the drama from the shackles
of verse; and for a heresy of this sort, couched as
it was in language that might even have been revolutionary enough for the French romanticists of
1830, the sixteenth century was not yet fully prepared. Faustino Summo, answering Beni in the
same year, asserts that not only is it improper for
tragedy and comedy to be written in prose, but
that no form of poetry whatever can properly be
composed without the accompaniment of verse.[2]
The result of the whole controversy was to fix the
metrical form of the drama throughout the period
of classicism. But it need not be said that the
same conclusion was not accepted by all for every
form of poetry. The remark of Cervantes in *Don
Quixote,* that epics can be written in prose as well as
in verse, is well known; and Julius Cæsar Scaliger[3]
speaks of Heliodorus's romance as a model epic.

Scaliger, however, regards verse as a fundamental part of poetry. For him, poetry and history have the forms of narration and ornament in

[1] Tiraboschi, vii. 1331.   [3] *Poet.* iii. 95.
[2] Summo, pp. 61–69.

common, but differ in that poetry adds fictions to
the things that are true, or imitates actual things
with fictitious ones, — *majore sane apparatu*, that
is, among other things, with verse. As a result of
this notion, Scaliger asserts that if the history of
Herodotus were versified, it would no longer be
history, but historical poetry. Under no circumstances, theoretically, will he permit the separation
of poetry from mere versification. He accordingly
dismisses with contempt the usual argument of the
period that Lucan was an historian rather than a
poet. "Take an actual history," says Scaliger;
"how does Lucan differ, for example, from Livy?
He differs in using verse. Well, then he is a poet."
Poetry, then, is imitation in verse;[1] but in imitating what ought to be rather than what is, the poet
creates another nature and other fortunes, as if he
were another God.[2]

It will be seen from these discussions that the
Renaissance always conceived of æsthetic imitation
in this ideal sense. There are scarcely any traces
of realism, in anything like its modern sense, in
the literary criticism of this period. Torquato
Tasso does indeed say that art becomes most perfect as it approaches most closely to nature;[3] and

---

[1] *Poet.* i. 1.

[2] Another critic of the time, Vettori, 1560, pp. 14, 93, attacks
poetic prose on the ground that in Aristotle's definition of the
various poetic forms, verse is always spoken of as an essential
part. It is interesting to note that the phrase "poetic prose"
is used, perhaps for the first time, in Minturno, *Arte Poetica*,
1564, p. 3, etc.

[3] *Opere*, x. 254. *Cf.* Minturno, *Arte Poetica*, p. 33.

Scaliger declares that the dramatic poet must beyond
all things aim at reproducing the actual conditions
of life.[1] But it is the appearance of reality, and
not the mere actuality itself, that the critics are
speaking of here. With the vast body of mediæval
literature before them, in which impossibilities follow upon impossibilities, and the sense of reality is
continually obscured, the critical writers of the
Renaissance were forced to lay particular stress on
the element of probability, the element of close
approach to the seeming realities of life; but the
imitation of life is for them, nevertheless, an imitation of things as they ought to be — in other words,
the imitation is ideal. Muzio says that nature is
adorned by art : —

> " Suol far l' opere sue roze, e tra le mani
>   Lasciarle a l' arte, che le adorni e limi ; " [2]

and he distinctly affirms that the poet cannot remain content with exact portraiture, with the mere
actuality of life : —

> " Lascia 'l vero a l' historia, e ne' tuoi versi
>   Sotto i nomi privati a l' universo
>   Mostra che fare e che non far si debbia."

In keeping with this idealized conception of art,
Muzio asserts that everything obscene or immoral
must be excluded from poetry; and this puristic
notion of art is everywhere emphasized in Renaissance criticism. It was the *verisimile*, as has been
said, that the writers of this period especially insisted upon. Poetry must have the appearance of

[1] *Poet*. iii. 96.   [2] Muzio, p. 69.

truth, that is, it must be probable; for unless the
reader believes what he reads, his spirit cannot be
moved by the poem.[1] This anticipates Boileau's
famous line : —

> " L'esprit n'est point ému de ce qu'il ne croit pas." [2]

But beyond and above the *verisimile*, the poet
must pay special regard to the ethical element
(*il lodevole e l'onesto*). A poet of the sixteenth
century, Palingenius, says that there are three
qualities required of every poem : —

> " Atqui scire opus est, triplex genus esse bonorum,
> Utile, delectans, majusque ambobus honestum." [3]

Poetry, then, is an ideal representation of life;
but should it be still further limited, and made an
imitation of only human life? In other words, are
the actions of men the only possible themes of
poetry, or may it deal, as in the *Georgics* and the
De Rerum Natura, with the various facts of external
nature and of science, which are only indirectly
connected with human life? May poetry treat of
the life of the world as well as of the life of men;
and if only of the latter, is it to be restricted to
the actions of men, or may it also depict their
passions, emotions, and character? In short, how
far may external nature on the one hand, and the
internal working of the human soul on the other
hand, be regarded as the subject-matter of poetry?
Aristotle says that poetry deals with the actions of

---

[1] Giraldi Cintio, i. 61.
[2] *Art Poét.* iii. 50. *Cf.* Horace, *Ars Poet.* 188.
[3] *Zodiac. Vitæ*, i. 143.

men, but he uses the word "actions" in a larger
sense than many of the Renaissance critics appear
to have believed. His real meaning is thus explained by a modern writer:—

"Everything that expresses the mental life, that reveals
a rational personality, will fall within this larger sense of
action. . . . The phrase is virtually an equivalent for ἤθη
(character), πάθη (emotion), πράξεις (action). . . . The
common original from which all the arts draw is human life,
— its mental processes, its spiritual movements, its outward
acts issuing from deeper sources ; in a word, all that constitutes the inward and essential activity of the soul. On
this principle landscape and animals are not ranked among
the objects of æsthetic imitation. The whole universe is not
conceived of as the raw material of art. Aristotle's theory
is in agreement with the practice of the Greek poets and
artists of the classical period, who introduce the external
world only so far as it forms a background of action, and
enters as an emotional element into man's life and heightens
the human interest." [1]

Aristotle distinctly says that "even if a treatise
on medicine or natural philosophy be brought out
in verse, the name of poet is by custom given to
the author; and yet Homer and Empedocles have
nothing in common except the material; the former,
therefore, is properly styled poet, the latter, physi-
cist rather than poet." [2]

The Aristotelian doctrine was variously conceived
during the Renaissance. Fracastoro, for example,
asserts that the imitation of human life alone is not
of itself a test of poetry, for such a test would
exclude Empedocles and Lucretius; it would make

[1] Butcher, pp. 117, 118.   [2] *Poet.* i. 8.

Virgil a poet in the *Æneid*, and not a poet in the
Georgics. All matters are proper material for the
poet, as Horace says, if they are treated poetically;
and although the imitation of men and women may
seem to be of higher importance for us who are
men and women, the imitation of human life is no
more the poet's end than the imitation of anything
else.[1] This portion of Fracastoro's argument may
be called apologetic, for the imitation of human
actions as a test of poetry would exclude most of
his own poems,[2] such as his famous *De Morbo
Gallico* (1529), written before the influence of
Aristotle was felt in anything but the mere external forms of creative literature. For Fracastoro,
all things poetically treated become poetry, and
Aristotle himself[3] says that everything becomes
pleasant when correctly imitated. So that not the
mere composition of verse, but the Platonic rapture, the delight in the true and essential beauty of
things, is for Fracastoro the test of poetic power.

Varchi, on the other hand, is more in accord with
Aristotle, in conceiving of "action," the subject-
matter of poetry, as including the passions and
habits of mind as well as the merely external
actions of mankind. By passions Varchi means
those mental perturbations which impel us to an
action at any particular time ($\pi\acute{a}\theta\eta$); while by
manners, or habits of mind, he means those mental
qualities which distinguish one man or one class
of men from another ($\accute{\eta}\theta\eta$). The exclusion of the

[1] Fracastoro, i. 335 *sq.*   [3] *Rhet.* i. 11.
[2] *Cf.* Castelvetro, *Poetica*, p. 27 *sq.*

emotional or introspective side of human life would
leave all lyric and, in fact, all subjective verse out
of the realms of poetry; and it was therefore essential, in an age in which Petrarch was worshipped,
that the subjective side of poetry should receive
its justification.[1]   There is also in Varchi a most interesting comparison between the arts of poetry and
painting.[2]   The basis of his distinction is Horace's
ut pictura poesis, doubtless founded on the parallel
of Simonides preserved for us by Plutarch; and
this distinction, which regarded painting as silent
poetry, and poetry as painting in language, may be
considered almost the keynote of Renaissance criticism, continuing even up to the time of Lessing.

In Capriano's *Della Vera Poetica* (1555) poetry is
given a preëminent place among all the arts, because
it does not merely deal with actions or with the objects of any single sense.   For Capriano, poetry is
an ideal representation of life, and as such " vere
nutrice e amatrice del nostro bene."[3]   All sensuous
or comprehensible objects are capable of being imitated by various arts.   The nobler of the imitative
arts are concerned with the objects of the nobler
senses, while the ignobler arts are concerned with
the objects of the senses of taste, touch, and smell.
Poetry is the finest of all the arts, because it comprehends in itself all the faculties and powers of
the other arts, and can in fact imitate anything, as,
for example, the form of a lion, its color, its feroc-
ity, its roar, and the like.   It is also the highest
form of art because it makes use of the most effi-

[1] *Cf.* A Segni, 1581, cap. i.   [2] Varchi, p. 227 *sq.*   [3] Capriano, cap. ii.

cacious means of imitation, namely, words, and especially since these receive the additional beauty and
power of rhythm. Accordingly, Capriano divides
poets into two classes: natural poets, who describe the
things of nature, and moral poets (such as epic and
tragic poets), who aim at presenting moral lessons
and indicating the uses of life; and of these two
classes the moral poets are to be rated above the
natural poets.

But if all things are the objects of poetic imitation, the poet must know everything; he must have
studied nature as well as life; and, accordingly,
Lionardi, in his dialogues on poetic imitation (1554),
says that to be a good poet, one must be a good
historian, a good orator, and a good natural and
moral philosopher as well;[1] and Bernardo Tasso
asserts that a thorough acquaintance with the art
of poetry is only to be gained from the study of
Aristotle's *Poetics*, combined with a knowledge of
philosophy and the various arts and sciences, and
vast experience of the world.[2] The Renaissance, with
its humanistic tendencies, never quite succeeded
in discriminating between erudition and genius.
Scaliger says that nothing which proceeds from
solid learning can ever be out of place in poetry,
and Fracastoro (1555) and Tomitano (1545) both
affirm that the good poet and the good orator must
essentially be learned scholars and philosophers.
Scaliger therefore distinguishes three classes of
poets, — first, the theological poets, such as Orpheus and Amphion; secondly, the philosophical

[1] Lionardi, p. 43 *sq.*   [2] *Lettere*, ii. 525.

poets, of two sorts, natural poets, such as Empedocles and Lucretius, and moral poets, who again are
either political, as Solon and Tyrtæus, economic, as
Hesiod, or common, as Phocyllides; and, thirdly,
the ordinary poets who imitate human life.[1] The
last are divided according to the usual Renaissance
classification into dramatic, narrative, and common
or mixed. Scaliger's classification is employed by
Sir Philip Sidney;[2] and a very similar subdivision
is given by Minturno.[3]

The treatment of Castelvetro, in his commentary
on the *Poetics* (1570), is at times much more in accord with the true Aristotelian conception than
most of the other Renaissance writers. While following Aristotle in asserting that verse is not of the
essence of poetry, he shows that Aristotle himself
by no means intended to class as poetry works that
imitated in prose, for this was not the custom of
Hellenic art. Prose is not suited to imitative or
imaginative subjects, for we expect themes treated
in prose to be actual facts.[4] " Verse does not distinguish poetry," says Castelvetro, " but clothes and
adorns it; and it is as improper for poetry to be
written in prose, or history in verse, as it is for
women to use the garments of men, and for men to
wear the garments of women." [5] The test of poetry
therefore is not the metre but the material. This
approximates to Aristotle's own view; since while
imitation is what distinguishes the poetic art, Aris-

---

[1] Scaliger, *Poet.* i. 2.
[2] *Defense*, pp. 10, 11.
[3] *De Poeta*, p. 53 *sq.*
[4] Castelvetro, *Poetica*, p. 23 *sq.*
[5] *Ibid.* p. 190.

totle, by limiting it to the imitation of human life
was, after all, making the matter the test of poetry.

Castelvetro, however, arrives at this conclusion
on different grounds. Science he regards as not
suitable material for poetry, and accordingly such
writers as Lucretius and Fracastoro are not poets.
They are good artists, perhaps, or good philosophers,
but not poets; for the poet does not attempt to discover the truth of nature, but to imitate the deeds
of men, and to bring delight to his audience by
means of this imitation. Moreover, poetry, as will
be seen later, is intended to give delight to the
populace, the untrained multitude, to whom the
sciences and the arts are dead letters;[1] if we con-
cede these to be fit themes for poetry, then poetry
is either not meant to delight, or not meant for the
ordinary people, but is intended for instruction and
for those only who are versed in sciences and arts.
Moreover, comparing poetry with history, Castelvetro finds that they resemble each other in many
points, but are not identical. Poetry follows, as it
were, in the footsteps of history, but differs from it
in that history deals with what has happened, poetry
with what is probable; and things that have happened, though probable, are never considered in
poetry as probable, but always as things that have
happened. History, accordingly, does not regard
verisimilitude or necessity, but only truth; poetry
must take care to establish the probability of its
subject in verisimilitude and necessity, since it
cannot regard truth. Castelvetro in common with

[1] *Cf.* T. Tasso, xi. 51.

most of the critics of the Renaissance seems to mis-
conceive the full meaning of ideal truth; for to the
Renaissance — nay, even to Shakespeare, if we are
to consider as his own various phrases which he has
put into the mouths of his dramatic characters —
truth was regarded as coincident with fact; and
nothing that was not actual fact, however subordinated to the laws of probability and necessity,
was ever called truth.

It is in keeping with this conception of the relations between history and poetry, that Castelvetro
should differ not only from Aristotle, but from most
of the critics of his own time, in asserting that the
order of the poetic narrative may be the same as
that of historical narrative. "In telling a story,"
he says, "we need not trouble ourselves whether it
has beginning, middle, and end, but only whether
it is fitted to its true purpose, that is, to delight its
auditors by the narration of certain circumstances
which could possibly happen but have not actually
happened."[1] Here the only vital distinction between history and poetry is that the incidents recounted in history have once happened, while those
recounted in poetry have never actually happened,
or the matter will not be regarded as poetry. Aristotle's fundamental requirement of the unity of the
fable is regarded as unessential, and is simply observed in order to show the poet's ingenuity. This
notion of poetic ingenuity is constant throughout
Castelvetro's commentary. Thus he explains Aristotle's statement that poetry is more philosophic

[1] *Poetica*, p. 158.

than history — more philosophic, according to Castelvetro, in the sense of requiring more thought,
more speculation in its composition — by showing
that it is a more difficult and more ingenious labor
to invent things that could possibly happen, than
merely to repeat things that have actually happened.[1]

III. *The Function of Poetry*

According to Strabo, it will be remembered, the
object or function of poetry is pleasurable instruction in reference to character, emotion, action.
This occasions the inquiry as to what is the function of the poetic art, and, furthermore, what are
its relations to morality. The starting-point of all
discussions on this subject in the Renaissance was
the famous verse of Horace : —

"Aut prodesse volunt aut delectare poetæ." [2]

This line suggests that the function of poetry may
be to please, or to instruct, or both to please and
instruct; and every one of the writers of the Renaissance takes one or other of these three positions. Aristotle, as we know, regarded poetry as
an imitation of human life, for the purpose of giving a certain refined pleasure to the reader or
hearer. "The end of the fine arts is to give pleasure (πρὸς ἡδονήν), or rational enjoyment (πρὸς
διαγωγήν)." [3] It has already been said that poetry,
in so far as it is an imitation of human life, and

[1] *Poetica*, p. 191.   [2] *Ars Poet.* 333.   [3] Butcher, p. 185.

attempts to be true to human life in its ideal aspects, must fundamentally be moral; but to give moral or scientific instruction is in no way the end or function of poetry. It will be seen that the Renaissance was in closer accord with Horace than with Aristotle, in requiring for the most part the *utile* as well as the *dulce* in poetry.

For Daniello, one of the earliest critical writers of the century, the function of the poet is to teach and delight. As the aim of the orator is to persuade, and the aim of the physician to cure, so the aim of the poet is equally to teach and delight; and unless he teaches and delights he cannot be called a poet, even as one who does not persuade cannot be called an orator, or one who does not cure, a physician.[1] But beyond profitableness and beauty, the poet must carry with him a certain persuasion, which is one of the highest functions of poetry, and which consists in moving and affecting the reader or hearer with the very passions depicted; but the poet must be moved first, before he can move others.[2] Here Daniello is renewing Horace's

"Si vis me flere, dolendum est
Primum ipsi tibi,"—

a sentiment echoed by poets as different as Vauquelin, Boileau, and Lamartine.

Fracastoro, however, attempts a deeper analysis of the proper function of the poetic art. What is the aim of the poet? Not merely to give delight, for the fields, the stars, men and women,

[1] Daniello, p. 25.   [2] *Ibid.* p. 40.

the objects of poetic imitation themselves do that; and poetry, if it did no more, could not be said to have any reason for existing. Nor is it merely to teach and delight, as Horace says; for the descriptions of countries, peoples, and armies, the scientific digressions and the historical events, which constitute the instructive side of poetry, are derived from cosmographers, scientists, and historians, who teach and delight as much as poets do. What, then, is the function of the poet? It is, as has already been pointed out, to describe the essential beauty of things, to aim at the universal and ideal, and to perform this function with every possible accompaniment of beautiful speech, thus affecting the minds of men in the direction of excellence and beauty. Portions of Fracastoro's argument have been alluded to before, and it will suffice here to state his own summing up of the aim of the poet, which is this, " Delectare et prodesse imitando in unoquoque maxima et pulcherrima per genus dicendi simpliciter pulchrum ex convenientibus." [1] This is a mingling of the Horatian and Platonic conceptions of poetic art.

By other critics a more practical function was given to poetry. Giraldi Cintio asserts that it is the poet's aim to condemn vice and to praise virtue, and Maggi says that poets aim almost exclusively at benefiting the mind. Poets who, on the contrary, treat of obscene matters for the corruption of youth, may be compared with infamous physicians who give their patients deadly poison

[1] Fracastoro, i. 363.

B

in the guise of wholesome medicine. Horace and
Aristotle, according to Maggi, are at one on this
point, for in the definition of tragedy Aristotle
ascribes to it a distinctly useful purpose, and whatever delight is obtainable is to be regarded as a
result of this moral function; for Maggi and the
Renaissance critics in general would follow the
Elizabethan poet who speaks of " delight, the fruit
of virtue dearly loved." Muzio, in his versified *Arte
Poetica* (1555), regards the end of poetry as pleasure
and profit, and the pleasurable aim of poetry as
attained by variety, for the greatest poems contain
every phase of life and art.

It has been seen that Varchi classed poetry with
rational philosophy. The end of all arts and sciences is to make human life perfect and happy;
but they differ in their modes of producing this
result. Philosophy attains its end by teaching;
rhetoric, by persuasion; history, by narration; poetry, by imitation or representation. The aim of
the poet, therefore, is to make the human soul perfect and happy, and it is his office to imitate, that
is, to invent and represent, things which render
men virtuous, and consequently happy. Poetry
attains this end more perfectly than any of the
other arts or sciences, because it does so, not by
means of precept, but by means of example. There
are various ways of making men virtuous, — by
teaching them what vice is and what virtue is,
which is the province of ethics; by actually chastising vices and rewarding virtues, which is the
province of law; or by example, that is, by the

representation of virtuous men receiving suitable
rewards for their virtue, and of vicious men receiving suitable punishments, which is the province of
poetry. This last method is the most efficacious,
because it is accompanied by delight. For men
either can not or will not take the trouble to study
sciences and virtues — nay, do not even like to be
told what they should or should not do; but in hear-
ing or reading poetic examples, not only is there no
trouble, but there is the greatest delight, and no
one can help being moved by the representation of
characters who are rewarded or punished according
to an ideal justice.

For Varchi, then, as for Sir Philip Sidney later,
the high importance of poetry is to be found in the
fact that it teaches morality better than any other
art, and the reason is that its instrument is not
precept but example, which is the most delightful
and hence the most efficacious of all means. The
function of poetry is, therefore, a moral one, and it
consists in removing the vices of men and inciting them to virtue. This twofold moral object of
poetry — the removal of vices, which is passive,
and the incitement to virtue, which is active — is
admirably attained, for example, by Dante in his
Divina Commedia; for in the *Inferno* evil men are
so fearfully punished that we resolve to flee from
every form of vice, and in the *Paradiso* virtuous
men are so gloriously rewarded that we resolve to
imitate every one of their perfections. This is the
expression of the extreme view of poetic justice;
and while it is in keeping with the common senti-

ment of the Renaissance, it is of course entirely
un-Aristotelian.

Scaliger's point of view is in accord with the
common Renaissance tradition. Poetry is imitation,
but imitation is not the end of poetry. Imitation
for its own sake — that is, art for art's sake — receives no encouragement from Scaliger. The pur.
pose of poetry is to teach delightfully (*docere cum
delectatione*); and, therefore, not imitation, as Aristotle says, but delightful instruction, is the test of
poetry.[1] Minturno (1559) adds a third element to
that of instruction and of delight.[2] The function
of poetry is not only to teach and delight, but also
to move, that is, beyond instruction and delight
the poet must impel certain passions in the reader
or hearer, and incite the mind to admiration of
what is described.[3] An ideal hero may be represented in a poem, but the poem is futile unless it
excites the reader to admiration of the hero depicted. Accordingly, it is the peculiar office of the
poet to move admiration for great men; for the
orator, the philosopher, and the historian need not
necessarily do so, but no one who does not incite
this admiration can really be called a poet.

This new element of admiration is the logical
consequence of the Renaissance position that philosophy teaches by precept, but poetry by example,
and that in this consists its superior ethical efficacy.
In Seneca's phrase, "longum iter per præcepta,

[1] Scaliger, *Poet.* vi. ii. 2.
[2] *De Poeta*, p. 102. *Cf.* Scaliger, *Poet.* iii. 96.
[3] *De Poeta*, p. 11.

breve per exempla." If poetry, therefore, attains
its end by means of example, it follows that to
arrive at this end the poet must incite in the
reader an admiration of the example, or the ethical
aim of poetry will not be accomplished. Poetry
is more than a mere passive expression of truth
in the most pleasurable manner; it becomes like
oratory an active exhortation to virtue, by attempting to create in the reader's mind a strong desire to
be like the heroes he is reading about. The poet
does not tell what vices are to be avoided and what
virtues are to be imitated, but sets before the
reader or hearer the most perfect types of the
various virtues and vices. It is, in Sidney's phrase
(a phrase apparently borrowed from Minturno),
"that feigning notable images of virtues, vices, or
what else, with that delightful instruction, which
must be the right describing note to know a poet
by." Dryden, a century later, seems to be insisting
upon this same principle of admiration when he
says that it is the work of the poet "to affect the
soul, and excite the passions, and above all to move
admiration, which is the delight of serious plays." [1]

But Minturno goes even further than this. If
the poet is fundamentally a teacher of virtue, it
follows that he must be a virtuous man himself;
and in pointing this out, Minturno has given the
first complete expression in modern times of the
consecrated conception of the poet's office. As no
form of knowledge and no moral excellence is foreign to the poet, so at bottom he is the truly wise

[1] *Essay of Dramatic Poesy*, p. 104.

and good man. The poet may, in fact, be defined
as a good man skilled in language and imitation;
not only ought he to be a good man, but no one will
be a good poet unless he is so.[1] This conception of
the moral nature of the poet may be traced henceforth throughout modern times. It is to be found
in Ronsard[2] and other French and Italian writers ;
it is especially noticeable in English literature, and
is insisted on by Ben Jonson,[3] Milton,[4] Shaftesbury,[5]
Coleridge,[6] and Shelley.[7] In this idea Plato's praise
of the philosopher, as well as Cicero's and Quintilian's praise of the orator, was by the Renaissance
transferred to the poet;[8] but the conception itself
goes back to a passage in Strabo's *Geography*, a work
well known to sixteenth-century scholars. This
passage is as follows : —

"Can we possibly imagine that the genius, power, and
excellence of a real poet consist in aught else than the just
imitation of life in formed discourse and numbers ? But
how should he be that just imitator of life, whilst he himself
knows not its measures, nor how to guide himself by judgment and understanding ? For we have not surely the same
notion of the poet's excellence as of the ordinary crafts-
man's, the subject of whose art is senseless stone or timber,

[1] *De Poeta*, p. 79.
[2] *Œuvres*, vii. 318.
[3] *Works*, i. 333.
[4] *Prose Works*, iii. 118.
[5] *Characteristicks*, 1711, i. 207.
[6] H. C. Robinson, *Diary*, May 29, 1812, "Coleridge talked of
the impossibility of being a good poet without being a good
man."
[7] *Defence of Poetry*, p. 42.
[8] Minturno plainly says as much, *De Poeta*, p. 105.

without life, dignity, or beauty ; whilst the poet's art turning principally on men and manners, he has his virtues and
excellence as poet naturally annexed to human excellence,
and to the worth and dignity of man, insomuch that it is
impossible he should be a great and worthy poet who is not
first a worthy and good man." [1]

Another writer of the sixteenth century, Bernardo
Tasso, tells us that in his poem of the *Amadigi* he
has aimed at delight rather than profitable instruction.[2] " I have spent most of my efforts," he says,
" in attempting to please, as it seems to me that
this is more necessary, and also more difficult to
attain ; for we find by experience that many poets
may instruct and benefit us very much, but certainly give us very little delight." This agrees
with what one of the sanest of English critics, John
Dryden (1668), has said of verse, " I am satisfied
if it caused delight, for delight is the chief if not
the only end of poesie; instruction can be admitted
but in the second place, for poesie only instructs as
it delights." [3]

It is this same end which Castelvetro (1570)
ascribes to poetic art. For Castelvetro, as in a
lesser degree for Robortelli also, the end of poetry
is delight, and delight alone.[4] This, he asserts, is
the position of Aristotle, and if utility is to be conceded to poetry at all, it is merely as an accident,
as in the tragic purgation of terror and compassion.[5]

---

[1] *Geog.* i. ii. 5, as cited by Shaftesbury.
[2] *Lettere*, ii. 195.
[3] *Essay of Dramatic Poesy*, p. 104.
[4] *Cf.* Piccolomini, p. 369.
[5] Castelvetro, *Poetica*, p. 505.   *Cf.* Twining, ii. 449, 450.

But he goes further than Aristotle would have been willing to go; for poetry, according to Castelvetro, is intended not merely to please, but to please the populace, in fact everybody, even the vulgar mob.[1] On this he insists throughout his commentary; indeed, as will be seen later, it is on this conception that his theory of the drama is primarily based. But it may be confidently asserted that Aristotle would have willingly echoed the conclusion of Shakespeare, as expressed in *Hamlet*, that the censure of one of the judicious must o'erweigh a whole theatre of others.   At the same time, Castelvetro's conception is in keeping with a certain modern feeling in regard to the meaning of poetic art.   Thus a recent writer regards literature as aiming " at the pleasure of the greatest possible number of the nation rather than instruction and practical effects," and as applying " to general rather than specialized knowledge." [2]   There is, then, in Castelvetro's argument this modicum of truth, that poetry appeals to no specialized knowledge, but that its function is, as Coleridge says, to give a definite and immediate pleasure.

Torquato Tasso, as might be expected, regards poetry in a more highly ideal sense.   His conception of the function of poets and of the poetic art may be explained as follows : The universe is beautiful in itself, because beauty is a ray from the Divine splendor; and hence art should seek to approach as closely as possible to nature, and to catch and

---

[1] *Poetica*, p. 29.
[2] Posnett, cited by Cook, p. 247.

express this natural beauty of the world.[1] Real beauty, however, is not so called because of any usefulness it may possess, but is primarily beautiful in itself; for the beautiful is what pleases every one, just as the good is what every one desires.[2] Beauty is therefore the flower of the good (*quasi un fiore del buono*); it is the circumference of the circle of which the good is the centre, and accordingly, poetry, as an expression of this beauty, imitates the outward show of life in its general aspects. Poetry is therefore an imitation of human actions, made for the guidance of life; and its end is delight, *ordinato al giovamento*.[3] It must essentially delight, either because delight is its aim, or because delight is the necessary means of effecting the ethical end of art.[4] Thus, for example, heroic poetry consists of imitation and allegory, the function of the former being to cause delight, and that of the latter to give instruction and guidance in life. But since difficult or obscure conceits rarely delight, and since the poet does not appeal to the learned only, but to the people, just as the orator does, the poet's idea must be, if not popular in the ordinary sense of the word, at least intelligible to the people. Now the people will not study difficult problems; but poetry, by appealing to them on the side of pleasure, teaches them whether they will or no; and this constitutes the true effectiveness of poetry, for it is the most delightful, and hence the most valuable, of teachers.[5]

[1] *Opere*, viii. 26 *sq*. [3] *Ibid*. xii. 13. [5] *Ibid*. xii. 212.
[2] *Ibid*. ix. 123. [4] *Ibid*. xi. 50.

Such, then, are the various conceptions of the function of poetry, as held by the critics of the Renaissance. On the whole, it may be said that at bottom the conception was an ethical one, for, with the exception of such a revolutionary spirit as Castelvetro, by most theorists it was as an effective guide to life that poetry was chiefly valued. Even when delight was admitted as an end, it was simply because of its usefulness in effecting the ethical aim.

In concluding this chapter, it may be well to say a few words, and only a few, upon the classification of poetic forms. There were during the Renaissance numerous attempts at distinguishing these forms, but on the whole all of them are fundamentally equivalent to that of Minturno, who recognizes three *genres*, — the lyric or melic, the dramatic or scenic, and the epic or narrative. This classification is essentially that of the Greeks, and it has lasted down to this very day. With lyric poetry this essay is scarcely concerned, for during the Renaissance there was no systematic lyric theory. Those who discussed it at all gave most of their attention to its formal structure, its style, and especially the conceit it contained. The model of all lyrical poetry was Petrarch, and it was in accordance with the lyrical poet's agreement or disagreement with the Petrarchan method that he was regarded as a success or a failure. Muzio's critical poem (1551) deals almost entirely with lyrical verse, and there are discussions on this subject in the works of Trissino, Equicola, Ruscelli,

Scaliger, and Minturno. But the real question at issue in all these discussions is merely that of external form, and it is with the question of principles, in so far as they regard literary criticism, that this essay is primarily concerned. The theory of dramatic and epic poetry, being fundamental, will therefore receive almost exclusive attention.

CHAPTER III

ARISTOTLE's definition of tragedy is the basis of the Renaissance theory of tragedy. That definition is as follows: "Tragedy is an imitation of an action that is serious, complete, and of a certain magnitude; in language embellished with each kind of artistic ornament, the several kinds being found in separate parts of the play; in the form of action, not of narration; through pity and fear effecting the proper *katharsis* or purgation of these emotions."[1]

To expand this definition, tragedy, in common with all other forms of poetry, is the imitation of an action; but the action of tragedy is distinguished from that of comedy in being grave and serious. The action is complete, in so far as it possesses perfect unity; and in length it must be of the proper magnitude. By embellished language, Aristotle means language into which rhythm, harmony, and song enter; and by the remark that the several kinds are to be found in separate parts of the play, he means that some parts of tragedy are rendered through the medium of verse alone, while others receive the aid of song. Moreover, tragedy is dis-

---

[1] *Poet.* vi. 2.

tinguished from epic poetry by being in the form
of action instead of that of narration.   The last por
tion of Aristotle's definition describes the peculiar
function of tragic performance.

I. *The Subject of Tragedy*

Tragedy is the imitation of a *serious* action, that
is, an action both grave and great, or, as the sixteenth century translated the word, illustrious.
Now, what constitutes a serious action, and what
actions are not suited to the dignified character of
tragedy ?   Daniello (1536) distinguishes tragedy
from comedy in that the comic poets " deal with the
most familiar and domestic, not to say base and
vile operations ; the tragic poets, with the deaths
of high kings and the ruins of great empires." [1]
Whichever of these matters the poet selects should
be treated without admixture of any other form; if
he resolves to treat of grave matters, mere loveliness should be excluded ; if of themes of loveliness,
he should exclude all grave themes.   Here, at the
very beginning of dramatic discussion, the strict
separation of themes or *genres* is advocated in as
formal a manner as ever during the period of classicism ; and this was never deviated from, at least
in theory, by any of the writers of the sixteenth
century.   Moreover, according to Daniello, the dignified character of tragedy demands that all un-
seemly, cruel, impossible, or ignoble incidents should
be excluded from the stage ; while even comedy

[1] Daniello, p. 34.

should not attempt to represent any lascivious act.[1]
This was merely a deduction from Senecan tragedy
and the general practice of the classics.

There is, in Daniello's theory of tragedy, no single Aristotelian element, and it was not until about
a decade later that Aristotle's theory of tragedy
played any considerable part in the literary criticism of the sixteenth century.   In 1543, however,
the *Poetics* had already become a part of university
study, for Giraldi Cintio, in his *Discorso sulle Comedie e sulle Tragedie*, written in that year, says that
it was a regular academic exercise to compare some
Greek tragedy, such as the *Œdipus* of Sophocles,
with a tragedy of Seneca on the same subject, using
the *Poetics* of Aristotle as a dramatic text-book.[2]
Giraldi distinguishes tragedy from comedy on somewhat the same grounds as Daniello.   "Tragedy and
comedy," he says, "agree in that they are both imi-
tations of an action, but they differ in that the
former imitates the illustrious and royal, the latter
the popular and civil.   Hence Aristotle says that
comedy imitates the worse sort of actions, not that
they are vicious and criminal, but that, as regards
nobility, they are worse when compared with royal
actions."   Giraldi's position is made clear by his
further statement that the actions of tragedy are
called illustrious, not because they are virtuous or
vicious, but merely because they are the actions
of people of the highest rank.[3]

This conception of the serious action of tragedy,

---

[1] *Cf.* Horace, *Ars Poet.* 182 *sq.*   [3] *Ibid.* ii. 30.
[2] Giraldi Cintio, ii. 6.

which makes its dignity the result of the rank of
those who are its actors, and thus regards rank as
the real distinguishing mark between comedy and
tragedy, was not only common throughout the Renaissance, but even throughout the whole period of
classicism, and had an extraordinary effect on the
modern drama, especially in France. Thus Dacier
(1692) says that it is not necessary that the action
be illustrious and important in itself : " On the contrary, it may be very ordinary or common ; but it
must be so by the quality of the persons who act.
. . . The greatness of these eminent men renders
the action great, and their reputation makes it cred-
ible and possible." [1]

Again, Robortelli (1548) maintains that tragedy
deals only with the greater sort of men (*præstanti-
ores*), because the fall of men of such rank into
misery and disgrace produces greater commiseration
(which is, as will be seen, one of the functions of
tragedy) than the fall of men of merely ordinary
rank. Another commentator on the *Poetics*, Maggi
(1550), gives a slightly different explanation of
Aristotle's meaning. Maggi asserts that Aristotle,[2]
in saying that comedy deals with the worse and
tragedy with the better sort of men, means to distinguish between those whose rank is lower or
higher than that of ordinary men; comedy dealing
with slaves, tradesmen, maidservants, buffoons, and
other low people, tragedy with kings and heroes.[3]
This explanation is defended on grounds similar to

[1] Cited by Butcher, p. 220.   [3] Maggi, p. 64.
[2] *Poet.* iv. 7.

those given by Robortelli, that is, the change from
felicity to infelicity is greater and more noticeable
in the greatest men.[1]

This conception of the rank of the characters as
the distinguishing mark between tragedy and comedy is, it need not be said, entirely un-Aristotelian.
"Aristotle does undoubtedly hold," says Professor
Butcher, "that actors in tragedy ought to be illustrious by birth and position. The narrow and trivial life of obscure persons cannot give scope for a
great and significant action, one of tragic consequence. But nowhere does he make outward rank
the distinguishing feature of tragic as opposed to
comic representation. Moral nobility is what he
demands; and this — on the French stage, or at
least with French critics — is transformed into an
inflated dignity, a courtly etiquette and decorum,
which seemed proper to high rank. The instance
is one of many in which literary critics have wholly
confounded the teaching of Aristotle." [2] This distinction, then, though common up to the end of the
eighteenth century, is not to be found in Aristotle;
but the fact is, that a similar distinction can be
traced, throughout the Middle Ages, throughout
classical antiquity, back almost to the time of Aristotle himself.

The grammarian, Diomedes, has preserved the
definition of tragedy formulated by Theophrastus,
Aristotle's successor as head of the Peripatetic
school. According to this definition, tragedy is

---

[1] Maggi, p. 154.
[2] Butcher, p. 220 *sq.*

"a change in the fortune of a hero."[1]   A Greek
definition of comedy preserved by Diomedes, and
ascribed to Theophrastus also,[2] speaks of comedy
as dealing with private and civil fortunes, without
the element of danger.   This seems to have been
the accepted Roman notion of comedy.   In the
treatise of Euanthius-Donatus, comedy is said to
deal with the common fortunes of men, to begin
turbulently, but to end tranquilly and happily ;
tragedy, on the other hand, has only mighty personages, and ends terribly ; its subject is often historical, while that of comedy is always invented by
the poet.[3]   The third book of Diomedes's *Ars Gram-
matica,* based on Suetonius's tractate *De Poetis* (written in the second century A.D.), distinguishes tragedy
from comedy in that only heroes, great leaders, and
kings are introduced in tragedy, while in comedy
the characters are humble and private persons ; in
the former, lamentations, exiles, bloodshed predominate, in the latter, love affairs and seductions.[4]
Isidore of Seville, in the seventh century, says very
much the same thing : "Comic poets treat of the
acts of private men, while tragic poets treat of
public matters and the histories of kings; tragic
themes are based on sorrowful affairs, comic themes
on joyful ones."[5]   In another place he speaks of
tragedy as dealing with the ancient deeds and mis-

---

[1] Butcher, p. 219, n. 1. — Müller, ii. 394, attempts to harmonize
the definition of Theophrastus with that of Aristotle.

[2] Egger, *Hist. de la Critique*, p. 344, n. 2.

[3] Cloetta, i. 29.   *Cf.* Antiphanes, cited by Egger, p. 72.

[4] Cloetta, p. 30.

[5] *Etymol.* viii. 7, 6.

deeds of infamous kings, and of comedy as dealing
with the actions of private men, and with the de-
filement of maidens and the love affairs of strum-
pets.[1] In the *Catholicon* of Johannes Januensis de
Balbis (1286) tragedy and comedy are distinguished
on similar grounds : tragedy deals only with kings
and princes, comedy with private citizens ; the style
of the former is elevated, that of the latter humble ;
comedy begins sorrowfully and ends joyfully, tragedy begins joyfully and ends miserably and terribly.[2]
For Dante, any poem written in an elevated and
sublime style, beginning happily and ending in misery and terror, is a tragedy ; his own great vision,
written as it is in the vernacular, and beginning in
hell and ending gloriously in paradise, he calls a
comedy.[3]

It appears, therefore, that during the post-classic
period and throughout the Middle Ages, comedy
and tragedy were distinguished on any or all of the
following grounds : —

i. The characters in tragedy are kings, princes,
or great leaders ; those in comedy, humble persons
and private citizens.

ii. Tragedy deals with great and terrible actions ;
comedy with familiar and domestic actions.

iii. Tragedy begins happily and ends terribly ;
comedy begins rather turbulently and ends joyfully.

---

[1] *Etymol.* xviii. 45 and 46.
[2] Cloetta, p. 28, and p. 31 *sq.*
[3] *Epist.* xi. 10.   *Cf.* Gelli's Lectures on the Divine Comedy,
ed. Negroni. 1887. i. 37 *sq.*

iv. The style and diction of tragedy are elevated
and sublime; while those of comedy are humble and
colloquial.

v. The subjects of tragedy are generally historical; those of comedy are always invented by the
poet.

vi. Comedy deals largely with love and seduc-
tion; tragedy with exile and bloodshed.

This, then, was the tradition that shaped the un-
Aristotelian conception of the distinctions between
comedy and tragedy, which persisted throughout
and even beyond the Renaissance. Giraldi Cintio
has followed most of these traditional distinctions,
but he is in closer accord with Aristotle [1] when he
asserts that the tragic as well as the comic plot
may be purely imaginary and invented by the
poet.[2] He explains the traditional conception that
the tragic fable should be historical, on the ground
that as tragedy deals with the deeds of kings and
illustrious men, it would not be probable that remarkable actions of such great personages should
be left unrecorded in history, whereas the private
events treated in comedy could hardly be known
to all. Giraldi, however, asserts that it does not
matter whether the tragic poet invents his story or
not, so long as it follows the law of probability.
The poet should choose an action that is probable
and dignified, that does not need the intervention
of a god in the unravelling of the plot, that does not
occupy much more than the space of a day, and
that can be represented on the stage in three or

[1] *Poet.* ix. 5–9.   [2] Giraldi Cintio, ii. 14.

four hours.[1] In respect to the dénouement of
tragedy, it may be happy or unhappy, but in
either case it must arouse pity and terror; and as
for the classic notion that no deaths should be represented on the stage, Giraldi declares that those
which are not excessively painful may be represented, for they are represented not for the sake of
commiseration but of justice.   The argument here
centres about Aristotle's phrase ἐν τῷ φανερῷ θάνατοι,[2]
but the common practice of classicism was based on
Horace's express prohibition: —

"Ne pueros coram populo Medea trucidet."[3]

Giraldi gives it as a universal rule of the drama
that nothing should be represented on the stage
which could not with propriety be done in one's
own house.[4]

Scaliger's treatment of the dramatic forms is particularly interesting because of its great influence
on the neo-classical drama.   He defines tragedy as
an imitation of an illustrious event, ending unhappily, written in a grave and weighty style, and
in verse.[5] Here he has discarded, or at least
disregarded, the Aristotelian definition of tragedy,
in favor of the traditional conception which had
come down through the Middle Ages.   Real tragedy, according to Scaliger, is entirely serious; and
although there are a few happy endings in ancient
tragedy, the unhappy ending is most proper to the

[1] Giraldi Cintio, ii. 20.   [4] Giraldi Cintio, ii. 119.
[2] *Poet.* xi. 6.   [5] Scaliger, *Poet.* i. 6.
[3] *Ars Poet.* 182–188.

spirit of tragedy itself. *Mortes aut exilia* — these
are the fit accompaniments of the tragic catastrophe.[1] The action begins tranquilly, but ends
horribly; the characters are kings and princes, from
cities, castles, and camps; the language is grave,
polished, and entirely opposed to colloquial speech;
the aspect of things is troubled, with terrors, menaces, exiles, and deaths on every hand. Taking as
his model Seneca, whom he rates above all the
Greeks in majesty,[2] he gives as the typical themes
of tragedy "the mandates of kings, slaughters, de-
spairs, executions, exiles, loss of parents, parricides,
incests, conflagrations, battles, loss of sight, tears,
shrieks, lamentations, burials, epitaphs, and funeral
songs."[3]   Tragedy is further distinguished from
comedy on the ground that the latter derives its
argument and its chief characters from history, inventing merely the minor characters; while comedy
invents its arguments and all its characters, and
gives them names of their own. Scaliger distinguishes men, for the purposes of dramatic poetry,
according to character and rank;[4] but it would seem
that he regarded rank alone as the distinguishing
mark between tragedy and comedy. Thus tragedy
is made to differ from comedy in three things: in
the rank of the characters, in the quality of the
actions, and in their different endings; and as a
result of these differences, in style also.

The definition of tragedy given by Minturno, in
his treatise *De Poeta* (1559), is merely a paraphrase

---

[1] Scaliger, i. 11; iii. 96.   [3] *Ibid.* iii. 96.
[2] *Ibid.* vi. 6.   [4] *Ibid.* i. 13.

of Aristotle's. He conceives of tragedy as describing *casus heroum cuius sibi quisque fortunæ fuerit
faber*, and it thus acts as a warning to men against
pride of rank, insolence, avarice, lust, and similar
passions.[1] It is grave and illustrious because its
characters are illustrious; and no variety of persons
or events should be introduced that are not in keeping
with the calamitous ending. The language throughout must be grave and severe; and Minturno has
expressed his censure in such matters by the phrase,
poema amatorio mollique sermone effœminat,[2] a censure which would doubtless apply to a large portion of classic French tragedy.

In Castelvetro (1570) we find a far more complete theory of the drama than had been attempted
by any of his predecessors. His work is by no
means a model of what a commentary on Aristotle's
Poetics should be. In the next century, Dacier,
whose subservience to Aristotle was even greater
than that of any of the Italians, accuses Castelvetro of lacking every quality necessary to a good
interpreter of Aristotle. " He knew nothing," says
Dacier, "of the theatre, or of character, or of the
passions; he understood neither the reasons nor
the method of Aristotle; and he sought rather to
contradict Aristotle than to explain him."[3] The
fact is that Castelvetro, despite considerable veneration for Aristotle's authority, often shows remark-

---

[1] *De Poeta*, p. 43 *sq.*

[2] *Ibid.* p. 173. *Cf.* Milton's phrase, " vain and amatorious
poem."

[3] Dacier, 1692, p. xvii.

able independence of thought; and so far from resting content, in his commentary, with the mere explanation of the details of the *Poetics*, he has attempted to deduce from it a more or less complete theory of poetic art.   Accordingly, though diverging from many of the details, and still more from the spirit of the *Poetics*, he has, as it were, built up a dramatic system of his own, founded upon certain modifications and misconceptions of the Aristotelian canons.   The fundamental idea of this system is quite modern; and it is especially interesting because it indicates that by this time the drama had become more than a mere academic exercise, and was actually regarded as intended primarily for representation on the stage.   Castelvetro examines the physical conditions of stage representation, and on this bases the requirements of dramatic literature.   The fact that the drama is intended for the stage, that it is to be acted, is at the bottom of his theory of tragedy, and it was to this notion, as will be seen later, that we are to attribute the origin of the unities of time and place.

But Castelvetro's method brings with it its own *reductio ad absurdum*.   For after all, stage representation, while essential to the production of dramatic literature, can never circumscribe the poetic power or establish its conditions.   The conditions of stage representation change, and must change, with the varying conditions of dramatic literature and the inventive faculty of poets, for truly great art makes, or at least fixes, its own conditions.   Besides, it is with what is permanent and

universal that the artist — the dramatic artist as
well as the rest — is concerned; and it is the
poetic, and not the dramaturgic, element that is
permanent and universal. " The power of tragedy,
we may be sure," says Aristotle, "is felt even apart
from representation and actors;"[1] and again: "The
plot [of a tragedy] ought to be so constructed that
even without the aid of the eye any one who is
told the incidents will thrill with horror and pity
at the turn of events."[2]

But what, according to Castelvetro, are the conditions of stage representation? The theatre is a
public place, in which a play is presented before a
motley crowd, — *la moltitudine rozza*, — upon a circumscribed platform or stage, within a limited
space of time. To this idea the whole of Castelvetro's dramatic system is conformed. In the first
place, since the audience may be great in number,
the theatre must be large, and yet the audience
must be able to hear the play; accordingly, verse is
added, not merely as a delightful accompaniment,
but also in order that the actors may raise their
voices without inconvenience and without loss of
dignity.[3] In the second place, the audience is not
a select gathering of choice spirits, but a motley
crowd of people, drawn to the theatre for the purpose of pleasure or recreation; accordingly, abstruse themes, and in fact all technical discussions,
must be eschewed by the playwright, who is thus
limited, as we should say to-day, to the elemental

---

[1] *Poet.* vi. 19.   [2] *Poet.* xiv. 1.
[3] Castelvetro, *Poetica*, p. 30.

passions and interests of man.[1] In the third place, the actors are required to move about on a raised and narrow platform; and this is the reason why deaths or deeds of violence, and many other things which cannot be acted on such a platform with convenience and dignity, should not be represented in the drama.[2] Furthermore, as will be seen later, it is on this conception of the circumscribed platform and the physical necessities of the audience and the actors, that Castelvetro bases his theory of the unities of time and place.

In distinguishing the different *genres*, Castelvetro openly differs with Aristotle. In the *Poetics*, Aristotle distinguishes men according as they are better than we are, or worse, or the same as we are; and from this difference the various species of poetry, tragic, comic, and epic, are derived. Castelvetro thinks this mode of distinction not only untrue, but even inconsistent with what Aristotle says later of tragedy. Goodness and badness are to be taken account of, according to Castelvetro, not to distinguish one form of poetry from another, but merely in the special case of tragedy, in so far as a moderate virtue, as Aristotle says, is best able to produce terror and pity. Poetry, as indeed Aristotle himself acknowledges, is not an imitation of character, or of goodness and badness, but of men acting; and the different kinds of poetry are distinguished, not by the goodness and badness, or the character, of the persons selected for imitation, but by their rank or condition alone. The great and all-pervading

---

[1] Castelvetro, *Poetica*, pp. 22, 23.   [2] *Ibid.* p. 57.

difference between royal and private persons is
what distinguishes tragedy and epic poetry on the
one hand from comedy and similar forms of poetry
on the other. It is rank, then, and not intellect,
character, action, — for these vary in men according
to their condition, — that differentiates one poetic
form from another; and the distinguishing mark
of rank on the stage, and in literature generally, is
the bearing of the characters, royal persons acting
with propriety, and meaner persons with impro-
priety.[1] Castelvetro has here escaped one pitfall,
only to fall into another; for while goodness and
badness cannot, from any æsthetic standpoint, be
made to distinguish the characters of tragedy from
those of comedy, — leaving out of consideration
here the question whether this was or was not the
actual opinion of Aristotle, — it is no less improper
to make mere outward rank or condition the distinguishing feature. Whether it be regarded as an
interpretation of Aristotle or as a poetic theory by
itself, Castelvetro's contention is, in either case,
equally untenable.

II. *The Function of Tragedy*

No passage in Aristotle's *Poetics* has been subjected to more discussion, and certainly no passage has been more misunderstood, than that in
which, at the close of his definition of tragedy, he
states its peculiar function to be that of effecting through pity and fear the proper purgation

[1] Castelvetro, *Poetica*, pp. 35, 36.

(κάθαρσις) of these emotions. The more probable
of the explanations of this passage are, as Twining
says,[1] reducible to two. The first of these gives to
Aristotle's *katharsis* an ethical meaning, attributing
the effect of the tragedy to its moral lesson and
example. This interpretation was a literary tradition of centuries, and may be found in such
diverse writers as Corneille and Lessing, Racine
and Dryden, Dacier and Rapin. According to the
second interpretation, the purgation of the emotions
produced by tragedy is an emotional relief gained
by the excitement of these emotions. Plato had
insisted that the drama excites passions, such as
pity and fear, which debase men's spirits; Aristotle in this passage answers that by the very
exaltation of these emotions they are given a pleasurable outlet, and beyond this there is effected a
purification of the emotions so relieved. That is,
the emotions are clarified and purified by being
passed through the medium of art, and by being, as
Professor Butcher points out, ennobled by objects
worthy of an ideal emotion.[2] This explanation
gives no direct moral purpose or influence to the
katharsis, for tragedy acts on the feelings and not
on the will. While the ethical conception, of course,
predominates in Italian criticism, as it does throughout Europe up to the very end of the eighteenth
century, a number of Renaissance critics, among
them Minturno and Speroni, even if they failed to
elaborate the further æsthetic meaning of Aristotle's
definition, at least perceived that Aristotle ascribed

[1] Twining, ii. 3.   [2] Butcher, ch. vi

to tragedy an emotional and not an ethical purpose.
It is unnecessary to give a detailed statement of the
opinions of the various Italian critics on this point;
but it is essential that the interpretations of the
more important writers should be alluded to, since
otherwise the Renaissance conception of the function of the drama could not be understood.

Giraldi Cintio points out that the aim of comedy
and of tragedy is identical, viz. to conduce to virtue; but they reach this result in different ways;
for comedy attains its end by means of pleasure
and comic jests, while tragedy, whether it ends
happily or unhappily, purges the mind of vice
through the medium of misery and terror, and thus
attains its moral end.[1] Elsewhere,[2] he affirms that
the tragic poet condemns vicious actions, and by
combining them with the terrible and the miserable
makes us fear and hate them.   In other words,
men who are bad are placed in such pitiable and
terrible positions that we fear to imitate their
vices; and it is not a purgation of pity and fear,
as Aristotle says, but an eradication of all vice and
vicious desire that is effected by the tragic *katharsis*.
Trissino, in the fifth section of his *Poetica* (1563),
cites Aristotle's definition of tragedy; but makes
no attempt to elucidate the doctrine of *katharsis*.
His conception of the function of the drama is
much the same as Giraldi's.   It is the office of the
tragic poet, through the medium of imitation, to
praise and admire the good, while that of the comic
poet is to mock and vituperate the bad; for tragedy,

---

[1] Giraldi Cintio, ii. 12.   [2] *Ibid.* i. 66 *sq.*

as Aristotle says, deals with the better sort of actions, and comedy with the worse.[1]

Robortelli (1548), however, ascribes a more æsthetic function to tragedy. By the representation of sad and atrocious deeds, tragedy produces terror and commiseration in the spectator's mind. The exercise of terror and commiseration purges the mind of these very passions; for the spectator, seeing things performed which are very similar to the actual facts of life, becomes accustomed to sorrow and pity, and these emotions are gradually diminished.[2] Moreover, by seeing the sufferings of others, men sorrow less at their own, recognizing such things as common to human nature. Robortelli's conception of the function of tragedy is, therefore, not an ethical one; the effect of tragedy is understood primarily as diminishing pity and fear in our minds by accustoming us to the sight of deeds that produce these emotions. A similar interpretation of the *katharsis* is given by Vettori (1560) and Castelvetro (1570).[3] The latter compares the process of purgation with the emotions which are excited by a pestilence. At first the infected populace is crazed by excitement, but gradually becomes accustomed to the sight of the disease, and the emotions of the people are thus tempered and allayed.

A somewhat different conception of *katharsis* is that of Maggi. According to him, we are to under-

[1] Trissino, ii. 93 *sq.*
[2] Robortelli, p. 52 *sq.*
[3] Vettori, p. 56 *sq.*, and Castelvetro, *Poetica*, p. 117 *sq.*

stand by purgation the liberation through pity and
fear of passions similar to these, but not pity and
fear themselves; for Maggi cannot understand how
tragedy, which induces pity and fear in the hearer,
should at the same time remove these perturbations.[1] Moreover, pity and fear are useful emotions,
while such passions as avarice, lust, anger, are
certainly not. In another place, Maggi, relying on
citations from Plato, Aristotle, and Alexander of
Aphrodisias, explains the pleasure we receive from
tragedy, by pointing out that we feel sorrow by
reason of the human heart within us, which is
carried out of itself by the sight of misery; while
we feel pleasure because it is human and natural to
feel pity. Pleasure and pain are thus fundamentally the same.[2] Varchi[3] is at one with Maggi in
interpreting the *katharsis* as a purgation, not of
pity and fear themselves, but of emotions similar
to them.

For Scaliger (1561) the aim of tragedy, like that
of all poetry, is a purely ethical one. It is not
enough to move the spectators to admiration and
dismay, as some critics say Æschylus does; it
is also the poet's function to teach, to move, and
to delight. The poet teaches character through
actions, in order that we should embrace and imitate the good, and abstain from the bad. The joy

[1] Maggi, p. 97 *sq.*

[2] *Cf.* Shelley, *Defence of Poetry*, p. 35, " Tragedy delights
by affording a shadow of that pleasure which exists in pain."
etc.

[3] *Lezzioni*, p. 660.

of evil men is turned in tragedy to bitterness, and
the sorrow of good men to joy.[1] Scaliger is here
following the extreme view of poetic justice which
we have found expressed in so many of the Renaissance writers. In the last century, Dr. Johnson,
in censuring Shakespeare for the tragic fate meted
out to Cordelia and other blameless characters,
showed himself an inheritor of this Renaissance
tradition, just as we shall see that Lessing was in
other matters. For Scaliger the moral aim of the
drama is attained both indirectly, by the representation of wickedness ultimately punished and
virtue ultimately rewarded, and more directly by
the enunciation of moral precepts throughout the
play. With the Senecan model before him, such
precepts (*sententiæ*) became the very props of
tragedy, — *sunt enim quasi columnæ aut pilæ quæ-
dam universæ fabricæ illius,* — and so they remained
in modern classical tragedy. Minturno points out
that these *sententiæ* are to be used most in tragedy
and least in epic poetry.[2]

Minturno also follows Scaliger in conceiving that
the purpose of tragedy is to teach, to delight, and
to move. It teaches by setting before us an example of the life and manners of superior men, who
by reason of human error have fallen into extreme
unhappiness. It delights us by the beauty of its
verse, its diction, its song, and the like. Lastly, it
moves us to wonder, by terrifying us and exciting
our pity, thus purging our minds of such matters.
This process of purgation is likened by Minturno

[1] Scaliger, *Poet.* vii. i. 3; iii. 96.   [2] *Arte Poetica,* p. 287.

to the method of a physician: "As a physician eradicates, by means of poisonous medicine, the perfervid poison of disease which affects the body, so tragedy purges the mind of its impetuous perturbations by the force of these emotions beautifully expressed in verse." [1]

According to this interpretation of the *katharsis*, tragedy is a mode of homœopathic treatment, effecting the cure of one emotion by means of a similar one ; and we find Milton, in the preface to *Samson Agonistes*, explaining the *katharsis* in much the same manner : —

"Tragedy, as it was anciently composed, hath been ever held the gravest, moralest, and most profitable of all other poems ; therefore said by Aristotle to be of power, by raising pity and fear, or terror, to purge the mind of those and such like passions ; that is, to temper and reduce them to just measure with a kind of delight, stirred up by reading or seeing those passions well imitated. Nor is nature wanting in her own effects to make good his assertion ; for so in physic, things of melancholic hue and quality are used against melancholy, sour against sour, salt to remove salt humours."

This passage has been regarded by Twining, Bernays, and other modern scholars as a remarkable indication of Milton's scholarship and critical insight ; [2] but after all, it need hardly be said, he was merely following the interpretation of the Italian commentators on the *Poetics*. Their writings he had studied and knew thoroughly, had imbibed all the critical ideas of the Italian Renaissance, and in the very preface from which we have just quoted

[1] *Arte Poetica*, p. 77.   [2] Butcher, pp. 229, 230.

filled as it is with ideas that may be traced back
to Italian sources, he acknowledges following " the
ancients and Italians," as of great "authority and
fame." Like Milton, Minturno conceived of tragedy
as having an ethical aim; but both Milton and Minturno clearly perceived that by *katharsis* Aristotle
had reference not to a moral, but to an emotional,
effect.

One of the most interesting discussions on the
meaning of the *katharsis* is to be found in a letter
of Sperone Speroni[1] written in 1565. His explanation of the passage itself is quite an impossible one, if
only on philological grounds; but his argument is
very interesting and very modern. He points out
that pity and fear may be conceived of as keeping the spirit of men in bondage, and hence it is
proper that we should be purged of these emotions.
But he insists that Aristotle cannot refer to the
complete eradication of pity and fear — a conception
which is Stoic rather than Peripatetic, for Aristotle
does not require us to free ourselves from emotions,
but to regulate them, since in themselves they are
not bad.

III. *The Characters of Tragedy*

Aristotle's conception of the ideal tragic hero
is based on the assumption that the function of
tragedy is to produce the *katharsis*, or purgation,
of pity and fear, — "pity being felt for a person
who, if not wholly innocent, meets with suffering

[1] *Opere*, v. 178.

G

beyond his deserts ; fear being awakened when the sufferer is a man of like nature with ourselves." [1] From this it follows that if tragedy represents the fall of an entirely good man from prosperity to adversity, neither pity nor fear is produced, and the result merely shocks and repels us. If an entirely bad man is represented as undergoing a change from distress to prosperity, not only do we feel no pity and no fear, but even the sense of justice is left unsatisfied.   If, on the contrary, such a man entirely bad falls from prosperity into adversity and distress, the moral sense is indeed satisfied, but without the tragic emotions of pity and fear.   The ideal hero is therefore morally between the two extremes, neither eminently good nor entirely bad, though leaning to the side of goodness ; and the misfortune which falls upon him is the result of some great flaw of character or fatal error of conduct.[2]

This conception of the tragic hero was the subject of considerable discussion in the Renaissance ; in fact, the first instance in Italian criticism of the application of Aristotelian ideas to the theory of tragedy is perhaps to be found in the reference of Daniello (1536) to the tragic hero's fate.   Daniello, however, understood Aristotle's meaning very incompletely, for he points out that tragedy, in order to imitate most perfectly the miserable and the terrible, should not introduce just and virtuous men fallen into vice and injustice through the adversity of fortune, for this is more wicked than it is miser-

[1] Butcher, p. 280 *sq*   [2] *Poet.* xiii. 2, 3.

able and terrible, nor should evil men, on the contrary, be introduced as changed by prosperity into good and just men.[1]　Here Daniello conceives of tragedy as representing the change of a man from vice to virtue, or from virtue to vice, through the medium of prosperity or misfortune.　This is a curious misconception of Aristotle's meaning.　Aristotle refers, not to the ethical effect of tragedy, but to the effect of the emotions of pity and terror upon the mind of the spectator, although of course he does not wish the catastrophe to shock the moral sense or the sense of justice.

Giraldi Cintio, some years after Daniello, follows Aristotle more closely in the conception of the tragic hero; and he affirms, moreover, that tragedy may end happily or unhappily so long as it inspires pity and terror.　Now, Aristotle has expressly stated his disapprobation of the happy ending of tragedy, for in speaking of tragedies with a double thread and a double catastrophe, that is, tragedies in which the good are ultimately rewarded and the bad punished, he shows that such a conclusion is decidedly against the general tragic effect.[2]　Scaliger's conception of the moral function of the tragic poet as rewarding virtue and punishing vice is therefore inconsistent with the Aristotelian conception; for, as Scaliger insists that every tragedy should end unhappily, it follows that only the good must survive and only the bad suffer.　Another critic of this time, Capriano (1555), points out that the fatal ending of tragedy is due to the inability

[1] Daniello, p. 38.　　　　[2] *Poet.* xiii. 7.

of certain illustrious men to conduct themselves
with prudence; and this is more in keeping with
Aristotle's true meaning.[1]

It has been seen that Aristotle regarded a perfectly good man as not fitted to be the ideal hero
of tragedy. Minturno, however, asserts that tragedy
is grave and illustrious because its characters are
illustrious, and that therefore he can see no reason,
despite Aristotle, why the lives of perfect men or
Christian saints should not be represented on the
stage, and why even the life of Christ would not
be a fit subject for tragedy.[2] This is, indeed, Corneille's opinion, and in the *examen* of his *Polyeucte*
he cites Minturno in justification of his own case.
As regards the other characters of tragedy, Minturno states a curious distinction between characters fit for tragedy and those fit for comedy.[3] In
the first place, he points out that no young girls,
with the exception of female slaves, should appear
in comedy, for the reason that the women of the
people do not appear in public until marriage, and
would be sullied by the company of the low characters of comedy, whereas the maidens of tragedy
are princesses, accustomed to meet and converse
with noblemen from girlhood. Secondly, married
women are always represented in comedy as faith-
ful, in tragedy as unfaithful to their husbands, for
the reason that comedy concludes with friendship

[1] *Della Vera Poetica*, cap. iii.
[2] *De Poeta*, p. 182 *sq*.
[3] *Arte Poetica*, p. 118 *sq*.; also in Scaliger and Giraldi
Cintio.

and tranquillity, and unfaithful relations could never end happily, while the love depicted in tragedy serves to bring about the tragic ruin of great houses. Thirdly, in comedy old men are often represented as in love, but never in tragedy, for an amorous old man is conducive to laughter, which comedy aims at producing, but which would be wholly out of keeping with the gravity required in tragedy. These distinctions are of course deduced from the practice of the Latin drama — the tragedies of Seneca on the one hand, and the comedies of Plautus and Terence on the other.

In a certain passage of Aristotle's *Poetics* there is a formulation of the requirements of character-drawing in the drama.[1] In this passage Aristotle says that the characters must be good; that they must be drawn with propriety, that is, in keeping with the type to which they belong; that they must be true to life, something quite distinct either from goodness or propriety; and that the characters must be self-consistent. This passage gave rise to a curious conception of character in the Renaissance and throughout the period of classicism. According to this, the conception of *decorum*, it was insisted that every old man should have such and such characteristics, every young man certain others, and so on for the soldier, the merchant, the Florentine or Parisian, and the like. This fixed and formal mode of regarding character was connected with the distinction of rank as the fundamental difference between the characters of

[1] *Poet.* xv. 1–5.

tragedy and comedy, and it was really founded on a passage in Horace's *Ars Poetica*, —

" Ætatis cujusque notandi sunt tibi mores," [1]

and on the rhetorical descriptions of the various characteristics of men in the second book of Aristotle's *Rhetoric*.

The explanation of the Renaissance conception of *decorum* may start from either of two points of view. In the first place, it is to be noted that Horace, and after him the critics of the Renaissance, set about to transpose to the domain of poetry the tentative distinctions of character formulated by Aristotle, in the *Rhetoric*, simply for the purposes of rhetorical exposition. These distinctions, it must be repeated, were rhetorical and not æsthetic, and they are therefore not alluded to by Aristotle in the *Poetics*. The result of the attempt to transpose them to the domain of poetry led to a hardening and crystallization of character in the classic drama. But the æsthetic misconception implied by such an attempt is only too obvious. In such a system poetry is held accountable, not to the ideal truth of human life, but to certain arbitrary, or at best merely empirical, formulæ of rhetorical theory. The Renaissance was in this merely doing for character what was being done for all the other elements of art. Every such element, when once discriminated and definitely formulated, became fixed as a necessary and inviolable substitute for the reality which had thus been analyzed.

[1] *Ars Poet.* 154 *sq.*

But we may look at the principle of *decorum* from another point of view.   A much deeper question — the question of social distinctions — is here involved.   The observance of *decorum* necessitated the maintenance of the social distinctions which formed the basis of Renaissance life and of Renaissance literature.   It was this same tendency which caused the tragedy of classicism to exclude all but characters of the highest rank.   Speaking of narrative poetry, Muzio (1551), while allowing kings to mingle with the masses, considers it absolutely improper for one of the people, even for a moment, to assume the sceptre.[1]   Accordingly, men as distinguished by the accidents of rank, profession, country, and not as distinguished by that only which art should take cognizance of, character, became the subjects of the literature of classicism; and in so far as this is true, that literature loses something of the profundity and the universality of the highest art.

This element of *decorum* is to be found in all the critics of the Renaissance from the time of Vida[2] and Daniello.[3]   So essential became the observance of *decorum* that Muzio and Capriano both considered it the most serious charge to be made against Homer, that he was not always observant of it.   Capriano, comparing Virgil with Homer, asserts that the Latin poet surpasses the Greek in eloquence, in dignity, in grandeur of style, but beyond everything in *decorum*.[4]   The seeming vulgarity

[1] Muzio, p. 80.   [3] *Poetica*, p. 36 *sq.*
[2] Pope, i. 165.   [4] Capriano, *op. cit.*, cap. v

of some of Homer's similes, and even of the
actions of some of his characters, appeared to the
Renaissance a most serious blemish; and it was
this that led Scaliger to rate Homer not only below
Virgil, but even below Musæus. In Minturno and
Scaliger we find every detail of character minutely
analyzed. The poet is told how young men and old
men should act, should talk, and should dress; and
no deviations from these fixed formulæ were allowed
under any circumstances. As a result of this, even
when the poet liberated himself from these conceptions, and aimed at depicting character in its true
sense, we find character, but never the development
of character, portrayed in the neo-classic drama.
The character was fixed from the beginning of the
play to the end; and it is here that we may find
the origin of Ben Jonson's conception of "humours." In one of Salviati's lectures, *Del Trattato
della Poetica*,[1] Salviati defines a humour as "a
peculiar quality of nature according to which every
one is inclined to some special thing more than to
any other." This would apply very distinctly to
the sense in which the Elizabethans used the word.
Thus Jonson himself, in the Induction of *Every
Man out of his Humour*, after expounding the med-
ical notion of a humour, says : —

> "It may, by metaphor, apply itself
> Unto the general disposition :
> As when some one peculiar quality
> Doth so possess a man, that it doth draw
> All his effects, his spirits, and his powers,

[1] Cod. Magliabechiano, vii. 7, 715.

> In their confluctions, all to run one way,
> This may be truly said to be a humour."

The origin of the term "humour," in Jonson's sense, has never been carefully studied. Jonson's editors speak of it as peculiar to the English language, and as first used in this sense about Jonson's period. It is not our purpose to go further into this question; but Salviati's definition is close enough to Jonson's to indicate that the origin of this term, as of all other critical terms and critical ideas throughout sixteenth-century Europe, must be looked for in the æsthetic literature of Italy.[1]

IV. *The Dramatic Unities*

In his definition of tragedy Aristotle says that the play must be complete or perfect, that is, it must have unity. By unity of plot he does not mean merely the unity given by a single hero, for, as he says, "infinitely various are the incidents in one man's life which cannot be reduced to unity; and so, too, there are many actions of one man out of which we cannot make one action. Hence the error, as it appears, of all poets who have composed a Heracleid, a Theseid, or other poems of the kind. They imagine that as Heracles was one man, the story of Heracles ought also to be a unity."[2] This is Aristotle's statement of the unity of action. But

---

[1] Another expression of Jonson's, "small Latin and less Greek," may perhaps be traced to Minturno's "poco del Latino e pochissimo del Greco," *Arte Poetica*, p. 158.

[2] *Poet.* viii. 1–4.

what is the origin of the two other unities, — the
unities of time and place?   There is in the *Poetics*
but a single reference to the time-limit of the tragic
action and none whatsoever to the so-called unity
of place.   Aristotle says that the action of tragedy and that of epic poetry differ in length, "for
tragedy endeavors, so far as possible, to confine
itself to a single revolution of the sun, or but
slightly to exceed this limit; whereas the epic
action has no limits of time." [1]   This passage is the
incidental statement of an historical fact; it is
merely a tentative deduction from the usual practice of Greek tragedy, and Aristotle never conceived of it as an inviolable law of the drama.   Of
the three unities which play so prominent a part in
modern classical drama, the unity of action was the
main, and, in fact, the only unity which Aristotle
knew or insisted on.   But from his incidental reference to the general time-limits of Greek tragedy,
the Renaissance formulated the unity of time, and
deduced from it also the unity of place, to which
there is absolutely no reference either in Aristotle
or in any other ancient writer whatever.   It is to the
Italians of the Renaissance, and not to the French
critics of the seventeenth century, that the world
owes the formulation of the three unities.   The
attention of scholars was first called to this fact
about twenty years ago, by the brochure of a Swiss
scholar, H. Breitinger, on the unities of Aristotle
before Corneille's *Cid;* but the gradual development and formulation of the three unities have

[1] *Poet.* v. 4.

never been systematically worked out. We shall endeavor here to trace their history during the sixteenth century, and to explain the processes by which they developed.

The first reference in modern literature to the doctrine of the unity of time is to be found in Giraldi Cintio's *Discorso sulle Comedie e sulle Tragedie*. He says that comedy and tragedy agree, among other things, in the limitation of the action to one day or but little more;[1] and he has thus for the first time converted Aristotle's statement of an historical fact into a dramatic law. Moreover, he has changed Aristotle's phrase, that tragedy limits itself "to a single revolution of the sun," into the more definite expression of "a single day." He points out that Euripides, in the *Heraclidœ*, on account of the long distance between the places in the action, had been unable to limit the action to one day. Now, as Aristotle must have known many of the best Greek dramas which are now lost, it was probably in keeping with the practice of such dramas that their actions were not strictly confined within the limits of one day. Aristotle, therefore, intentionally allowed the drama a slightly longer space of time than a single day. The unity of time, accordingly, becomes a part of the theory of the drama between 1540 and 1545, but it was not until almost exactly a century later that it became an invariable rule of the dramatic literature of France and of the world.

In Robortelli (1548) we find Aristotle's phrase,

[1] Giraldi Cintio, ii. 10 *sq.*

"a single revolution of the sun," restricted to the
artificial day of twelve hours; for as tragedy can
contain only one single and continuous action, and as
people are accustomed to sleep in the night, it follows
that the tragic action cannot be continued beyond
one artificial day. This holds good of comedy as
well as tragedy, for the length of the fable in each is
the same.[1] Segni (1549) differs from Robortelli,
however, in regarding a single revolution of the sun
as referring not to the artificial day of twelve hours,
but to the natural day of twenty-four hours, because
various matters treated in tragedy, and even in
comedy, are such as are more likely to happen
in the night (adulteries, murders, and the like);
and if it be said that night is naturally the time for
repose, Segni answers that unjust people act contrary to the laws of nature.[2] It was about this
time, then, that there commenced the historic controversy as to what Aristotle meant by limiting
tragedy to one day; and three-quarters of a century
later, in 1623, Beni could cite thirteen different
opinions of scholars on this question.

Trissino, in his *Poetica* (1563), paraphrases as
follows the passage in Aristotle which refers to
the unity of time: "They also differ in length,
for tragedy terminates in one day, that is, one
period of the sun, or but little more, while there is
no time determined for epic poetry, as indeed was
the custom with tragedy and comedy at their be-

[1] Robortelli, pp. 50, 275, and appendix, p. 45. *Cf.* Luisino's
Commentary on Horace's *Ars Poetica*, 1554, p. 40.
[2] B. Segni, p. 170 v.

ginning, and is even to-day among ignorant poets." [1]
Here for the first time, as a French critic remarks,
the observance of the unity of time is made a distinction between the learned and the ignorant
poet.[2] It is evident that Trissino conceives of the
unity of time as an artistic principle which has
helped to save dramatic poetry from the formlessness and chaotic condition of the mediæval drama.
So that the unity of time became not only a dramatic law, but one the observation of which distinguished the dramatic artist from the mere ignorant
compiler of popular plays.

There is in none of the writers we have mentioned so far any reference to the unity of place,
for the simple reason that there is no allusion to
such a requirement for the drama in Aristotle's
Poetics. Maggi's discussion of the unity of time,
in his commentary on the *Poetics* (1550), is of
particular interest as preparing the way for the
third unity. Maggi attempts to explain logically
the reason for the unity of time.[3] Why should
tragedy be limited as to time, and not epic poetry?
According to him, this difference is to be explained
by the fact that the drama is represented on the
stage before our eyes, and if we should see the actions of a whole month performed in about the
time it takes to perform the play, that is, two or
three hours, the performance would be absolutely
incredible. For example, says Maggi, if in a tragedy we should send a messenger to Egypt, and he
would return in an hour, would not the spectator

[1] Trissino, ii. 95.   [2] Brunetière, i. 69.   [3] Maggi, p. 94.

regard this as ridiculous ? In the epic, on the contrary, we do not see the actions performed, and so
do not feel the need of limiting them to any particular time. Now, it is to be noted here that this
limitation of time is based on the idea of representation. The duration of the action of the drama
itself must fairly coincide with the duration of its
representation on the stage. This is the principle
which led to the acceptance of the unity of place,
and upon which it is based. Limit the time of the
action to the time of representation, and it follows
that the place of the action must be limited to the
place of representation. Such a limitation is of
course a piece of realism wholly out of keeping
with the true dramatic illusion ; but it was almost
exclusively in the drama that classicism tended
toward a minuter realism than could be justified by
the Aristotelian canons. In Maggi the beginnings
of the unity of place are evident, inasmuch as he
finds that the requirements of the representation
do not permit a messenger or any character in the
drama to be sent very far from the place where the
action is being performed. The closer action and
representation coincide, the clearer becomes the necessity of a limitation in place as well as in time ;
and it was on this principle that Scaliger and
Castelvetro, somewhat later, formulated the three
unities.

There is, indeed, in Scaliger (1561) no direct
statement of the unity of time ; but the reference
to it is nevertheless unmistakable. First of all,
Scaliger requires that the events be so arranged

and disposed that they approach nearest to actual
truth (*ut quam proxime accedant ad veritatem*).[1]
This is equivalent to saying that the duration of
the action, its place, its mode of procedure, must
correspond more or less exactly with the representation itself. The dramatic poet must aim, beyond
all things, at reproducing the actual conditions of
life. The *verisimile*, the *vraisemblable*, in the ety-
mological sense of these words, must be the final
criterion of dramatic composition. It is not sufficient that the spectator should be satisfied with
the action as typical of similar actions in life. An
absolutely perfect illusion must prevail; the spectator must be moved by the actions of the play
exactly as if they were those of real life.

This notion of the *verisimile*, and of its effect of
perfect illusion on the spectator's mind, prevailed
throughout the period of classicism, and was vigorously defended by no less a critic than Voltaire
himself. Accordingly, as Maggi first pointed out,
if the playwright, in the few hours it takes to
represent the whole play, requires one of his characters to perform an action that cannot be done in
less than a month, this impression of actual truth
and perfect illusion will not be left on the spectator's mind. "Therefore," says Scaliger, "those
battles and assaults which take place about Thebes
in the space of two hours do not please me; no sensible poet should make any one move from Delphi
to Thebes, or from Thebes to Athens, in a mo-

<hr />

[1] Scaliger, iii. 96. So Robortelli, p. 53, speaks of tragedy as
representing things *quæ multum accedunt ad veritatem ipsam.*

ment's time. Agamemnon is buried by Æschylus
after being killed, and Lichas is hurled into the
sea by Hercules; but this cannot be represented
without violence to truth. Accordingly, the poet
should choose the briefest possible argument, and
should enliven it by means of episodes and details.
. . . Since the whole play is represented on the
stage in six or eight hours, it is not in accordance
with the exact appearance of truth (*haud verisimile
est*) that within that brief space of time a tempest
should arise and a shipwreck occur, out of sight of
land."

The observance of the unity of time could not
be demanded in clearer or more forcible terms
than this. But it is a mistake to construe this
passage into a statement of the unity of place.[1]
When Scaliger says that the poet should not move
any one of the characters from Delphi to Thebes,
or from Thebes to Athens, in a moment's time, he
is referring to the exigencies, not of place, but of
time. In this, as in many other things, he is merely
following Maggi, who, as we have seen, says that
it is ridiculous for a dramatist to have a messenger
go to Egypt with a message and return in an hour.
The characters, according to Scaliger, should not
move from Delphi to Thebes in a moment, not
because the action need necessarily occur in one
single place, but because the characters cannot
with any appearance of truth go a great distance
in a short space of time. This is an approach to
the unity of place, and had Scaliger followed his

---

[1] *E.g.* Lintilhac, *De Scal. Poet.* p. 32.

contention to its logical conclusion, he must certainly have formulated the three unities. But by requiring the action to be disposed with the greatest possible approach to the actual truth, or, in other words, by insisting that the action must coincide with the representation, Scaliger helped more than any of his predecessors to the final recognition of the unity of place.

In Minturno [1] and in Vettori [2] we find a tendency to restrict the duration of the epic as well as the tragic action. It has been seen that Aristotle distinctly says that while the action of tragedy generally endeavors to confine itself within a period of about one day, that of epic poetry has no determined time. Minturno, however, alludes to the unity of time in the following words: "Whoever examines well the works of the most esteemed ancient writers, will find that the action represented on the stage is terminated in one day, or does not pass beyond the space of two days; while the epic has a longer period of time, except that its action cannot exceed one year in duration." [3] This limitation Minturno deduces from the practice of Homer and Virgil. [4] The action of the *Iliad* begins in the tenth year of the Trojan war, and lasts one year; the action of the *Æneid* begins in the seventh year after the departure of Æneas from Troy, and also lasts one year.

Castelvetro, however, was the first theorist to formulate the unity of place, and thus to give the

[1] *De Poeta*, pp. 185, 281.   [3] *Arte Poet.* pp. 71, 117.
[2] Vettori, p. 250.   [4] *Ibid.* p. 12.

H

three unities their final form. We have seen that
Castelvetro's theory of the drama was based entirely
upon the notion of stage representation. All the
essentials of dramatic literature are thus fixed by
the exigencies of the stage. The stage is a circumscribed space, and the play must be performed upon
it within a period of time limited by the physical
necessities of the spectators. It is from these two
facts that Castelvetro deduces the unities of time
and place. While asserting that Aristotle held it
as *cosa fermissima e verissima* that the tragic action
cannot exceed the length of an artificial day of
twelve hours, he does not think that Aristotle himself understood the real reason of this limitation.[1]
In the seventh chapter of the *Poetics* Aristotle says
that the length of the plot is limited by the possibility of its being carried in the memory of the
spectator conveniently at one time. But this, it is
urged, would restrict the epic as well as the tragic
fable to one day. The difference between epic and
dramatic poetry in this respect is to be found in the
essential difference between the conditions of narrative and scenic poetry.[2] Narrative poetry can in
a short time narrate things that happen in many
days or months or even years; but scenic poetry,
which spends as many hours in representing things
as it actually takes to do them in life, does quite
otherwise. In epic poetry words can present to
our intellect things distant in space and time; but
in dramatic poetry the whole action occurs before
our eyes, and is accordingly limited to what we can

[1] Castelvetro, *Poetica*, pp 157, 170.   [2] *Ibid.* pp 57, 109.

actually see with our own senses, that is, to that
brief duration of time and to that small amount of
space in which the actors are occupied in acting, and
not any other time or place.   But as the restricted
place is the stage, so the restricted time is that in
which the spectators can at their ease remain sitting
through a continuous performance; and this time,
on account of the physical necessities of the spectators, such as eating, drinking, and sleeping, cannot
well go beyond the duration of one revolution of the
sun.   So that not only is the unity of time an
essential dramatic requirement, but it is in fact impossible for the dramatist to do otherwise even
should he desire to do so — a conclusion which is
of course the *reductio ad absurdum* of the whole
argument.

In another place Castelvetro more briefly formulates the law of the unities in the definitive form
in which it was to remain throughout the period
of classicism: " La mutatione tragica non può
tirar con esso seco se non una giornata e un
luogo. " [1]   The unities of time and place are for
Castelvetro so very important that the unity of
action, which is for Aristotle the only essential of
the drama, is entirely subordinated to them.   In
fact, Castelvetro specifically says that the unity of
action is not essential to the drama, but is merely
made expedient by the requirements of time and
place.   " In comedy and tragedy," he says, " there
is usually one action, not because the fable is un-
fitted to contain more than one action, but because

[1] Castelvetro, *Poetica*, p. 534.   *Cf.* Boileau, *Art Poét.* iii. 45.

the restricted space in which the action is represented, and the limited time, twelve hours at the
very most, do not permit of a multitude of actions."[1] In a similar manner Castelvetro applies
the law of the unities to epic poetry. Although
the epic action can be accomplished in many places
and at diverse times, yet as it is more commendable
and pleasurable to have a single action, so it is
better for the action to confine itself to a short time
and to but few places. In other words, the more
the epic attempts to restrict itself to the unities of
place and time, the better, according to Castelvetro,
it will be.[2] Moreover, Castelvetro was not merely
the first one to formulate the unities in their definitive form, but he was also the first to insist upon
them as inviolable laws of the drama; and he
refers to them over and over again in the pages of
his commentary on the *Poetics*.[3]

This then is the origin of the unities. Our discussion must have made it clear how little they
deserve the traditional title of Aristotelian unities,
or as a recent critic with equal inaccuracy calls
them, the Scaligerian unities (*unités scaligériennes*).[4]
Nor were they, as we have seen, first formulated in
France, though this was the opinion of the seventeenth and eighteenth centuries. Thus Dryden
says that "the unity of place, however it might be

[1] Castelvetro, *Poetica*, p. 179.

[2] *Ibid.* pp. 534, 535.

[3] Other allusions to the unities, besides those already mentioned, will be found in Castelvetro, *Poetica*, pp. 163-165, 168-
171, 191, 397, 501, 527, 531-536, 692, 697, etc.

[4] Lintilhac, in the *Nouvelle Revue*, lxiv. 541.

practised by the ancients, was never one of their rules: we neither find it in Aristotle, Horace, or any who have written of it, till in our age the French poets first made it a precept of the stage." [1] It may be said, therefore, that just as the unity of action is *par excellence* the Aristotelian unity, so the unities of time and place are beyond a doubt the Italian unities. They enter the critical literature of Europe from the time of Castelvetro, and may almost be said to be the last contributions of Italy to literary criticism. Two years after their formulation by Castelvetro they were introduced into France, and a dozen years after this formulation, into England. It was not until 1636, however, that they became fixed in modern dramatic literature, as a result of the *Cid* controversy. This is approximately a hundred years after the first mention of the unity of time in Italian criticism.

V. *Comedy*

The treatment of comedy in the literary criticism of this period is entirely confined to a discussion and elaboration of the little that Aristotle says on the subject of comedy in the *Poetics*. Aristotle, it will be remembered, had distinguished tragedy from comedy in that the former deals with the nobler, the latter with the baser, sort of actions. Comedy is an imitation of characters of a lower type than those of tragedy, — characters of a lower type indeed, but not in the full sense of the word bad.

---

[1] *Essay of Dramatic Poesy*, p. 31.

"The ludicrous is merely a subdivision of the ugly. It may be defined as a defect or ugliness which is not painful or destructive. Thus, for example, the comic mask is ugly and distorted, but does not cause pain."[1] From these few hints the Italian theorists constructed a body of comic doctrine. There is, however, in the critical literature of this period no attempt to explain the theory of the indigenous Italian comedy, the *commedia dell' arte*. The classical comedies of Plautus and Terence were the models, and Aristotle's *Poetics* the guide, of all the discussions on comedy during the Renaissance. The distinction between the characters of comedy and tragedy has already been explained in sufficient detail. All that remains to be done in treating of comedy is to indicate as briefly as possible such definitions of it as were formulated by the Renaissance, and the special function which the Renaissance understood comedy to possess.

According to Trissino (1563), the comic poet deals only with base things, and for the single purpose of chastising them. As tragedy attains its moral end through the medium of pity and fear, comedy does so by means of the chastisement and vituperation of things that are base and evil.[2] The comic poet, however, is not to deal with all sorts of vices, but only such as give rise to ridicule, that is, the jocose actions of humble and unknown persons. Laughter proceeds from a certain delight or pleasure arising from the sight of objects of ugliness.

[1] *Poet.* v. 1. *Cf. Rhet.* iii. 18.
[2] Trissino, ii. 120. *Cf.* Butcher, p. 203 *sq.*

We do not laugh at a beautiful woman, a gorgeous
jewel, or beautiful music; but a distortion or de-
formity, such as a silly speech, an ugly face, or a
clumsy movement, makes us laugh. We do not
laugh at the benefits of others; the finder of a
purse, for example, arouses not laughter but envy.
But we do laugh at some one who has fallen into
the mud, because, as Lucretius says, it is sweet to
find in others some evil not to be found in ourselves.
Yet great evils, so far from causing us to laugh,
arouse pity and fear, because we are apprehensive
lest such things should happen to us. Hence we
may conclude that a slight evil which is neither sad
nor destructive, and which we perceive in others but
do not believe to be in ourselves, is the primary
cause of the ludicrous.[1] In Maggi's treatise, *De
Ridiculis*, appended to his commentary on the
Poetics, the Aristotelian conception of the ridiculous
is accepted, with the addition of the element of
admiratio. Maggi insists on the idea of suddenness
or novelty; for we do not laugh at painless ugliness
if it be very familiar or long continued.[2]

According to Robortelli (1548), comedy, like all
other forms of poetry, imitates the manners and
actions of men, and aims at producing laughter and

---

[1] Trissino, ii. 127–130. Trissino seems to follow Cicero, *De Orat.*
ii. 58 *sq.* It is to these Italian discussions of the ludicrous that
the theory of laughter formulated by Hobbes, and after him by
Addison, owes its origin. For Renaissance discussions of wit
and humor before the introduction of Aristotle's *Poetics*, *cf.* the
third and fourth books of Pontano's *De Sermone*, and the second
book of Castiglione's *Cortigiano*.

[2] Maggi, p. 307. *Cf.* Hobbes, *Human Nature*, 1650, ix. 13.

light-heartedness. But what produces laughter ?
The evil and obscene merely disgust good men ; the
sad and miserable cause pity and fear. The basis
of laughter is therefore to be found in what is only
slightly mean or ugly (*subturpiculum*). The object
of comedy, according to the consensus of Renaissance opinion, is therefore to produce laughter for
the purpose of rendering the minor vices ridiculous.
Muzio (1551) indeed complains, as both Sidney and
Ben Jonson do later, that the comic writers of his
day were more intent on producing laughter than
on depicting character or manners : —

> " Intenta al riso
> Più ch' a i costumi."

But Minturno points out that comedy is not to be
contemned because it excites laughter ; for by comic
hilarity the spectators are kept from becoming
buffoons themselves, and by the ridiculous light in
which amours are placed, are made to avoid such
things in future. Comedy is the best corrective
of men's morals; it is indeed what Cicero calls it,
*imitatio vitæ, speculum consuetudinis, imago verita-
tis.* This phrase, ascribed by Donatus to Cicero,
runs through all the dramatic discussions of the
Renaissance,[1] and finds its echo in a famous passage in *Hamlet.* Cervantes cites the phrase in *Don
Quixote* ;[2] and Il Lasca, in the prologue to *L'Arzi-
goglio,* berates the comic writers of his day after
this fashion : " They take no account of the absurdities, the contradictions, the inequalities, and

---

[1] *Cf.* B. Tasso, ii. 515; Robortelli, p. 2; etc.
[2] *Don Quix.* iv. 21.

the discrepancies of their pieces; for they do not seem to know that comedy should be truth's image, the ensample of manners, and the mirror of life."

This is exactly what Shakespeare is contending for when he makes Hamlet caution the players not to " o'erstep the modesty of nature; for anything so overdone is from the purpose of playing, whose end, both at the first and now, was and is, to hold as 'twere the mirror up to nature; to show virtue her own feature, scorn her own image, and the very age and body of the time his form and pressure." [1]

The high importance which Scaliger (1561) gives to comedy, and in fact to satiric and didactic poetry in general, is one of many indications of the incipient formation of neo-classical ideals during the Renaissance. He regards as absurd the statement which he conceives Horace to have made, that comedy is not really poetry; on the contrary, it is the true form of poetry, and the first and highest of all, for its matter is entirely invented by the poet.[2] He defines comedy as a dramatic poem filled with intrigue (*negotiosum*), written in popular style, and ending happily.[3] The characters in comedy are chiefly old men, slaves, courtesans, all in humble station or from small villages. The action begins rather turbulently, but ends happily, and the

[1] *Hamlet*, iii. 2.

[2] Scaliger, *Poet.* i. 2. Castiglione, in the second book of the *Cortigiano*, says that the comic writer, more than any other, expresses the true image of human life.

[3] *Poet.* i. 5.

style is neither high nor low. The typical themes
of comedy are " sports, banquets, nuptials, drunken
carousals, the crafty wiles of slaves, and the decep-
tion of old men." [1]

The theory of comedy in sixteenth-century Italy
was entirely classical, and the practice of the time
agrees with its theory. There are indeed to be
heard occasional notes of dissatisfaction and revolt,
especially in the prologues of popular plays. Il
Lasca, in the prologue to the *Strega*, defiantly protests against the inviolable authority of Aristotle
and Horace, and in the prologue to his *Gelosia* re-
serves the right to copy the manners of his own time,
and not those of Plautus and Terence. Cecchi,
Aretino, Gelli, and other comic writers give expression to similar sentiments.[2] But on the whole
these protests availed nothing. The authors of
comedy, and more especially the literary critics,
were guided by classical practice and classical theory. Dramatic forms like the improvised *commedia
dell' arte* had marked influence on the practice of
European comedy in general, especially in France,
but left no traces of their influence on the literary
criticism of the Italian Renaissance.

[1] *Poet.* iii. 96.

[2] Symonds, *Ren. in Italy*, v. 124 *sq.*, 533 *sq.* For Castelvetro's
theory of comedy, see A. Fusco, *La Poetica di Lodovico
Castelvetro*, Naples, 1904, p. 228 *sq.* Ben Jonson derived his
theory of laughter in comedy from Daniel Heinsius; *cf.* my
article in *Modern Philology*, 1905, ii. 451 *sq.*

CHAPTER IV

THE THEORY OF EPIC POETRY

EPIC poetry was held in the highest esteem during the Renaissance and indeed throughout the
period of classicism. It was regarded by Vida as
the highest form of poetry,[1] and a century later,
despite the success of tragedy in France, Rapin
still held the same opinion.[2] The reverence for
the epic throughout the Renaissance may be
ascribed in part to the mediæval veneration of
Virgil as a poet, and his popular apotheosis as
prophet and magician, and also in part to the
decay into which dramatic literature had fallen
during the Middle Ages in the hands of the wan-
dering players, the *histriones* and the *vagantes.*
Aristotle[3] indeed had regarded tragedy as the highest form of poetry; and as a result, the traditional
reverence for Virgil and Homer, and the Renaissance subservience to Aristotle, were distinctly at
variance. Trissino (1561) paraphrases Aristotle's
argument in favor of tragedy, but points out, not-
withstanding this, that the whole world is unani-
mous in considering Virgil and Homer greater than
any tragic poet before or after them.[4] Placed in

[1] Pope, i. 133.   [3] *Poet.* xxvi.
[2] Rapin, 1674, ii. 2.   [4] Trissino, ii. 118 *sq.*

this quandary, he concludes by leaving the reader
to judge for himself whether epic or tragedy be the
nobler form.

I. *The Theory of the Epic Poem*

Vida's *Ars Poetica*, written before 1520, although
no edition prior to that of 1527 is extant, is the
earliest example in modern times of that class
of critical poems to which belong Horace's *Ars
Poetica*, Boileau's *Art Poétique*, and Pope's *Essay
on Criticism*. Vida's poem is entirely based on that
of Horace; but he substitutes epic for Horace's
dramatic studies, and employs the *Æneid* as the
model of an epic poem. The incompleteness of the
treatment accorded to epic poetry in Aristotle's
Poetics led the Renaissance to deduce the laws of
heroic poetry and of poetic artifice in general from
the practice of Virgil; and it is to this point of
view that the critical works on the *Æneid* by Regolo
(1563), Maranta (1564), and Toscanella (1566) owe
their origin. The obvious and even accidental
qualities of Virgil's poem are enunciated by Vida
as fundamental laws of epic poetry. The precepts
thus given are purely rhetorical and pedagogic in
character, and deal almost exclusively with questions of poetic invention, disposition, polish, and
style. Beyond this Vida does not attempt to go.
There is in his poem no definition of the epic, no
theory of its function, no analysis of the essentials
of narrative structure. In fact, no theory of poetry
in any real sense is to be found in Vida's treatise.

Daniello (1536) deals only very cursorily with epic poetry, but his definition of it strikes the key-note of the Renaissance conception. Heroic poetry is for him an imitation of the illustrious deeds of emperors and other men magnanimous and valorous in arms,[1] — a conception that goes back to Horace's

" Res gestae regumque ducumque et tristia bella." [2]

Trissino (1563) first introduced the Aristotelian theory of the epic into modern literary criticism; and the sixth section of his *Poetica* is given up almost exclusively to the treatment of heroic poetry. The epic agrees with tragedy in dealing with illustrious men and illustrious actions. Like tragedy it must have a single action, but it differs from tragedy in not having the time of the action limited or determined. While unity of action is essential to the epic, and is indeed what distinguishes it from narrative poems that are not really epics, the Renaissance conceived of vastness of design and largeness of detail as necessary to the grandiose character of the epic poem.[3] Thus Muzio says: —

" Il poema sovrano è una pittura
De l' universo, e però in sè comprende
Ogni stilo, ogni forma, ogni ritratto."

Trissino regards *versi sciolti* as the proper metre for an heroic poem, since the stanzaic form impedes the continuity of the narrative. In this point he finds fault with Boccaccio, Boiardo, and Ariosto, whose romantic poems, moreover, he does not regard as epics, because they do not obey Aristotle's invio-

[1] Daniello, p. 34. [2] *Ars Poet.* 73. [3] Trissino, ii. 112 *sq.*

lable law of the single action. He also finds fault
with the romantic poets for describing the improbable, since Aristotle expressly prefers an impossible probability to an improbable possibility.

Minturno's definition of epic poetry is merely a
modification or paraphrase of Aristotle's definition
of tragedy. Epic poetry is an imitation of a grave
and noble deed, perfect, complete, and of proper
magnitude, with embellished language, but without
music or dancing; at times simply narrating and
at other times introducing persons in words and
actions; in order that, through pity and fear of the
things imitated, such passions may be purged from
the mind with both pleasure and profit.[1] Here
Minturno, like Giraldi Cintio, ascribes to epic
poetry the same purgation of pity and fear effected
by tragedy. Epic poetry he rates above tragedy,
since the epic poet, more than any other, arouses
that admiration of great heroes which it is the peculiar function of the poet to excite, and therefore
attains the end of poetry more completely than any
other poet. This, however, is true only in the highest form of narrative poetry; for Minturno distinguishes three classes of narrative poets, the lowest,
or *bucolici*, the mediocre, or *epici*, who have nothing
beyond verse, and the highest, or *heroici*, who imitate the life of a single hero in noble verse.[2] Minturno insists fundamentally on the unity of the
epic action; and directly against Aristotle's statement, as we have seen, he restricts the duration of
the action to one year. The license and prolixity

[1] *Arte Poetica*, p. 9.   [2] *De Poeta*, pp. 105, 106.

of the *romanzi* led the defenders of the classical
epic to this extreme of rigid circumspection. According to Scaliger, the epic, which is the norm by
which all other poems may be judged and the chief
of all poems, describes *heroum genus, vita, gesta.*[1]
This is the Horatian conception of the epic, and
there is in Scaliger little or no trace of the Aristotelian doctrine.   He also follows Horace closely in
forbidding the narrative poet to begin his poem
from the very beginning of his story (*ab ovo*), and
in various other details.

Castelvetro (1570) differs from Aristotle in regard
to the unity of the epic fable, on the ground that
poetry is merely imaginative history, and can
therefore do anything that history can do.   Poetry
follows the footsteps of history, differing merely in
that history narrates what has happened, while
poetry narrates what has never happened but yet
may possibly happen ; and therefore, since history
recounts the whole life of a single hero, without
regard to its unity, there is no reason why poetry
should not do likewise.   The epic may in fact deal
with many actions of one person, one action of a
whole race, or many actions of many people; it
need not necessarily deal with one action of one
person, as Aristotle enjoins, but if it does so it is
simply to show the ingenuity and excellence of the
poet.[2]

---

[1] *Poet.* iii. 95.
[2] Castelvetro, *Poetica*, p. 178 *sq.*

II. *Epic and Romance*

This discussion of epic unity leads to one of the most important critical questions of the sixteenth century, — the question of the unity of romance. Ariosto's *Orlando Furioso* and Boiardo's *Orlando Innamorato* were written before the Aristotelian canons had become a part of the critical literature of Italy. When it became clear that these poems diverged from the fundamental requirements of the epic as expounded in the *Poetics*, Trissino set out to compose an heroic poem which would be in perfect accord with the precepts of Aristotle. His *Italia Liberata*, which was completed by 1548, was the result of twenty years of study, and it is the first modern epic in the strict Aristotelian sense. With Aristotle as his guide, and Homer as his model, he had studiously and mechanically constructed an epic of a single action; and in the dedication of his poem to the Emperor Charles V. he charges all poems which violate this primary law of the single action with being merely bastard forms. The *romanzi*, and among them the *Orlando Furioso*, in seemingly disregarding this fundamental requirement, came under Trissino's censure; and this started a controversy which was not to end until the commencement of the next century, and in a certain sense may be said to remain undecided even to this day.

The first to take up the cudgels in defence of the writers of the *romanzi* was Giraldi Cintio, who in his youth had known Ariosto personally, and who wrote his *Discorso intorno al comporre dei Romanzi*, in April, 1549. The grounds of his defence are twofold. In the first place, Giraldi maintains that the romance is a poetic form of which Aristotle did not know, and to which his rules therefore do not apply; and in the second place, Tuscan literature, differing as it does from the literature of Greece in language, in spirit, and in religious feeling, need not and indeed ought not to follow the rules of Greek literature, but rather the laws of its own development and its own traditions. With Ariosto and Boiardo as models, Giraldi sets out to formulate the laws of the *romanzi*. The *romanzi* aim at imitating illustrious actions in verse, with the purpose of teaching good morals and honest living, since this ought to be the aim of every poet, as Giraldi conceives Aristotle himself to have said.[1] All heroic poetry is an imitation of illustrious actions, but Giraldi, like Castelvetro twenty years later, recognizes several distinct forms of heroic poetry, according as to whether it imitates one action of one man, many actions of many men, or many actions of one man. The first of these is the epic poem, the rules of which are given in Aristotle's *Poetics*. The second is the romantic poem, after the manner of Boiardo and Ariosto. The third is the biographical poem, after the manner of the *Theseid* and similar works dealing with the whole life of a single hero.

These forms are therefore to be regarded as three distinct and legitimate species of heroic poetry, the

[1] Giraldi Cintio, i. 11, 64.

I

first of them being an epic poem in the strict Aristotelian sense, and the two others coming under the
general head of *romanzi*. Of the two forms of
romanzi, the biographical deals preferably with an
historical subject, whereas the noblest writers of
the more purely romantic form, dealing with many
actions of many men, have invented their subject-
matter. Horace says that an heroic poem should
not commence at the very beginning of the hero's
life; but it is difficult to understand, says Giraldi,
why the whole life of a distinguished man, which
gives us so great and refined a pleasure in the works
of Plutarch and other biographers, should not please
us all the more when described in beautiful verse
by a good poet.[1] Accordingly, the poet who is
composing an epic in the strict sense should, in
handling the events of his narrative, plunge immediately *in medias res*. The poet dealing with
many actions of many men should begin with the
most important event, and the one upon which all
the others may be said to hinge; whereas the poet
describing the life of a single hero should begin at
the very beginning, if the hero spent a really heroic
youth, as Hercules for example did. The poem
dealing with the life of a hero is thus a separate
genre, and one for which Aristotle does not attempt
to lay down any laws. Giraldi even goes so far as
to say that Aristotle [2] censured those who write the
life of Theseus or Hercules in a single poem, not
because they dealt with many actions of one man,
but because they treated such a poem in exactly

[1] Giraldi Cintio, i. 24.   [2] *Poet.* viii. 2.

the same manner as those who dealt with a single
action of a single hero, — an assertion which is of
course utterly absurd. Giraldi then proceeds to
deal in detail with the disposition and composition
of the *romanzi,* which he rates above the classical
epics in the efficacy of ethical teaching. It is the
office of the poet to praise virtuous actions and to
condemn vicious actions; and in this the writers of
the *romanzi* are far superior to the writers of the
ancient heroic poems.[1]

Giraldi's discourse on the *romanzi* gave rise to a
curious dispute with his own pupil, Giambattista
Pigna, who published a similar work, entitled *I
Romanzi,* in the same year (1554). Pigna asserted
that he had suggested to Giraldi the main argument
of the discourse, and that Giraldi had adopted it as
his own. Without entering into the details of this
controversy, it would seem that the priority of
Giraldi cannot fairly be contested.[2] At all events,
there is a very great resemblance between the works
of Giraldi and Pigna. Pigna's treatise, however,
is more detailed than Giraldi's. In the first book,
Pigna deals with the general subject of the *romanzi;*
in the second he gives a life of Ariosto, and discusses the *Furioso,* point by point; in the third he
demonstrates the good taste and critical acumen of
Ariosto by comparing the first version of the *Furioso* with the completed and perfected copy.[3] Both

---

[1] Giraldi, i. 66 *sq.*

[2] *Cf.* Tiraboschi, vii. 947 *sq.*, and Giraldi, ii. 153 *sq.* Pigna's
own words are cited in Giraldi, i. p. xxiii.

[3] Canello, p. 306 *sq.*

Pigna and Giraldi consider the *romanzi* to constitute a new *genre*, unknown to the ancients, and
therefore not subject to Aristotle's rules. Giraldi's
sympathies were in favor of the biographical form
of the *romanzi*, and his poem, the *Ercole* (1557),
recounts the whole life of a single hero. Pigna,
who keeps closer to the tradition of Ariosto, regards the biographical form as not proper to poetry,
because too much like history.

These arguments, presented by Giraldi and Pigna,
were answered by Speroni, Minturno, and others.
Speroni pointed out that while it is not necessary
for the romantic poets to follow the rules prescribed
by the ancients, they cannot disobey the fundamental laws of poetry. "The *romanzi*," says
Speroni, "are epics, which are poems, or they are
histories in verse, and not poems."[1] That is, how
does a poem differ from a well-written historical
narrative, if the former be without organic unity?[2]
As to the whole discussion, it may be said here,
without attempting to pass judgment on Ariosto, or
any other writer of *romanzi*, that unity of some
sort every true poem must necessarily have; and,
flawless as the *Orlando Furioso* is in its details, the
unity of the poem certainly has not the obviousness
of perfect, and especially classical, art. A work of
art without organic unity may be compared with
an unsymmetrical circle; and, while the *Furioso* is
not to be judged by any arbitrary or mechanical
rules of unity, yet if it has not that internal unity
which transcends all mere external form, it may be

[1] Speroni, v. 521.   [2] *Cf.* Minturno, *De Poeta*, p. 151.

considered, as a work of art, hardly less than a
failure; and the farther it is removed from perfect unity, the more imperfect is the art. "Poetry
adapts itself to its times, but cannot depart from its
own fundamental laws." [1]

Minturno's answer to the defenders of the *romanzi*
is more detailed and explicit than Speroni's, and it
is of considerable importance because of its influence on Torquato Tasso's conception of epic poetry.
Minturno does not deny — and in this his point of
view is identical with Tasso's — that it is possible
to employ the matter of the *romanzi* in the composition of a perfect poem. The actions they describe
are great and illustrious, their knights and ladies
are noble and illustrious, too, and they contain in a
most excellent manner that element of the marvellous which is so important an element in the epic
action. It is the structure of the *romanzi* with
which Minturno finds fault. They lack the first
essential of every form of poetry, — unity. In
fact, they are little more than versified history or
legend; and, while expressing admiration for the
genius of Ariosto, Minturno cannot but regret that
he so far yielded to the popular taste of his time as
to employ the method of the *romanzi*. He approves
of the suggestion of Bembo, who had tried to persuade Ariosto to write an epic instead of a romantic
poem,[2] just as later, and for similar reasons, Gabriel
Harvey attempted to dissuade Spenser from con-

---

[1] Minturno, *Arte Poetica*, p. 31. For various opinions on the
unity of the *Orlando Furioso*, *cf.* Canello, p. 106, and Foffano,
p. 59 *sq.*   [2] *Arte Poetica*, p. 31.

tinuing the *Faerie Queene*. Minturno denies that
the Tuscan tongue is not well adapted to the composition of heroic poetry ; on the contrary, there is
no form of poetry to which it is not admirably
fitted. He denies that the romantic poem can be
distinguished from the epic on the ground that the
actions of knights-errant require a different and
broader form of narrative than do those of the
classical heroes. The celestial and infernal gods
and demi-gods of the ancients correspond with the
angels, saints, anchorites, and the one God of Christianity ; the ancient sibyls, oracles, enchantresses,
and divine messengers correspond with the modern
necromancers, fates, magicians, and celestial angels.
To the claim of the romantic poets that their poems
approximate closer to that magnitude which Aristotle enjoins as necessary for all poetry, Minturno
answers that magnitude is of no avail without proportion ; there is no beauty in the giant whose limbs
and frame are distorted. Finally, the *romanzi* are
said to be a new form of poetry unknown to Aristotle and Horace, and hence not amenable to their
laws. But time, says Minturno, cannot change
the truth ; in every age a poem must have unity,
proportion, magnitude. Everything in nature is
governed by some specific law which directs its
operation ; and as it is in nature so it is in art, for
art tries to imitate nature, and the nearer it approaches nature in her essential laws, the better it
does its work. In other words, as has already been
pointed out, poetry adapts itself to its times, but
cannot depart from its own laws.

Bernardo Tasso, the father of Torquato, had originally been one of the defenders of the classical epic; but he seems to have been converted to the opposite view by Giraldi Cintio, and in his poem of the *Amadigi* he follows romantic models. His son Torquato, in his *Discorsi dell' Arte Poetica*, originally written one or two years after the appearance of Minturno's *Arte Poetica*, although not published until 1587, was the first to attempt a reconciliation of the epic and romantic forms; and he may be said to have effected a solution of the problem by the formulation of the theory of a narrative poem which would have the romantic subject-matter, with its delightful variety, and the epic form, with its essential unity. The question at issue, as we have seen, is that of unity; that is, does the heroic poem need unity? Tasso denies that there is any difference between the epic poem and the romantic poem as poems. The reason why the latter is more pleasing, is to be found in the fact of the greater delightfulness of the themes treated.[1] Variety in itself may be pleasing, for even a variety of disagreeable things may possibly please. But the perfect and at the same time most pleasing form of heroic poem would deal with the chivalrous themes of the *romanzi*, yet would possess that unity of structure which, according to the precepts of Aristotle and the practice of Homer and Virgil, is essential to every epic. There are two sorts of unity possible in art as in nature, — the simple unity of a chemical element, and the complex unity of an organism

[1] T. Tasso, xii. 219 *sq*.

like an animal or plant, — and of these the latter
is the sort of unity that the heroic poet should aim
at.[1]   Capriano (1555) had referred to this same distinction, when he pointed out that poetry ought not
to be the imitation of a single act, such as a single
act of weeping in the elegy, or a single act of pastoral life in the eclogue, for such a sporadic imitation is to be compared to a picture of a single hand
without the rest of the body; on the contrary,
poetry ought to be the representation of a number
of attendant or dependent acts, leading from a
given beginning to a suitable end.[2]

Having settled the general fact that the attrac-
tive themes of the *romanzi* should be employed in a
perfect heroic poem, we may inquire what particular
themes are most fitted to the epic, and what must
be the essential qualities of the epic material.[3]   In
the first place, the subject of the heroic poem must
be historical, for it is not probable that illustrious
actions such as are dealt with in the epic should be
unknown to history.   The authority of history gains
for the poet that semblance of truth necessary to
deceive the reader and make him believe that what
the poet writes is true.   Secondly, the heroic poem,
according to Tasso, must deal with the history, not
of a false religion, but of the true one, Christianity.
The religion of the pagans is absolutely unfit for
epic material; for if the pagan deities are not introduced, the poem will lack the element of the
marvellous, and if they are introduced it will lack

[1] T. Tasso, xii. 234.   [3] T. Tasso, xii. 199 *sq*.
[2] *Della Vera Poetica*, cap. iii.

the element of probability. Both the marvellous
and the *verisimile* must exist together in a perfect
epic, and difficult as the task may seem, they must
be reconciled.   Another reason why paganism is
unfit for the epic is to be found in the fact that the
perfect knight must have piety as well as other
virtues.   In the third place, the poem must not
deal with themes connected with the articles of
Christian faith, for such themes would be unalter-
able, and would allow no scope to the free play of
the poet's inventive fancy.   Fourthly, the material
must be neither too ancient nor too modern, for the
latter is too well known to admit of fanciful changes
with probability, and the former not only lacks
interest but requires the introduction of strange
and alien manners and customs.   The times of
Charlemagne and Arthur are accordingly best fitted
for heroic treatment.   Finally, the events themselves must possess nobility and grandeur.   Hence
an epic should be a story derived from some event
in the history of Christian peoples, intrinsically
noble and illustrious, but not of so sacred a character as to be fixed and immutable, and neither
contemporary nor very remote.   By the selection
of such material the poem gains the authority of
history, the truth of religion, the license of fiction,
the proper atmosphere in point of time, and the
grandeur of the events themselves.[1]

   Aristotle says that both epic and tragedy deal
with illustrious actions.   Tasso points out that if
the actions of tragedy and of epic poetry were both

[1] T. Tasso, xii. 208.

illustrious in the same way, they would both produce the same results; but tragic actions move
horror and compassion, while epic actions as a rule
do not and need not arouse these emotions. The
tragic action consists in the unexpected change of
fortune, and in the grandeur of the events carrying
with them horror and pity; but the epic action is
founded upon undertakings of lofty martial virtue,
upon deeds of courtesy, piety, generosity, none of
which is proper to tragedy. Hence the characters
in epic poetry and in tragedy, though both of the
same regal and supreme rank, differ in that the
tragic hero is neither perfectly good nor entirely
bad, as Aristotle says, while the epic hero must
have the very height of virtue, such as Æneas, the
type of piety, Amadis, the type of loyalty, Achilles,
of martial virtue, and Ulysses, of prudence.

Having formulated these theories of heroic poetry
in his youth, Tasso set out to carry them into practice, and his famous *Gerusalemme Liberata* was the
result. This poem, almost immediately after its
publication, started a violent controversy, which
raged for many years, and which may be regarded
as the legitimate outcome of the earlier dispute in
connection with the *romanzi*.[1] The *Gerusalemme*
was in fact the centre of critical activity during the
latter part of the century. Shortly after its publication, Camillo Pellegrino published a dialogue, en-

---

[1] Accounts of this famous controversy will be found in Tiraboschi, Canello, Serassi, etc.; but the latest and most complete
is that given in the twentieth chapter of Solerti's monumental
Vita di Torquato Tasso, Torino, 1895.

titled *Il Caraffa* (1583), in which the *Gerusalemme* is compared with the *Orlando Furioso*, much to the advantage of the former. Pellegrino finds fault with Ariosto on account of the lack of unity of his poem, the immoral manners imitated, and various imperfections of style and language; and in all of these things, unity, morality, and style, he finds Tasso's poem perfect. This was naturally the signal for a heated and long-continued controversy. The Accademia della Crusca had been founded at Florence, in 1582, and it seems that the members of the new society felt hurt at some sarcastic remarks regarding Florence in one of Tasso's dialogues. Accordingly, the head of the academy, Lionardo Salviati, in a dialogue entitled *L' Infarinato*, wrote an ardent defence of Ariosto; and an acrid and undignified dispute between Tasso and Salviati was begun.[1] Tasso answered the Accademia della Crusca in his *Apologia;* and at the beginning of the next century, Paolo Beni, the commentator on Aristotle's *Poetics,* published his *Comparazione di Omero, Virgilio, e Torquato,* in which Tasso is rated above Homer, Virgil, and Ariosto, not only in dignity, in beauty of style, and in unity of fable, but in every other quality that may be said to constitute perfection in poetry. Before dismissing this whole matter, it should be pointed out that the defenders of Ariosto had absolutely abandoned the position of Giraldi and Pigna, that the *romanzi*

---

[1] Nearly all the important documents of the Tasso controversy are reprinted in Rosini's edition of Tasso, *Opere,* vols. xviii.-xxiii.

constitute a *genre* by themselves, and are therefore
not subject to Aristotle's law of unity.   The question as Giraldi had stated it was this: Does every
poem need to have unity?   The question as discussed in the Tasso controversy had changed to
this form: What is unity? It was taken for
granted by both sides in the controversy that every
poem must have organic unity; and the authority
of Aristotle, in epic as in dramatic poetry, was
henceforth supreme.   It was to the authority of
Aristotle that Tasso's opponents appealed; and
Salviati, merely for the purpose of undermining
Tasso's pretensions, wrote an extended commentary
on the *Poetics*, which still lies in Ms. at Florence,
and which has been made use of in the present
essay.[1]

[1] The question of unity was also raised in another controversy
of the second half of the sixteenth century.   A passage in
Varchi's *Ercolano* (1570), rating Dante above Homer, started
a controversy on the *Divine Comedy*.   The most important outcome of this dispute was Mazzoni's *Difesa di Dante* (1573), in
which a more or less novel theory of poetry is expounded in
order to defend the great Tuscan poet.

CHAPTER V

THE growth of classicism in Renaissance criticism was due to three causes, — humanism, or the imitation of the classics, Aristotelianism, or the influence of Aristotle's *Poetics*, and rationalism, or the authority of the reason, the result of the growth of the modern spirit in the arts and sciences. These three causes are at the bottom of Italian classicism, as well as of French classicism during the seventeenth century.

I. *Humanism*

The progress of humanism may be distinguished by an arbitrary but more or less practical division into four periods. The first period was characterized by the discovery and accumulation of classical literature, and the second period was given up to the arrangement and translation of the works thus discovered. The third period is marked by the formation of academies, in which the classics were studied and humanized, and which as a result produced a special cult of learning. The fourth and last period is marked by the decline of pure erudition, and the beginning of æsthetic and stylistic scholarship.[1] The practical result of the revival of learning and the progress of humanism was thus the study and imitation of the classics. To this imitation of classical literature all that humanism gave to the modern world may be ultimately traced. The problem before us, then, is this: What was the result of this imitation of the classics, in so far as it regards the literary criticism of the Renaissance?

In the first place, the imitation of the classics resulted in the study and cult of external form. Elegance, polish, clearness of design, became objects of study for themselves; and as a result we have the formation of æsthetic taste, and the growth of a classic purism, to which many of the literary tendencies of the Renaissance may be traced.[2] Under Leo X. and throughout the first half of the sixteenth century, the intricacies of style and versification were carefully studied. Vida was the first to lay down laws of imitative harmony;[3] Bembo, and after him Dolce and others, studied the poetic effect of different sounds, and the onomatopœic value of the various vowels and consonants;[4] Claudio Tolomei attempted to introduce classical metres into the vernacular;[5] Trissino published subtle and systematic researches in Tuscan

[1] Symonds, ii. 161, based on Voigt.

[2] *Cf.* Woodward, p. 210 *sq.*

[3] Hallam, *Lit. of Europe*, i. 8. 1. *Cf.* Pope, i. 182: "Omnia sed numeris vocum concordibus aptant," etc.

[4] Bembo, *Le Prose*, 1525; Dolce, *Osservationi*, 1550, lib. iv.; etc.

[5] *Versi e Regole de la Nuova Poesia Toscana*, 1539.

language and versification.[1]   Later, the rhetorical
treatises of Cavalcanti (1565), Lionardi (1554), and
Partenio (1560), and the more practical manuals of
Fanucci (1533), Equicola (1541), and Ruscelli (1559),
all testify to the tremendous impulse which the imitation of the classics had given to the study of form
both in classical and vernacular literatures.

In Vida's *Ars Poetica* there are abundant evidences of the rhetorical and especially the puristic
tendencies of modern classicism.   The mechanical
conception of poetic expression, in which imagination, sensibility, and passion are subjected to the
elaborate and intricate precepts of art, is everywhere found in Vida's poem.   Like Horace, Vida
insists on long preparation for the composition of
poetry, and warns the poet against the indulgence
of his first impulses.   He suggests as a preparation
for the composition of poetry, that the poet should
prepare a list of phrases and images for use when-
ever occasion may demand.[2]   He impresses upon
the poet the necessity of euphemistic expressions
in introducing the subject of his poem; for example, the name of Ulysses should not be mentioned, but he should be referred to as one who
has seen many men and many cities, who has suf-
fered shipwreck on the return from Troy, and the
like.[3]   In such mechanical precepts as these, the
rhetoric of seventeenth-century classicism is antici-

[1] Trissino, *Poética*, lib. i.–iv., 1529; Tomitano, *Della Lingua
Toscana*, 1545; etc.
[2] Pope, i. 134.   *Cf.* De Sanctis, ii. 153 *sq.*
[3] Pope, i. 152.

pated. Its restraint, its purity, its mechanical side,
are everywhere visible in Vida. A little later, in
Daniello, we find similar puristic tendencies. He
requires the severe separation of *genres*, decorum
and propriety of characterization, and the exclusion
of everything disagreeable from the stage. In Partenio's *Della Imitatione Poetica* (1560), the poet is
expressly forbidden the employment of the ordinary
words in daily use,[1] and elegance of form is especially
demanded. Partenio regards form as of superior
importance to subject or idea; for those who hear
or read poetry care more for beauty of diction than
for character or even thought.[2]

It is on merely rhetorical grounds that Partenio
distinguishes excellent from mediocre poetry. The
good poet, unlike the bad one, is able to give splendor and dignity to the most trivial idea by means
of adornments of diction and disposition. This
conception seems to have particularly appealed to
the Renaissance; and Tasso gives expression to a
similar notion when he calls it the poet's noblest
function " to make of old concepts new ones, to
make of vulgar concepts noble ones, and to make
common concepts his own." [3] In a higher and more
ideal sense, poetry, according to Shelley, " makes
familiar objects be as if they were not familiar." [4]

It is in keeping with this rhetorical ideal of
classicism that Scaliger makes *electio et sui fastidium* the highest virtues of the poet.[5] All that is

---

[1] Partenio, p. 80.   [4] *Defence*, p. 13.
[2] *Ibid.* p. 95.   [5] *Poet.* v. 3.
[3] *Opere*, xi. 51.

merely popular (*plebeium*) in thought and expression is to be minutely avoided; for only that which proceeds from solid erudition is proper to art. The basis of artistic creation is imitation and judgment; for every artist is at bottom somewhat of an echo.[1] Grace, decorum, elegance, splendor are the chief excellences of poetry and the life of all excellence lies in measure, that is, moderation and proportion. It is in the spirit of this classical purism that Scaliger minutely distinguishes the various rhetorical and grammatical figures, and carefully estimates their proper place and function in poetry. His analysis and systematization of the figures were immediately accepted by the scholars and grammarians of his time, and have played a large part in French education ever since. Another consequence of Scaliger's dogmatic teaching, the Latinization of culture, can only be referred to here in passing.[2]

A second result of the imitation of the classics was the paganization of Renaissance culture. Classic art is at bottom pagan, and the Renaissance sacrificed everything in order to appear classical.[3] Not only did Christian literature seem contemptible when compared with classic literature, but the mere treatment of Christian themes offered numerous difficulties in itself. Thus Muzio declares that the ancient fables are the best poetic materials, since they permit the introduction of the deities into poetry, and a poem, being something divine, should not dispense with the association of divinity.[4] To

---

[1] *Poet.* v. 1 ; vi. 4.
[2] *Cf.* Brunetière, p. 53.
[3] Symonds, ii. 395 *sq.*
[4] Muzio, p. 94.

ĸ

bring the God of Israel into poetry, to represent him, as it were, in the flesh, discoursing and arguing with men, was sacrilege; and to give the events of poetic narrative divine authoritativeness, the pagan deities became necessities of Renaissance poetry. Savonarola, in the fifteenth century, and the Council of Trent, in the sixteenth, reacted against the paganization of literature, but in vain. Despite the Council of Trent, despite Tasso and Du Bartas, the pagan gods held sway over Parnassus until the very end of the classical period; and in the seventeenth century, as will be seen, Boileau expressly discourages the treatment of Christian themes, and insists that the ancient pagan fables alone must form the basis of neo-classical art.

A third result of the imitation of the classics was the development of applied, or concrete, criticism. If the foundations of literature, if the formation of style, can result only from a close and judicious imitation of classical literature, this problem confronts us: Which classical authors are we to imitate? An answer to this question involves the application of concrete criticism. A reason must be given for one's preferences; in other words, they must be justified on principle. The literary controversies of the humanists, the disputes on the subject of imitation, of Ciceronianism, and what not, all tended in this direction. The judgment of authors was dependent more or less on individual impressions. But the longer these controversies continued, the nearer was the approach to a literary criticism, justified by appeals to general principles, which became more and more fixed and determined; so that the growth of principles, or criteria of judgment in matters of literature, is in reality coterminous with the history of the growth of classicism.[1]

But one of the most important consequences of the imitation of the classics was that this imitation became a dogma of criticism, and radically changed the relations of art and nature in so far as they touch letters and literary criticism. The imitation of the classics became, in a word, the basis of literary creation. Vida, for example, affirms that the poet must imitate classical literature, for only by such imitation is perfection attainable in modern poetry. In fact, this notion is carried to such an extreme that the highest originality becomes for Vida merely the ingenious translation of passages from the classic poets : —

> " Haud minor est adeo virtus, si te audit Apollo,
> Inventa Argivûm in patriam convertere vocem,
> Quam si tute aliquid intactum inveneris ante." [2]

Muzio, echoing Horace, urges the poet to study the classics by day and by night; and Scaliger, as has been seen, makes all literary creation depend ultimately on judicious imitation: "Nemo est qui non aliquid de Echo." As a result, imitation gradually acquired a specialized and almost esoteric meaning, and became in this sense the starting-point of all the educational theories of the later

[1] *Cf.* Dennis, *Select Works*, 1718, ii. 417 *sq.*
[2] Pope, i. 167.

humanists. The doctrine of imitation set forth by John Sturm, the Strasburg humanist, was particularly influential.[1] According to Sturm, imitation is not the servile copying of words and phrases; it is "a vehement and artistic application of mind," which judiciously uses and transfigures all that it imitates. Sturm's theory of imitation is not entirely original, but comes through Agricola and Melanchthon from Quintilian.[2] Quintilian had said that the greater part of art consists in imitation; but for the humanists imitation became the chief and almost the only element of literary creation, since the literature of their own time seemed so vastly inferior to that of the ancients.

The imitation of the classics having thus become essential to literary creation, what was to be its relation to the imitation of nature? The ancient poets seemed to insist that every writer is at bottom an imitator of nature, and that he who does not imitate nature diverges from the purpose and principle of art. A lesson coming from a source so authoritative as this could not be left unheeded by the writers of the Renaissance, and the evolution of classicism may be distinguished by the changing point of view of the critics in regard to the relations between nature and art. This evolution may be traced in the neo-classical period through three distinct stages, and these three stages may be indicated by the doctrines respectively of Vida, Scaliger, and Boileau.

---

[1] Laas, *Die Paedagogik des Johannes Sturm*, Berlin, 1872, p. 65 *sq.*   [2] *Inst. Orat.* x. 2.

Vida says that it is the first essential of literary art to imitate the classics. This, however, does not prevent him from warning the poet that it is his first duty to observe and copy nature: —

> " Præterea haud lateat te, nil conarier artem,
>   Naturam nisi ut assimulet, propiusque sequatur."

For Vida, however, as for the later classicists, nature is synonymous with civilized men, perhaps even further restricted to the men of the city and the court; and the study of nature was hardly more for him than close observation of the differences of human character, more especially of the external differences which result from diversity of age, rank, sex, race, profession, and which may be designated by the term *decorum*.[1] The imitation of nature even in this restricted sense Vida requires on the authority of the ancients. The modern poet should imitate nature because the great classical poets have always acknowledged her sway: —

> " Hanc unam vates sibi proposuere magistram."

Nature has no particular interest for Vida in itself. He accepts the classics as we accept the Scriptures; and nature is to be imitated and followed because the ancients seem to require it.

In Scaliger this principle is carried one stage farther. The poet creates another nature and other fortunes as if he were another God.[2] Virgil especially has created another nature of such beauty and perfection that the poet need not concern him

---

[1] Pope, i. 165.   [2] *Poet.* i. 1.

self with the realities of life, but can go to the
second nature created by Virgil for the subject-
matter of his imitation. " All the things which
you have to imitate, you have according to another
nature, that is, Virgil." [1]   In Virgil, as in nature,
there are the most minute details of the foundation
and government of cities, the management of armies,
the building and handling of ships, and in fact all
the secrets of the arts and sciences.   What more
can the poet desire, and indeed what more can he
find in life, and find there with the same certainty
and accuracy ?   Virgil has created a nature far
more perfect than that of reality, and one compared
with which the actual world and life itself seem
but pale and without beauty.   What Scaliger
stands for, then, is the substitution of the world of
art instead of life as the object of poetic imitation.
This point of view finds expression in many of the
theorists of his time.   Partenio, for example, asserts
that art is a firmer and safer guide than nature ;
with nature we can err, but scarcely with art, for
art eradicates from nature all that is bad, while
nature mingles weeds with flowers, and does not
distinguish vices from virtues.[2]

Boileau carries the neo-classical ideal of nature
and art to its ultimate perfection.   According to
him, nothing is beautiful that is not true, and nothing is true that is not in nature.   Truth, for classicism, is the final test of everything, including beauty ;
and hence to be beautiful poetry must be founded
on nature.   Nature should therefore be the poet's

[1] *Poet*. iii. 4.   [2] Partenio, p. 39 *sq*.

sole study, although for Boileau, as for Vida, nature
is one with the court and the city. Now, in what
way can we discover exactly how to imitate nature,
and perceive whether or not we have imitated it
correctly? Boileau finds the guide to the correct
imitation of nature, and the very test of its correct-
ness, in the imitation of the classics. The ancients
are great, not because they are old, but because
they are true, because they knew how to see and
to imitate nature; and to imitate antiquity is therefore to use the best means the human spirit has
ever found for expressing nature in its perfection.[1]
The advance of Boileau's theory on that of Vida
and Scaliger is therefore that he founded the
rules and literary practice of classical literature on
reason and nature, and showed that there is nothing
arbitrary in the authority of the ancients. For
Vida, nature is to be followed on the authority
of the classics; for Boileau, the classics are to
be followed on the authority of nature and reason.
Scaliger had shown that such a poet as Virgil
had created another nature more perfect than that
of reality, and that therefore we should imitate
this more beautiful nature of the poet. Boileau, on
the contrary, showed that the ancients were simply
imitating nature itself in the closest and keenest
manner, and that by imitating the classics the poet
was not imitating a second and different nature, but
was being shown in the surest way how to imitate
the real and only nature. This final reconciliation

---

[1] *Cf.* Brunetière, p. 102 *sq.*, and Lanson, *Hist. de la Litt. fr.*,
p. 494 *sq.*

of the imitation of nature and the imitation of the classics was Boileau's highest contribution to the literary criticism of the neo-classical period.

II. *Aristotelianism*

The influence of Aristotle's *Poetics* is first visible in the dramatic literature of the early sixteenth century. Trissino's *Sofonisba* (1515), usually accounted the first regular modern tragedy, Rucellai's *Rosmunda* (1516), and innumerable other tragedies of this period, were in reality little more than mere attempts at putting the Aristotelian theory of tragedy into practice. The Aristotelian influence is evident in many of the prefaces of these plays, and in a few contemporary works of scholarship, such as the *Antiquæ Lectiones* (1516) of Cælius Rhodiginus, whom Scaliger called *omnium doctissimus præceptor noster.* At the same time, the *Poetics* did not immediately play an important part in the critical literature of Italy. From the time of Petrarch, Aristotle, identified in the minds of the humanists with the mediæval scholasticism so obnoxious to them, had lost somewhat of his supremacy; and the strong Platonic tendencies of the Renaissance had further contributed to lower the prestige of Aristotelianism among the humanists. At no time of the Renaissance, however, did Aristotle lack ardent defenders, and Filelfo, for example, wrote in 1439, "To defend Aristotle and the truth seems to me one and the same thing."[1] In the domain of philosophy the influence of Aristotle

[1] *Lettres grecques*, ed. Legrand, 1892, p. 31.

was temporarily sustained by the liberal Peripateticism of Pomponazzi; and numerous others, among them Scaliger himself, continued the traditions of a modernized Aristotelianism. From this time, however, Aristotle's position as the supreme philosopher was challenged more and more; and he was regarded by the advanced thinkers of the Renaissance as the representative of the mediæval obscurantism that opposed the progress of modern scientific investigation.

But whatever of Aristotle's authority was lost in the domain of philosophy was more than regained in the domain of literature. The beginning of the Aristotelian influence on modern literary theory may be said to date from the year 1536, in which year Trincaveli published a Greek text of the *Poetics*, Pazzi his edition and Latin version, and Daniello his own *Poetica*. Pazzi's son, in dedicating his father's posthumous work, said that in the *Poetics* "the precepts of poetic art are treated by Aristotle as divinely as he has treated every other form of knowledge." In the very year that this was said, Ramus gained his Master's degree at the University of Paris by defending victoriously the thesis that Aristotle's doctrines without exception are all false.[1] The year 1536 may therefore be regarded as a turning-point in the history of Aristotle's influence. It marks the beginning of his supremacy in literature, and the decline of his dictatorial authority in philosophy.

[1] "Quæcunque ab Aristotele dicta sint falsa et commentitia esse;" Bayle, *Dict.* s. v. Ramus, note C.

Between the year 1536 and the middle of the century the lessons of Aristotle's *Poetics* were being gradually learned by the Italian critics and poets. By 1550 the whole of the *Poetics* had been incorporated in the critical literature of Italy, and Fracastoro could say that "Aristotle has received no less fame from the survival of his *Poetics* than from his philosophical remains."[1] According to Bartolommeo Ricci, in a letter to Prince Alfonso, son of Hercules II., Duke of Ferrara, Maggi was the first person to interpret Aristotle's *Poetics* in public.[2] These lectures were delivered some time before April, 1549. As early as 1540, Bartolommeo Lombardi, the collaborator of Maggi in his commentary on the *Poetics*, had intended to deliver public lectures on the *Poetics* before a Paduan academy, but died before accomplishing his purpose.[3] Numerous public readings on the subject of Aristotle and Horace followed those of Maggi, — among them those by Varchi, Giraldi Cintio, Luisino, and Trifone Gabrielli; and the number of public readings on topics connected with literary criticism, and on the poetry of Dante and Petrarch, increased greatly from this time.

The number of commentaries on the *Poetics* itself, published during the sixteenth century, is really remarkable. The value of these commentaries in general is not so much that they add anything to the literary criticism of the Renaissance, but that their explanations of Aristotle's meaning

[1] Fracastoro, i. 321.   [2] Tiraboschi, vii. 1465.
[3] Maggi, dedication.

were accepted by contemporary critics, and became in a way the source of all the literary arguments of the sixteenth century. Nor was their influence restricted merely to this particular period. They were, one might almost say, living things to the critics and poets of the classical period in France. Racine, Corneille, and other distinguished writers possessed copies of these commentaries, studied them carefully, cited them in their prefaces and critical writings, and even annotated their own copies of the commentaries with marginal notes, of which some may be seen in the modern editions of their works. In the preface to Rapin's *Réflexions sur l'Art Poétique* (1674) there is a history of literary criticism, which is almost entirely devoted to these Italian commentators; and writers like Chapelain and Balzac eagerly argued and discussed their relative merits.

Several of these Italian commentators have been alluded to already.[1] The first critical edition of the *Poetics* was that of Robortelli (1548), and this was followed by those of Maggi (1550) and Vettori (1560), both written in Latin, and both exhibiting great learning and acumen. The first translation of the *Poetics* into the vernacular was that by Segni (1549), and this was followed by the Italian commentaries of Castelvetro (1570) and Piccolomini (1575). Tasso, after comparing the works of these two commentators, concluded that while Castelvetro

---

[1] In an appendix to this essay will be found an excerpt from Salviati's unpublished commentary on the *Poetics*, giving his judgment of the commentators who had preceded him.

had greater erudition and invention, Piccolomini had greater maturity of judgment, more learning, perhaps, with less erudition, and certainly learning more Aristotelian and more suited to the interpretation of the *Poetics*.[1] The two last sections of Trissino's *Poetica*, published in 1563, are little more than a paraphrase and transposition of Aristotle's treatise. But the curious excesses into which admiration of Aristotle led the Italian scholars may be gathered from a work published at Milan in 1576, an edition of the *Poetics* expounded in verse, Baldini's *Ars Poetica Aristotelis versibus exposita*. The *Poetics* was also adapted for use as a practical manual for poets and playwrights in such works as Riccoboni's brief *Compendium Artis Poeticæ Aristotelis ad usum conficiendorum poematum* (1591). The last of the great Italian commentaries on the *Poetics* to have a general European influence was perhaps Beni's, published in 1613; but this carries us beyond the confines of the century. Besides the published editions, translations, and commentaries, many others were written which may still be found in Ms. in the libraries of Italy. Reference has already been made to Salviati's (1586). There are also two anonymous commentaries dating from this period in Ms. at Florence, — one in the Magliabechiana and the other in the Riccardiana. The last work which may be mentioned here is Buonamici's *Discorsi Poetici in difesa d' Aristotele*, in which Aristotle is ardently defended against the attacks of his detractors.

[1] Tasso, xv. 20.

It was in Italy during this period that the literary
dictatorship of Aristotle first developed, and it was
Scaliger to whom the modern world owes the formulation of the supreme authority of Aristotle as a
critical theorist. Fracastoro had likened the importance of Aristotle's *Poetics* to that of his philosophical treatises. Trissino had followed Aristotle
verbally and almost literally. Varchi had spoken of
years of Aristotelian study as an essential prerequi-
site for every one who entered the field of literary
criticism. Partenio, a year before the publication
of Scaliger's *Poetics*, had asserted that everything
relating to tragedy and epic poetry had been settled
by Aristotle and Horace. But Scaliger went farther
still. He was the first to regard Aristotle as the
perpetual lawgiver of poetry. He was the first to
assume that the duty of the poet is first to find out
what Aristotle says, and then to obey these precepts
without question. He distinctly calls Aristotle the
perpetual dictator of all the arts: "Aristoteles im-
perator noster, omnium bonarum artium dictator
perpetuus."[1] This is perhaps the first occasion in
modern literature in which Aristotle is definitely
regarded as a literary dictator, and the dictatorship
of Aristotle in literature may, therefore, be dated
from the year 1561.

But Scaliger did more than this. He was the
first apparently to attempt to reconcile Aristotle's
Poetics, not only with the precepts of Horace and
the definitions of the Latin grammarians, but with
the whole practice of Latin tragedy, comedy, and

[1] *Poet.* vii. ii. 1.

epic poetry. It was in the light of this recon ciliation, or concord of Aristotelianism with the Latin spirit, that Aristotle became for Scaliger a literary dictator. It was not Aristotle that primarily interested him, but an ideal created by himself, and founded on such parts of the doctrine of Aristotle as received confirmation from the theory or practice of Roman literature; and this new ideal, harmonizing with the Latin spirit of the Renaissance, became in the course of time one of the foundations of classicism. The influence of Aristotelianism was further augmented by the Council of Trent, which gave to Aristotle's doctrine the same degree of authority as Catholic dogma.

All these circumstances tended to favor the importance of Aristotle in Italy during the sixteenth century, and as a result the literary dictatorship of Aristotle was by the Italians foisted on Europe for two centuries to come. From 1560 to 1780 Aristotle was regarded as the supreme authority in letters throughout Europe. At no time, even in England, during and after that period, was there a break in the Aristotelian tradition, and the influence of the *Poetics* may be found in Sidney and Ben Jonson, in Milton and Dryden, as well as in Shelley and Coleridge. Lessing, even in breaking away from the classical practice of the French stage, defended his innovations on the authority of Aristotle, and said of the *Poetics*, " I do not hesitate to acknowledge, even if I should therefore be held up to scorn in these enlightened times, that I consider the work as infallible as the Elements of

Euclid."[1] In 1756, a dozen years before Lessing, one of the precursors of the romantic movement in England, Joseph Warton, had also said of the *Poetics*, "To attempt to understand poetry without having diligently digested this treatise would be as absurd and impossible as to pretend to a skill in geometry without having studied Euclid."[2]

One of the first results of the dictatorship of Aristotle was to give modern literature a body of inviolable rules for the drama and the epic; that is, the dramatic and heroic poets were restricted to a certain fixed form, and to certain fixed characters. Classical poetry was of course the ideal of the Renaissance, and Aristotle had analyzed the methods which these works had employed. The inference seems to have been that by following these rules a literature of equal importance could be created. These formulæ were at the bottom of classical literature, and rules which had created such literatures as those of Greece and Rome could hardly be disregarded. As a result, these rules came to be considered more and more as essentials, and finally, almost as the very tests of literature; and it was in consequence of their acceptance as poetic laws that the modern classical drama and epic arose. The first modern tragedies and the first modern epics were hardly more than such attempts at putting the Aristotelian rules into practice. The cult of form during the Renaissance had produced a reaction against the

[1] *Hamburg. Dramat.* 101–104.
[2] *Essay on Pope*, 3d ed., i. 171.

formlessness and invertebrate character of mediæval literature. The literature of the Middle Ages was infinitely inferior to that of the ancients; mediæval literature lacked form and structure, classical literature had a regular and definite form. Form then came to be regarded as the essential difference between the perfect literatures of Greece and Rome, and the imperfect and vulgar literature of the Middle Ages; and the deduction from this was that, to be classical, the poet must observe the form and structure of the classics. Minturno indeed says that "the precepts given of old by the ancient masters, and now repeated by me here, are to be regarded merely as common usage, and not as inviolable laws which must serve under all circumstances."[1]   But this was not the general conception of the Renaissance. Muzio, for example, specifically says:—

> "Queste legge ch' io scrivo e questi esempi
> Sian, lettore, al tuo dir perpetua norma;"

and in another place he speaks of a precept he has given, as "vera, ferma, e inevitabil legge."[2]   Scaliger goes still further than this; for, according to him, even the classics themselves are to be judged by these standards and rules. "It seems to me," says Scaliger, "that we ought not to refer everything back to Homer, just as though he were the norm, but Homer himself should be referred to the norm."[3]   In the modern classical period somewhat

---

[1] *Arte Poetica*, p. 158.   [2] Muzio, pp. 81 v., 76 v.
[3] *Poet.* i. 5.

later, these rules were found to be based on
reason : —

> "These rules of old, discovered not devised,
> Are nature still, but nature methodized." [1]

But during the Renaissance they were accepted *ex
cathedra* from classical literature.

The formulation of a fixed body of critical
rules was not the only result of the Aristotelian
influence.   One of the most important of these
results, as has appeared, was the rational justification of imaginative literature.   With the introduction of Aristotle's *Poetics* into modern Europe the
Renaissance was first able to formulate a systematic
theory of poetry; and it is therefore to the redis-
covery of the *Poetics* that we may be said to owe
the foundation of modern criticism.   It was on the
side of Aristotelianism that Italian criticism had
its influence on European letters; and that this
influence was deep and widespread, our study of
the critical literatures of France and England will
in part show.   The critics with whom we have been
dealing are not merely dead provincial names;
they influenced, for two whole centuries, not only
France and England, but Spain, Portugal, and
Germany as well.

Literary criticism, in any real sense, did not begin in Spain until the very end of the sixteenth
century, and the critical works that then appeared
were wholly based on those of the Italians.   Ren-
gifo's *Arte Poética Española* (1592), in so far as it

---

[1] Pope, *Essay on Criticism*, 88.

L

deals with the theory of poetry, is based on Aristotle, Scaliger, and various Italian authorities,
according to the author's own acknowledgment.
Pinciano's *Philosophia Antigua Poética* (1596) is
based on the same authorities. Similarly, Cascales,
in his *Tablas Poéticas* (1616), gives as his authorities Minturno, Giraldi Cintio, Maggi, Riccoboni,
Castelvetro, Robortelli, and his own countryman
Pinciano. The sources of these and all other works
written at this period are Italian; and the following passage from the *Egemplar Poético*, written
about 1606 by the Spanish poet Juan de la Cueva,
is a good illustration, not only of the general influence of the Italians on Spanish criticism, but of the
high reverence in which the individual Italian
critics were held by Spanish men of letters: —

" De los primeros tiene Horacio el puesto,
    En numeros y estilo soberano,
    Qual en su Arte al mundo es manifesto.
    Escaligero [*i.e.* Scaliger] hace el paso llano
    Con general enseñamiento y guia,
    Lo mismo el docto Cintio [*i.e.* Giraldi Cintio] y Biperano.[1]
    Maranta[2] es egemplar de la Poesia,
    Vida el norte, Pontano[3] el ornamento,
    La luz Minturno qual el sol del dia . . . . .
    Acuden todos a colmar sus vasos

[1] Viperano, author of *De Poetica libri tres*, Antwerp, 1579.

[2] Maranta, author of *Lucullanæ Quæstiones*, Basle, 1564.

[3] Three writers of the Renaissance bore this name: G. Pontano, the famous Italian humanist and Latin poet, who died in
1503; P. Pontano, of Bruges, the author of an *Ars Versificatoria*,
published in 1520; and J. Pontanus, a Bohemian Jesuit, author
of *Institutiones Poeticæ*, first published at Ingolstadt in 1594,
and several times reprinted.

Al oceano sacro de Stagira [*i.e.* Aristotle],
Donde se afirman los dudosos pasos,
Se eterniza la trompa y tierna lira." [1]

The influence of the Italians was equally great
in Germany. From Fabricius to Opitz, the critical ideas of Germany were almost all borrowed,
directly or indirectly, from Italian sources. Fabricius in his *De Re Poetica* (1584) acknowledges his
indebtedness to Minturno, Partenio, Pontanus, and
others, but above all to Scaliger; and most of the
critical ideas by which Opitz renovated modern German literature go back to Italian sources, through
Scaliger, Ronsard, and Daniel Heinsius. No better
illustration of the influence of the Italian critics
upon European letters could be afforded than that
given by Opitz's *Buch von der deutschen Poeterei.*[2]

The influence of Italian criticism on the critical
literature of France and England will be more or
less treated in the remaining portions of this essay.
It may be noted here, however, that in the critical
writings of Lessing there is represented the climax
of the Italian tradition in European letters, especially on the side of Aristotelianism. Shelley represents a similar culmination of the Italian tradition
in England. His indebtedness to Sidney and Mil-

[1] Sedano, *Parnaso Español*, Madrid, 1774, viii. 40, 41.

[2] *Cf.* Berghoeffer, *Opitz' Buch von der Poeterei*, 1888, and
Beckherrn, *Opitz, Ronsard, und Heinsius*, 1888. The first reference to Aristotle's *Poetics*, north of the Alps, is to be found in
Luther's *Address to the Christian Nobles of the German Nation*,
1520. Schosser's *Disputationes de Tragœdia*, published in 1559,
two years before Scaliger's work appeared, is entirely based on
Aristotle's *Poetics.*

ton, who represent the Italian influence in the Elizabethan age, and especially to Tasso, whom he continually cites, is very marked. The debt of modern literature to Italian criticism is therefore not slight. In the half century between Vida and Castelvetro, Italian criticism formulated three things: a theory of poetry, a rigid form for the epic, and a rigid form for the drama. These rigid forms for drama and epic governed the creative imagination of Europe for two centuries, and then passed away. But while modern æsthetics for over a century has studied the processes of art, the theory of poetry, as enunciated by the Italians of the sixteenth century, has not diminished in value, but has continued to pervade the finer minds of men from that time to this.

III. *Rationalism*

The rationalistic temper may be observed in critical literature almost at the very beginning of the sixteenth century. This spirit of rationalism is observable throughout the Renaissance; and its general causes may be looked for in the liberation of the human reason by the Renaissance, in the growth of the sciences and arts, and in the reaction against mediæval sacerdotalism and dogma. The causes of its development in literary criticism may be found not only in these but in several other influences of the period. The paganization of culture, the growth of rationalistic philosophies, with their all-pervading influence on arts and letters, and moreover the influence of Horace's *Ars Poetica*, with its ideal of "good sense," all tended to make the element of reason predominate in literature and in literary criticism.

In Vida the three elements which are at the bottom of classicism, the imitation of the classics, the imitation of nature, and the authority of reason, may all be found. Reason is for him the final test of all things: —

"Semper nutu rationis eant res." [1]

The function of the reason in art is, first, to serve as a standard in the choice and carrying out of the design, a bulwark against the operation of mere chance,[2] and secondly, to moderate the expression of the poet's own personality and passion, a bulwark against the morbid subjectivity which is the horror of the classical temperament.[3]

It has been said of Scaliger that he was the first modern to establish in a body of doctrine the principal consequences of the sovereignty of the reason in literature.[4] That was hardly his aim, and certainly not his attainment. But he was, at all events, one of the first modern critics to affirm that there is a standard of perfection for each specific form of literature, to show that this standard may be arrived at *a priori* through the reason, and to attempt a formulation of such standard for each literary form. "Est in omni rerum genere unum

---

[1] Pope, i. 155.
[2] *Loc. cit.*, beginning, "Nec te fors inopina regat."
[3] Pope, i. 164, beginning, "Ne tamen ah nimium."
[4] Lintilhac, in *Nouvelle Revue*, lxiv. 543.

primum ac rectum ad cuius tum normam, tum ratio-
nem cætera dirigenda sunt." [1] This, the funda
mental assumption of Scaliger's *Poetics*, is also one
of the basic ideas of classicism. Not only is there
a standard, a norm, in every species of literature,
but this norm can be definitely formulated and defined by means of the reason; and it is the duty of
the critic to formulate this norm, and the duty of
the poet to study and follow it without deviating
from the norm in any way. Even Homer, as we
have seen, is to be judged according to this standard arrived at through the reason. Such a method
cuts off all possibility of novelty of form or expression, and holds every poet, ancient or modern, great
or small, accountable to one and the same standard
of perfection.

The growth and influence of rationalism in Italian criticism may be best observed by the gradual
effect which its development had on the element
of Aristotelianism.   In other words, rationalism
changed the point of view according to which the
Aristotelian canons were regarded in the Italian
Renaissance. The earlier Italian critics accepted
their rules and precepts on the authority of Aristotle alone. Thus Trissino, at the beginning of the
fifth section of his *Poetica*, finished in 1549, although begun about twenty years before, says, "I
shall not depart from the rules and precepts of the
ancients, and especially Aristotle." [2]   Somewhat
later, in 1553, Varchi says, "Reason *and* Aristotle
are my *two* guides." [3]   Here the element of the

[1] Scaliger, *Poet.* iii. 11.   [2] Trissino, ii. 92.   [3] Varchi, p. 600

reason first asserts itself, but there is no intimation
that the Aristotelian canons are in themselves
reasonable. The critic has two guides, the individual reason and the Aristotelian rules, and each of
these two guides is to serve wherever the other is
found wanting. This same point of view is found
a decade later in Tasso, who says that the defenders
of the unity of the epic poem have made " a shield
of the authority of Aristotle, nor do they lack the
arms afforded by the reason; " [1] and similarly, in
1583, Sir Philip Sidney says that the unity of time
is demanded "both by Aristotle's precept and
common reason." [2] Here both Tasso and Sidney,
while contending that the particular law under discussion is in itself reasonable, speak of Aristotle's
Poetics and the reason as separate and distinct
authorities, and fail to show that Aristotle himself
based all his precepts upon the reason. In Denores,
a few years later, the development is carried one
stage farther in the direction of the ultimate classical attitude, as when he speaks of "reason and
Aristotle's *Poetics,* which is indeed founded on
naught save reason." [3] This is as far as Italian
criticism ever went. It was the function of neo-
classicism in France, as will be seen, to show that
such a phrase as "reason *and* Aristotle" is a con-
tradiction in itself, that the Aristotelian canons
and the reason are ultimately reducible to the same
thing, and that not only what is in Aristotle will

[1] Tasso, xii. 217.
[2] *Defense of Poesy*, p. 48.
[3] *Discorso*, 1587, p. 39 v.

be found reasonable, but all that reason dictates for literary observance will be found in Aristotle.

Rationalism produced several very important results in literature and literary criticism during the sixteenth century. In the first place, it tended to give the reason a higher place in literature than imagination or sensibility. Poetry, it will be remembered, was often classified by Renaissance critics as one of the logical sciences; and nothing could be in greater accord with the neo-classical ideal than the assertion of Varchi and others that the better logician the poet is, the better he will be as a poet. Sainte-Beuve gives Scaliger the credit of having first formulated this theory of literature which subordinates the creative imagination and poetic sensibility to the reason; [1] but the credit or discredit of originating it does not belong exclusively to Scaliger. This tendency toward the apotheosis of the reason was diffused throughout the sixteenth century, and does not characterize any individual author. The Italian critics of this period were the first to formulate the classical ideal that the standard of perfection may be conceived of by the reason, and that perfection is to be attained only by the realization of this standard.

The rationalistic spirit also tended to set the seal of disapprobation on extravagances of any sort. Subjectivity and individualism came to be regarded more and more, at least in theory, as out of keeping with classical perfection. Clearness, reasonableness, sociableness, were the highest requirements

[1] *Causeries du Lundi*, iii. 44.

of art; and any excessive expression of the poet's individuality was entirely disapproved of. Man, not only as a reasonable being, but also as a social being, was regarded as the basis of literature. Boileau's lines : —

> " Que les vers ne soient pas votre éternel emploi ;
> Cultivez vos amis, soyez homme de foi ;
> C'est peu d'être agréable et charmant dans un livre,
> Il faut savoir encore et converser et vivre," [1]

were anticipated in Berni's *Dialogo contra i Poeti*, written in 1526, though not published until 1537. This charming invective is directed against the fashionable literature of the time, and especially against all professional poets. Writing from the standpoint of a polished and rationalistic society, Berni lays great stress on the fact that poetry is not to be taken too seriously, that it is a pastime, a recreation for cultured people, a mere bagatelle; and he professes to despise those who spend all their time in writing verses. The vanity, the uselessness, the extravagances, and the ribaldry of the professional poets receive his hearty contempt; only those who write verses for pastime merit approbation. "Are you so stupid," he cries, "as to think that I call any one who writes verses a poet, and that I regard such men as Vida, Pontano, Bembo, Sannazaro, as mere poets? I do not call any one a poet, and condemn him as such, unless he does nothing but write verses, and wretched ones at that, and is good for nothing else. But the men I have mentioned are not

[1] *Art Poét.* iv. 121.

poets by profession." [1]   Here the sentiments expressed are those of a refined and social age, —
the age of Louis XIV. no less than that of Leo X.

The irreligious character of neo-classic art may
also be regarded as one of the consequences of this
rationalistic temper. The combined effect of humanism, essentially pagan, and rationalism, essentially sceptical, was not favorable to the growth
of religious feeling in literature. Classicism, the
result of these two tendencies, became more and
more rationalistic, more and more pagan; and in
consequence, religious poetry in any real sense
ceased to flourish wherever the more stringent forms
of classicism prevailed. In Boileau these tendencies result in a certain distinct antagonism to the
very forms of Christianity in literature : —

> " C'est donc bien vainement que nos auteurs déçus,
>   Bannissant de leurs vers ces ornemens reçus,
>   Pensent faire agir Dieu, ses saints et ses prophètes,
>   Comme ces dieux éclos du cerveau des poëtes ;
>   Mettent à chaque pas le lecteur en enfer ;
>   N'offrent rien qu'Astaroth, Belzébuth, Lucifer.
>   De la foi d'un chrétien les mystères terribles
>   D'ornemens égayés ne sont point susceptibles ;
>   L'Évangile à l'esprit n'offre de tous côtés
>   Que pénitence à faire et tourmens mérités ;
>   Et de vos fictions le mélange coupable
>   Même à ses vérités donne l'air de la fable." [2]

[1] Berni, p. 249.
[2] *Art Poét.* iii. 193. *Cf.* Dryden, *Discourse on Satire*, in
Works, xiii. 23 *sq.*

CHAPTER VI

In the Italian critical literature of the sixteenth century there are to be found the germs of romantic as well as classical criticism. The development of romanticism in Renaissance criticism is due to various tendencies, of ancient, of mediæval, and of modern origin. The ancient element is Platonism; the mediæval elements are Christianity, and the influence of the literary forms and the literary subject-matter of the Middle Ages; and the modern elements are the growth of national life and national literatures, and the opposition of modern philosophy to Aristotelianism.

I. *The Ancient Romantic Element*

As the element of reason is the predominant feature of neo-classicism, so the element of imagination is the predominant feature of romanticism; and according as the reason or the imagination predominates in Renaissance literature, there results neo-classicism or romanticism, while the most perfect art finds a reconciliation of both elements in the imaginative reason. According

155

to the faculty of reason, when made the basis of literature, the poet is, as it were, held down to earth, and art becomes the mere reasoned expression of the truth of life. By the faculty of imagination, the poet is made to create a new world of his own, — a world in which his genius is free to mould whatever its imagination takes hold of. This romantic doctrine of the freedom of genius, of inspiration and the power of imagination, in so far as it forms a part of Renaissance criticism, owes its origin to Platonism. The influence of the Platonic doctrines among the humanists has already been alluded to. Plato was regarded by them as their leader in the struggle against mediævalism, scholasticism, and Aristotelianism. The Aristotelian dialectic of the Middle Ages appealed exclusively to the reason; Platonism gave opportunities for the imagination to soar to vague and sublime heights, and harmonize with the divine mysteries of the universe. As regards poetry and imaginative literature in general, the critics of the Renaissance appealed from the Plato of the *Republic* and the *Laws* to the Plato of the *Ion*, the *Phædrus*, and the *Symposium*. Beauty being the subject-matter of art, Plato's praise of beauty was transferred by the Renaissance to poetry, and his praise of the philosopher was transferred to the poet.

The Aristotelian doctrine defines beauty according to its relations to the external world; that is, poetry is an imitation of nature, expressed in general terms. The Platonic doctrine, on the contrary, is concerned with poetry, or beauty, in so far as it concerns the poet's own nature; that is, the poet is divinely inspired and is a creator like God.   Fracastoro, as has been seen, makes the Platonic rapture, the delight in the true and essential beauty of things, the true tests of poetic power. In introducing this Platonic ideal of poetic beauty into modern literary criticism, he defines and distinguishes poetry according to a subjective criterion; and it is according to whether the objective or the subjective conception of art is insisted upon, that we have the classic spirit or the romantic spirit.   The extreme romanticists, like the Schlegels and their contemporaries in Germany, entirely eliminate the relation of poetry to the external world, and in this extreme form romanticism becomes identified with the exaggerated subjective idealism of Fichte and Schelling.   The extreme classicists entirely eliminate the poet's personality; that is, poetry is merely reasoned expression, a perfected expression of what all men can see in nature, for the poet has no more insight into life — no more imagination — than any ordinary, judicious person.

The effects of this Platonic element upon Renaissance criticism were various.   In the first place, it was through the Platonic influence that the relation of beauty to poetry was first made prominent.[1]   According to Scaliger, Tasso, Sidney, another world of beauty is created by the poet, — a world that possesses beauty in its perfection as this world

[1] De Sanctis, ii. 193 *sq.*

never can. The reason alone leaves no place for beauty; and accordingly, for the neo-classicists, ar was ultimately restricted to moral and psychological observation. Moreover, Platonism raised the question of the freedom of genius and of the imagination. Of all men, only the poet, as Sidney and others pointed out, is bound down and restricted by no laws. But if poetry is a matter of inspiration, how can it be called an art? If genius alone suffices, what need is there of study and artifice? For the extreme romanticists of this period, genius alone was accounted sufficient to produce the greatest works of poetry; for the extreme classicists, studious and labored art unaided by genius fulfilled all the functions of poetic creation; but most of the critics of the sixteenth century seem to have agreed with Horace that genius, or an inborn aptitude, is necessary to begin with, but that it needs art and study to regulate and perfect it. Genius cannot suffice without restraint and cultivation.

Scaliger, curiously, reconciles both classic and romantic elements. The poet, according to Scaliger, is inspired, is in fact a creator like God; but poetry is an imitation (that is, re-creation) of nature, according to certain fixed rules obtained from the observation of the anterior expression of nature in great art. It is these rules that make poetry an art; and these rules form a distinct neo-classic element imposed on the Aristotelian doctrine.

II. *Mediæval Elements*

The Middle Ages contributed to the poetic
ideal of the Renaissance two elements: romantic
themes and the Christian spirit. The forms and
subjects of mediæval literature are distinctly romantic. Dante's *Divine Comedy* is an allegorical
vision; it is almost unique in form, and has no
classical prototype.[1] The tendency of Petrarchism
was also in the direction of romanticism. Its
"conceits" and its subjectivity led to an unclassical
extravagance of thought and expression; and the
Petrarchistic influence made lyric poetry, and accordingly the criticism of lyric poetry, more romantic than any other form of literature or literary
criticism during the period of classicism. It was
for this reason that there was little lyricism in the
classical period, not only in France, but wherever
the classic temper predominated. The themes of
the *romanzi* are also mediæval and romantic; but
while they are mediæval contributions to literature,[2]
they became contributions to literary criticism
only after the growth of national life and the development of the feeling of nationality, both distinctly modern.

Some reference has already been made to the
paganization of culture by the humanists. But
with the growth of that revival of Christian sentiment which led to the Reformation, there were
numerous attempts to reconcile Christianity with

[1] *Cf.* Bosanquet, *Hist. of Æsthetic*, p. 152 *sq.*
[2] *Cf.* Foffano, p. 151 *sq.*

pagan culture.[1] Such men as Ficino and Pico della Mirandola attempted to harmonize Christianity and Platonic philosophy; and under the great patron of letters, Pope Leo X., there were various attempts to harmonize Christianity with the classic spirit in literature. In such poems as Vida's *Christiad* and Sannazaro's *De Partu Virginis*, Christianity is covered with the drapery of paganism or classicism.

The first reaction against this paganization of culture was, as has been seen, effected by Savonarola. This reaction was reënforced, in the next century, by the influence and authority of the Council of Trent; and after the middle of the sixteenth century the Christian ideal plays a prominent part in literary criticism. The spirit of both Giraldi Cintio and Minturno is distinctly Christian. For Giraldi the *romanzi* are Christian, and hence superior to the classical epics. He allows the introduction of pagan deities only into epics dealing with the ancient classical subjects; but Tasso goes further, and says that no modern heroic poet should have anything to do with them. According to Tasso, the heroes of an heroic poem must be Christian knights, and the poem itself must deal with a true, not a false, religion. The subject is not to be connected with any article of Christian faith or dogma, because that was fixed by the Council of Trent; but paganism in any form is altogether unfit for a modern epic. Tasso even goes so far as to assert that piety shall be numbered among the virtues of the knightly heroes of epic poetry.

[1] Symonds, ii. 470.

At the same time also, Lorenzo Gambara wrote his
work, *De Perfecta Poeseos Ratione*, to prove that it
is essential for every poet to exclude from his
poems, not only everything that is wicked or obscene, but also everything that is fabulous or that
deals with pagan divinities.[1]   It was to this religious reaction that we owe the Christian poetry of
Tasso, Du Bartas, and Spenser. But humanism
was strong, and rationalism was rife; and the religious revival was hardly more than temporary.
Neo-classicism throughout Europe was essentially
pagan.

III. *Modern Elements*

The literature of the Middle Ages constitutes, as
it were, one vast body of European literature; only
with the Renaissance did distinctly national literatures spring into existence.   Nationalism as well as
individualism was subsequent to the Renaissance;
and it was at this period that the growth of a
national literature, of national life, — in a word,
patriotism in its widest sense, — was first effected.

The linguistic discussions and controversies of
the sixteenth century prepared the way for a higher
appreciation of national languages and literatures.
These controversies on the comparative merits of
the classical and vernacular tongues had begun in
the time of Dante, and were continued in the sixteenth century by Bembo, Castiglione, Varchi, Muzio,
Tolomei, and many others; and in 1564 Salviati
summed up the Italian side of the question in an

[1] Baillet, iii. 70.

M

oration in which he asserted that the Tuscan, or, as
he called it, the Florentine language and the Florentine literature are vastly superior to any other
language or literature, whether ancient or modern.
However extravagant this claim may appear, the
mere fact that Salviati made such a claim at all is
enough to give him a place worthy of serious consideration in the history of Italian literature. The
other side of the controversy finds its extremest
expression in a treatise of Celio Calcagnini addressed to Giraldi Cintio, in which the hope is
expressed that the Italian language, and all the
literature composed in that language, would be
absolutely abandoned by the world.[1]

In Giraldi Cintio we find the first traces of purely
national criticism. His purpose, in writing the
discourse on the *romanzi*, was primarily to defend
Ariosto, whom he had known personally in his
youth. The point of view from which he starts is
that the *romanzi* constitute a new form of poetry
of which Aristotle did not know, and to which,
therefore, Aristotle's rules do not apply. Giraldi
regarded the romantic poems of Ariosto and Boiardo both as national and as Christian works; and
Italian literature is thus for the first time critically
distinguished from classical literature in regard to
language, religion, and nationality. In Giraldi's
discourse there is no apparent desire either to un-
derrate or to disregard the *Poetics* of Aristotle; the
fact was simply that Aristotle had not known the
poems which deal with many actions of many men,

[1] Tiraboschi, vii. 1559.

and hence it would be absurd to demand that such
poems should conform to his rules. The *romanzi*
deal with phases of poetry, and phases of life,
which Aristotle could not be expected to understand.

A similar feeling of the distinct nationality of
Italian literature is to be found in many of the
prefaces of the Italian comedies of this period. Il
Lasca, in the preface of the *Strega* (*c.* 1555), says
that "Aristotle and Horace knew their own times,
but ours are not the same at all. We have other
manners, another religion, and another mode of
life; and it is therefore necessary to make comedies after a different fashion." As early as 1534,
Aretino, in the prologue of his *Cortegiana*, warned
his audience "not to be astonished if the comic
style is not observed in the manner required, for
we live after a different fashion in modern Rome
than they did in ancient Athens." Similarly, Gelli,
in the dedication of the *Sporta* (1543), justifies the
use of language not to be found in the great sources
of Italian speech, on the ground that "language,
together with all other natural things, continually
varies and changes." [1]

Although there is in Giraldi Cintio no fundamental opposition to Aristotle, it is in his discourse on
the *romanzi* that there may be found the first attempt to wrest a province of art from Aristotle's
supreme authority. Neither Salviati, who had
rated the Italian language above all others, nor
Calcagnini, who had regarded it as the meanest of

[1] Several similar extracts from Italian comic prologues **may
be found in Symonds, v. 533 *sq*.**

all, had understood the discussion of the importance of the Tuscan tongue to be concerned with
the question of Aristotle's literary supremacy. It
was simply a national question — a question as to the
national limits of Aristotle's authority, just as was
the case in the several controversies connected with
Tasso, Dante, and Guarini's *Pastor Fido*.[1] Castelvetro, in his commentary on the *Poetics*, differs
from Aristotle on many occasions, and does not
hesitate even to refute him. Yet his reverence for
Aristotle is great; his sense of Aristotle's supreme
authority is strong; and on one occasion, where
Horace, Quintilian, and Cicero seem to differ from
Aristotle, Castelvetro does not hesitate to assert
that they could not have seen the passage of the
Poetics in question, and that, in fact, they did not
thoroughly understand the true constitution of a
poet.[2]

The opposition to Aristotelianism among the
humanists has already been alluded to. This opposition increased more and more with the development of modern philosophy. In 1536 Ramus had
attacked Aristotle's authority at Paris. A few
years later, in 1543, Ortensio Landi, who had been
at the Court of France for some time, published his
Paradossi, in which it is contended that the works
which pass under the name of Aristotle are not
really Aristotle's at all, and that Aristotle himself
was not only an ignoramus, but also the most vil-
lanous man of his age. "We have, of our own
accord," he says, "placed our necks under the yoke,

[1] Foffano, p. 154 *sq*.   [2] *Poetica*, p. 32.

putting that vile beast of an Aristotle on a throne, and depending on his conclusions as if he were an oracle." [1] It is the philosophical authority of Aristotle that Landi is attacking. His attitude is not that of a humanist, for Cicero and Boccaccio do not receive more respectful treatment at his hands than Aristotle does. Landi, despite his mere eccentricities, represents the growth of modern free thought and the antagonism of modern philosophy to Aristotelianism.

The literary opposition and the philosophical opposition to Aristotelianism may be said to meet in Francesco Patrizzi, and, in a less degree, in Giordano Bruno. Patrizzi's bitter Antiperipateticism is to be seen in his *Nova de Universis Philosophia* (1591), in which the doctrines of Aristotle are shown to be false, inconsistent, and even opposed to the doctrines of the Catholic Church. His literary antagonism to Aristotle is shown in his remarkable work, *Della Poetica*, published at Ferrara in 1586. This work is divided into two parts, — the first historical, *La Deca Istoriale*, and the second controversial, *La Deca Disputata*. In the historical section he attempts to derive the norm of the different poetic forms, not from one or two great works as Aristotle had done, but from the whole history of literature. It is thus the first work in modern times to attempt the philosophical study of literary history, and to trace out the evolution of literary forms. The second or controversial section is directed against the *Poetics* of Aristotle, and in part

1 *Paradossi*, Venetia, 1545, ii. 29.

also against the critical doctrines of Torquato
Tasso. In this portion of his work Patrizzi sets out
to demonstrate — *per istoria, e per ragioni, e per
autorità de' grandi antichi* — that the accepted critical opinions of his time were without foundation ;
and the *Poetics* of Aristotle himself he exhibits
as obscure, inconsistent, and entirely unworthy of
credence.

Similar antagonism to the critical doctrines of
Aristotle is to be found in passages scattered here
and there throughout the works of Giordano Bruno.
In the first dialogue of the *Eroici Furori,* published
at London in 1585, while Bruno was visiting England, he expresses his contempt for the mere pedants who judge poets by the rules of Aristotle's
Poetics. His contention is that there are as many
sorts of poets as there are human sentiments and
ideas, and that poets, so far from being subservient
to rules, are themselves really the authors of all
critical dogma. Those who attack the great poets
whose works do not accord with the rules of Aristotle are called by Bruno stupid pedants and beasts.
The gist of his argument may be gathered from the
following passage : —

"Tans. Thou dost well conclude that poetry is not born
in rules, or only slightly and accidentally so ; the rules are
derived from the poetry, and there are as many kinds and
sorts of true rules as there are kinds and sorts of true poets.

Cic. How then are the true poets to be known ?

Tans. By the singing of their verses ; in that singing
they give delight, or they edify, or they edify and delight
together.

CIC. To whom then are the rules of Aristotle useful?

TANS. To him who, unlike Homer, Hesiod, Orpheus, and others, could not sing without the rules of Aristotle, and who, having no Muse of his own, would coquette with that of Homer." [1]

A similar antagonism to Aristotle and a similar literary individualism are to be found in a much later work by Benedetto Fioretti, who under the pseudonym of Udeno Nisieli published the five volumes of his *Proginnasmi Poetici* between 1620 and 1639.[2] Just before the close of the sixteenth century, however, the *Poetics* had obtained an ardent defender against such attacks in the person of Francesco Buonamici, in his *Discorsi Poetici;* and three years later, in 1600, Faustino Summo published a similar defence of Aristotle. The attacks on Aristotle's literary dictatorship were of little avail ; it was hardly necessary even to defend him. For two centuries to come he was to reign supreme on the continent of Europe ; and in Italy this supremacy was hardly disturbed until the days of Goldoni and Metastasio.

[1] *Opere*, ii. 315 (Williams's translation).

[2] *Cf.* the diverse opinions of Tiraboschi, viii. 516, and Hallam, *Lit. of Europe*, pt. iii. ch. 7.

PART SECOND

LITERARY CRITICISM IN FRANCE

LITERARY CRITICISM IN FRANCE

CHAPTER I

LITERARY criticism in France, while beginning somewhat later than in Italy, preceded the birth of criticism in England and in Spain by a number of years. Critical activity in nearly all the countries of western Europe seems to have been ushered in by the translation of Horace's *Ars Poetica* into the vernacular tongues. Critical activity in Italy began with Dolce's Italian version of the *Ars Poetica* in 1535; in France, with the French version of Pelletier in 1545; in England, with the English version of Drant in 1567; and in Spain, with the Spanish versions of Espinel and Zapata in 1591 and 1592, respectively. Two centuries of literary discussion had prepared the way for criticism in Italy; and lacking this period of preparation, French criticism during the sixteenth century was necessarily of a much more practical character than that of Italy during the same age. The critical works of France, and of England also, were on the whole designed for those whose immediate intention it

171

was to write verse themselves. The disinterested
and philosophic treatment of æsthetic problems,
wholly aside from all practical considerations, characterized much of the critical activity of the Italian
Renaissance, but did not become general in France
until the next century. For this reason, in the
French and English sections of this essay, it will
be necessary to deal with various rhetorical and
metrical questions which in the Italian section
could be largely disregarded. In these matters, as in
the more general questions of criticism, it will be seen
that sixteenth-century Italy furnished the source
of all the accepted critical doctrines of western
Europe. The comparative number of critical works
in Italy and in France is also noteworthy. While
those of the Italian Renaissance may be counted by
the score, the literature of France during the sixteenth century, exclusive of a few purely rhetorical
treatises, hardly offers more than a single dozen.
It is evident, therefore, that the treatment of
French criticism must be more limited in extent
than that of Italian criticism, and somewhat different in character.

The literature of the sixteenth century in France
is divided into two almost equal parts by Du
Bellay's *Défense et Illustration de la Langue française*, published in 1549. In no other country of
Europe is the transition from the Middle Ages to
the Renaissance so clearly marked as it is in France
by this single book. With the invasion of Italy by
the army of Charles VIII. in 1494, the influence of
Italian art, of Italian learning, of Italian poetry,

had received its first impetus in France.   But over
half a century was to elapse before the effects of
this influence upon the creative literature of France
was universally and powerfully felt.   During this
period the activity of Budæus, Erasmus, Dolet, and
numerous other French and foreign humanists
strengthened the cause and widened the influence
of the New Learning.   But it is only with the birth
of the Pléiade that modern French literature may
be said to have begun.   In 1549 Du Bellay's
Défense, the manifesto of the new school, appeared.
Ronsard's *Odes* were published in the next year;
and in 1552 Jodelle inaugurated French tragedy
with his *Cléopâtre*, and first, as Ronsard said,

" Françoisement chanta la grecque tragédie."

The *Défense* therefore marks a distinct epoch in the
critical as well as the creative literature of France.
The critical works that preceded it, if they may be
called critical in any real sense, did not attempt to
do more than formulate the conventional notions of
rhetorical and metrical structure common to the
French poets of the later Middle Ages.   The
Pléiade itself, as will be more clearly understood
later, was also chiefly concerned with linguistic and
rhetorical reforms; and as late as 1580 Montaigne
could say that there were more poets in France
than judges and interpreters of poetry.[1]   The creative reforms of the Pléiade lay largely in the direction of the formation of a poetic language, the
introduction of new *genres*, the creation of new

[1] *Essais*, i. 36.

rhythms, and the imitation of classical literature. But with the imitation of classical literature there came the renewal of the ancient subjects of inspiration; and from this there proceeded a high and dignified conception of the poet's office. Indeed, many of the more general critical ideas of the Pléiade spring from the desire to justify the function of poetry, and to magnify its importance. The new school and its epigones dominate the second half of the sixteenth century; and as the first half of the century was practically unproductive of critical literature, a history of French Renaissance criticism is hardly more than an account of the poetic theories of the Pléiade.

The series of rhetorical and metrical treatises that precede Du Bellay's *Défense* begins with *L'Art de dictier et de fere chançons, balades, virelais et rondeaulx*, written by the poet Eustache Deschamps in 1392, over half a century after the similar work of Antonio da Tempo in Italy.[1] Toward the close of the fifteenth century a work of the same nature, the *Fleur de Rhétorique*, by an author who refers to himself as L'Infortuné, seems to have had some influence on later treatises. Three works of this sort fall within the first half of the sixteenth century: the *Grand et vrai Art de pleine Rhétorique* of Pierre Fabri, published at Rouen in 1521; the *Rhétorique metrifiée* of Gracien du Pont, published at Paris in 1539; and the *Art Poétique* of Thomas Sibilet, published at Paris in 1548. The second

---

[1] On these early works, see Langlois, *De Artibus Rhetoricæ Rhythmicæ*, Parisiis, 1890.

part of Fabri's *Rhétorique* deals with questions of
versification — of rhyme, rhythm, and the complex
metrical form of such poets as Crétin, Meschinot,
and Molinet, in whom Pasquier found *prou de rime
et équivoque, mais peu de raison.* As the *Rhétorique*
of Fabri is little more than an amplification of
the similar work of L'Infortuné, so the work of
Gracien du Pont is little more than a reproduc-
tion of Fabri's. Gracien du Pont is still chiefly
intent on *rime équivoquée, rime entrelacée, rime
retrograde, rime concatenée,* and the various other
mediæval complexities of versification. Sibilet's
Art Poétique is more interesting than any of its
predecessors. It was published a year before
the *Défense* of Du Bellay, and discusses many
of the new *genres* which the latter advocates.
Sibilet treats of the sonnet, which had recently
been borrowed from the Italians by Mellin de
Saint-Gelais, the ode, which had just been employed
by Pelletier, and the epigram, as practised by
Marot. The eclogue is described as "Greek by
invention, Latin by usurpation, and French by imitation." But one of the most interesting passages
in Sibilet's book is that in which the French morality is compared with the classical drama. This
passage exhibits perhaps the earliest trace of the
influence of Italian ideas on French criticism; it
will be discussed later in connection with the dramatic theories of this period.

It is about the middle of the sixteenth century,
then, that the influence of Italian criticism is first
visible. The literature of Italy was read with

avidity in France. Many educated young French-
men travelled in Italy, and several Italian men of
letters visited France. Girolamo Muzio travelled
in France in 1524, and again in 1530 with Giulio
Cammillo.[1] Aretino mentions the fact that a Vin-
cenzo Maggi was at the Court of France in 1548,
but it has been doubted whether this was the
author of the commentary on the *Poetics*.[2] In 1549,
after the completion of the two last parts of his
Poetica, dedicated to the Bishop of Arras, Trissino
made a tour about France.[3] Nor must we forget
the number of Italian scholars called to Paris by
Francis I.[4] The literary relations between the
two countries do not concern us here; but it is no
insignificant fact that the great literary reforms of
the Pléiade should take place between 1548 and
1550, the very time when critical activity first
received its great impetus in Italy. This Italian
influence is just becoming apparent in Sibilet, for
whom the poets between Jean le Maire de Belges
and Clément Marot are the chief models, but who
is not wholly averse to the moderate innovations
derived by France from classical antiquity and the
Italian Renaissance.

M. Brunetière, in a very suggestive chapter of
his History of French Criticism, regards the *Défense* of Du Bellay, the *Poetics* of Scaliger, and the
Art Poétique of Vauquelin de la Fresnaye as the
most important critical works in France during

---

[1] Tiraboschi, vii. 350.
[2] *Ibid*. vii. 1465.
[3] Morsolin, *Trissino*, p. 358.
[4] Egger, *Hellénisme*, ch. vii.

the sixteenth century.[1] It may indeed be said that Du Bellay's *Défense* (1549) is not in any true sense a work of literary criticism at all; that Scaliger's *Poetics* (1561) is the work, not of a French critic, but of an Italian humanist; and that Vauquelin's *Art Poétique* (not published until 1605), so far as any influence it may have had is concerned, does not belong to the sixteenth century, and can hardly be called important. At the same time these three works are interesting documents in the literary history of France, and represent three distinct stages in the development of French criticism in the sixteenth century. Du Bellay's work marks the beginning of the introduction of classical ideals into French literature; Scaliger's work, while written by an Italian and in Latin, was composed and published in France, and marks the introduction of the Aristotelian canons into French criticism; and Vauquelin's work indicates the sum of critical ideas which France had gathered and accepted in the sixteenth century.

With Du Bellay's *Défense et Illustration de la Langue française* (1549) modern literature and modern criticism in France may be said to begin. The *Défense* is a monument of the influence of Italian upon French literary and linguistic criticism. The purpose of the book, as its title implies, is to defend the French language, and to indicate the means by which it can approach more closely to dignity and perfection. The fundamental contention of Du Bellay is, first, that the French

---

[1] Brunetière, i. 43.

N

language is capable of attaining perfection; and, secondly, that it can only hope to do so by imitating Greek and Latin. This thesis is propounded and proved in the first book of the *Défense;* and the second book is devoted to answering the question: By what specific means is this perfection, based on the imitation of the perfection of Greek and Latin, to be attained by the French tongue? Du Bellay contends that as the diversity of language among the different nations is ascribable entirely to the caprice of men, the perfection of any tongue is due exclusively to the diligence and artifice of those who use it. It is the duty, therefore, of every one to set about consciously to improve his native speech. The Latin tongue was not always as perfect as it was in the days of Virgil and Cicero; and if these writers had regarded language as incapable of being polished and enriched, or if they had imagined that their language could only be perfected by the imitation of their own national predecessors, Latin would never have arrived at a higher state of perfection than that of Ennius and Crassus. But as Virgil and Cicero perfected Latin by imitating Greek, so the French tongue can only be made beautiful by imitating Greek, Latin, and Italian, all of which have attained a certain share of perfection.[1]

At the same time, two things must be guarded against. The French tongue cannot be improved by merely translating the classic and Italian tongues. Translation has its value in popularizing ideas; but

[1] *Cf.* Horace, *Ars Poet.* 53 *sq.*

by mere translation no language or literature can
hope to attain perfection. Nor is a mere bald imitation sufficient; but, in Du Bellay's oft-cited phrase,
the beauties of these foreign tongues "must be converted into blood and nourishment."[1] The classics
have "blood, nerves, and bones," while the older
French writers have merely "skin and color."[2]
The modern French writer should therefore dis-
miss with contempt the older poets of France, and
set about to imitate the Greeks, Latins, and Italians.
He should leave off composing rondeaux, ballades,
virelays, and such *épiceries*, which corrupt the taste
of the French language, and serve only to show its
ignorance and poverty; and in their stead he should
employ the epigram, which mingles, in Horace's
words, the profitable with the pleasant, the tearful
elegy, in imitation of Ovid and Tibullus, the ode,
one of the sublimest forms of poetry, the eclogue, in
imitation of Theocritus, Virgil, and Sannazaro,
and the beautiful sonnet, an Italian invention no
less learned than pleasing.[3] Instead of the morality
and the farce, the poet should write tragedies and
comedies; he should attempt another *Iliad* or
Æneid for the glory and honor of France. This
is the gist of Du Bellay's argument in so far as it
deals in general terms with the French language
and literature. The six or seven concluding chapters treat of more minute and detailed questions of
language and versification. Du Bellay advises the
adoption of classical words as a means of enriching
the French tongue, and speaks with favor of the

---

[1] *Défense*, i. 7.   [2] *Ibid.* ii. 2.   [3] *Ibid.* ii. 4.

use of rhymeless verse in imitation of the classics
The *Défense* ends with an appeal to the reader not
to fear to go and despoil Greece and Rome of their
treasures for the benefit of French poetry.[1]

From this analysis it will be seen that the *Défense* is really a philological polemic, belonging to
the same class as the long series of Italian discussions on the vulgar tongue which begins with
Dante, and which includes the works of Bembo,
Castiglione, Varchi, and others. It is, as a French
critic has said, a combined pamphlet, defence, and
ars poetica ;[2] but it is only an *ars poetica* in so far
as it advises the French poet to employ certain
poetic forms, and treats of rhythm and rhyme in a
concluding chapter or two. But curiously enough,
the source and inspiration of Du Bellay's work have
never been pointed out. The actual model of the
Défense was possibly Dante's *De Vulgari Eloquio*,
which, in the Italian version of Trissino, had
been given to the world for the first time in 1529,
exactly twenty years before the *Défense*. The
two works, allowing for the difference in time and
circumstance, resemble each other somewhat in
spirit and purpose as well as in contents and design. Du Bellay's work, like Dante's, is divided
into two books, each of which is again divided into
about the same number of chapters. The first book
of both works deals with language in general, and
the relations of the vulgar tongue to the ancient
and modern languages; the second book of both
works deals with the particular practices of the

[1] *Cf.* Vida. in Pope. i. 167.   [2] Lanson. *op. cit.*, p. **274**.

vulgar tongue concerning which each author is
arguing. Both works begin with a somewhat
similar theory of the origin of language; both
works close with a discussion of the versification of
the vernacular. The purpose of both books is the
justification of the vulgar tongue, and the consideration of the means by which it can attain perfection; the title of *De Vulgari Eloquio* might be
applied with equal force to either treatise. The
Défense, by this justification of the French language
on rational if not entirely cogent and consistent
grounds, prepared the way for critical activity in
France; and it is no insignificant fact that the first
critical work of modern France should have been
based on the first critical work of modern Italy.
Thirty years later, Henri Estienne, in his *Précel-
lence du Langage françois*, could assert that French
is the best language of ancient or modern times,
just as Salviati in 1564 had claimed that preëminent position for Italian.[1]

It is not to be expected that so radical a break
with the national traditions of France as was implied by Du Bellay's innovations would be left
unheeded by the enemies of the Pléiade. The answer came soon, in an anonymous pamphlet, entitled *Le Quintil Horatian sur la Défense et Illustration
de la Langue françoise*. Until a very few years ago,
this treatise was ascribed to a disciple of Marot,
Charles Fontaine. But in 1883 an autograph letter
of Fontaine's was discovered, in which he strenu-
ously denies the authorship of the *Quintil Horatian*;

[1] *Cf.* T. Tasso, xxiii. 97.

and more recent researches have shown pretty con-
clusively that the real author was a friend of Fontaine's, Barthélemy Aneau, head of the College of
Lyons.[1] The *Quintil Horatian* was first published
in 1550, the year after the appearance of the *Défense*.[2] The author informs us that he had translated the whole of Horace's *Ars Poetica* into
French verse "over twenty years ago, before Pelletier or any one else," that is, between 1525 and
1530.[3] This translation was never published, but
fragments of it are cited in the *Quintil Horatian*.
The pamphlet itself takes up the arguments of Du
Bellay step by step, and refutes them. The author
finds fault with the constructions, the metaphors,
and the neologisms of Du Bellay. Aneau's temperament was dogmatic and pedagogic; his judgment was not always good; and modern French
critics cannot forgive him for attacking Du Bellay's
use of such a word as *patrie*.

But it is not entirely just to speak of the *Quintil
Horatian*, in the words of a modern literary historian, as full of futile and valueless criticisms. The
author's minute linguistic objections are often hy-
percritical, but his work represents a natural reaction
against the Pléiade. His chief censure of the *Défense* was directed against the introduction of classical and Italian words into the French language.
"Est-ce là défense et illustration," he exclaims, "ou

[1] H. Chamard, "Le Date et l'Auteur du Quintil Horatian,"
in the *Revue d'Histoire littéraire de la France*, 1898, v. 59 *sq*.
[2] *Ibid*. v. 54 *sq*.
[3] *Ibid*. v. 62; 63, n. 1.

plus tost offense et dénigration?"   He charges
the Pléiade with having contemned the classics of
French poetry; the new school advocated the dis-
use of the complicated metrical forms merely because they were too difficult.   The sonnet, the ode,
and the elegy he dismisses as useless innovations.
The object of poetry, according to Horace, is to
gladden and please, while the elegy merely saddens
and brings tears to the eyes.   "Poetry," he says,
"is like painting; and as painting is intended to
fill us with delight, and not to sadden us, so the
mournful elegy is one of the meanest forms of
poetry."   Aneau is unable to appreciate the high
and sublime conception of the poet's office which
the Pléiade first introduced into French literature;
for him the poet is a mere versifier who amuses his
audience.   He represents the general reaction of
the national spirit against the classical innovations
of the Pléiade; and the *Quintil Horatian* may therefore be called the last representative work of the
older school of poetry.

It was at about this period that Aristotle's *Poetics*
first influenced French criticism.   In one of the
concluding chapters of the *Défense* Du Bellay
remarks that "the virtues and vices of a poem have
been diligently treated by the ancients, such as
Aristotle and Horace, and after them by Hierony-
mus Vida."[1]   Horace is mentioned and cited in
numerous other places, and the influence of the
general rhetorical portions of the *Ars Poetica* is
very marked throughout the *Défense ;* there are

[1] *Défense*, ii. 9.

also many traces of the influence of Vida. But
there is no evidence whatsoever of any knowledge
of Aristotle's *Poetics*. Of its name and importance
Du Bellay had probably read in the writings of the
Italians, but of its contents he knew little or nothing. There is indeed no well-established allusion
to the *Poetics* in France before this time. None of
the French humanists seems to have known it. Its
title is cited by Erasmus in a letter dated February
27, 1531, and it was published by him without any
commentary at Basle in the same year, though
Simon Grynæus appears to have been the real edi-
tor of this work. An edition of the *Poetics* was
also published at Paris in 1541, but does not seem
to have had any appreciable influence on the critical
activity of France. Several years after the publication of the *Défense*, in the satirical poem, *Le Poëte
Courtisan*, written shortly after his return from
Italy in 1555, Du Bellay shows a somewhat more
definite knowledge of the contents of the *Poetics* : —

" Je ne veux point ici du maistre d'Alexandre [*i.e.* Aristotle],
  Touchant l'art poétic, les preceptes t'apprendre
  Tu n'apprendras de moy comment jouer il faut
  Les miseres des rois dessus un eschaffaut :
  Je ne t'enseigne l'art de l'humble comœdie
  Ni du Méonien la muse plus hardie :
  Bref je ne monstre ici d'un vers horacien
  Les vices et vertus du poëme ancien :
  Je ne depeins aussi le poëte du Vide." [1]

In 1555 Guillaume Morel, the disciple of Turne-
bus, published an edition of Aristotle's *Poetics* at

[1] Du Bellay, p. 120.

Paris. It is interesting to note, however, that the reference in the *Défense* is the first allusion to the *Poetics* to be found in the critical literature of France; by 1549 the Italian Renaissance, and Italian criticism, had come into France for good. In 1560, the year before the publication of Scaliger's *Poetics*, Aristotle's treatise had acquired such prominence that in a volume of selections from Aristotle's works, published at Paris in that year, *Aristotelis Sententiæ*, the selections from the *Poetics* are placed at the head of the volume.[1] In 1572 Jean de la Taille refers his readers to what "the great Aristotle in his *Poetics*, and after him Horace though not with the same subtlety, have said more amply and better than I."[2]

The influence of Scaliger's *Poetics* on the French dramatic criticism of this period has generally been overestimated. Scaliger's influence in France was not inconsiderable during the sixteenth century, but it was not until the very end of the century that he held the dictatorial position afterward accorded to him. No edition of his *Poetics* was ever published at Paris. The first edition appeared at Lyons, and subsequent editions appeared at Heidelberg and Leyden. It was in Germany, in Spain, and in England that his influence was first felt; and it was largely through the Dutch scholars, Heinsius and Vossius, that his influence was carried into France in the next century. It is a mistake to say that he had any primary influence on

---

[1] Parisiis, apud Hieronymum de Marnaf, 1560.
[2] Robert, appendix iii.

the formulation and acceptance of the unities of
time and place in French literature; there is in his
Poetics, as has been seen, no such definite and formal
statement of the unities as may be found in Castelvetro, in Jean de la Taille, in Sir Philip Sidney, or
in Chapelain. At the same time, while Scaliger's
Poetics did not assume during the sixteenth century
the dictatorial supremacy it attained during the
seventeenth, and while the particular views enunciated in its pages had no direct influence on the cur-
rent of sixteenth-century ideas, it certainly had an
indirect influence on the general tendency of the
critical activity of the French Renaissance. This
indirect influence manifests itself in the gradual
Latinization of culture during the second half of
the sixteenth century, and, as will be seen later, in
the emphasis on the Aristotelian canons in French
dramatic criticism. Scaliger was a personal
friend of several members of the Pléiade, and
there is every reason to believe that he wielded
considerable, even if merely indirect, influence
on the development of that great literary movement.

The last expression of the poetic theories of the
Pléiade is to be found in the didactic poem of
Vauquelin de la Fresnaye, *L'Art Poétique françois,
où l'on peut remarquer la perfection et le défaut
des anciennes et des modernes poésies.* This poem,
though not published until 1605, was begun in
1574 at the command of Henry III., and, augmented by successive additions, was not yet complete by 1590. Vauquelin makes the following

explicit acknowledgment of his indebtedness to the critical writers that preceded him: —

> " Pour ce ensuivant les pas du fils de Nicomache [*i.e.* Aristotle],
>   Du harpeur de Calabre [*i.e.* Horace], et tout ce que remache
>   Vide et Minturne aprés, j'ay cet œuvre apresté." [1]

Aristotle, Horace, Vida, and Minturno are thus his acknowledged models and sources. Nearly the whole of Horace's *Ars Poetica* he has translated and embodied in his poem; and he has borrowed from Vida a considerable number of images and metaphors.[2] His indebtedness to Aristotle and to Minturno brings up several intricate questions. It has been said that Vauquelin simply mentioned Minturno in order to put himself under the protection of a respectable Italian authority.[3] On the contrary, exclusive of Horace, Ronsard, and Du Bellay, the whole of whose critical discussions he has almost incorporated into his poem, Minturno is his chief authority, his model, and his guide. In fact, it was probably from Minturno that he derived his entire knowledge of the Aristotelian canons; it is not Aristotle, but Minturno's conception of Aristotle, that Vauquelin has adhered to. Many points in his poem are explained by this fact; here only one can be mentioned. Vauquelin's account, in the second canto of his *Art Poétique*, of the origin of

[1] *Art Poét.* i. 63.

[2] Pellissier, pp. 57–63.

[3] Lemercier, *Étude sur Vauquelin*, 1887, p. 117, and Pellissier, p. 57.

the drama from the songs at the altar of Bacchus at the time of the vintage, is undoubtedly derived from Minturno.[1] It may have been observed that during the Renaissance there were two distinct conceptions of the origin of poetry. One, which might be called ethical, was derived from Horace, according to whom the poet was originally a law-giver, or divine prophet; and this conception per-sists in modern literature from Poliziano to Shelley. The other, or scientific conception, was especially applied to the drama, and was based on Aristotle's remarks on the origin of tragedy; this attempt to discover some scientific explanation for poetic phe-nomena may be found in the more rationalistic of Renaissance critics, such as Scaliger and Viperano. Vauquelin de la Fresnaye, the disciple of Ronsard and the last exponent of the critical doctrines of the Pléiade, thus represents the incorporation of the body of Italian ideas into French criticism.

With Vauquelin de la Fresnaye and De Laudun Daigaliers (1598) the history of French criticism during the sixteenth century is at an end. The critical activity of this period, as has already been remarked, is of a far more practical character than that of Italy. Literary criticism in France was created by the exigencies of a great literary move-ment; and throughout the century it never lost its connection with this movement, or failed to serve it in some practical way. The poetic criticism was carried on by poets, whose desire it was to further

---

[1] Minturno, *Arte Poetica*, p. 73; *De Poeta*, p. 252. *Cf.* Vauquelin, Pellissier's introduction, p. xliv.

a cause, to defend their own works, or to justify their own views. The dramatic criticism was for the most part carried on by dramatists, sometimes even in the prefaces of their plays. In the sixteenth century, as ever since, the interrelation of the creative and the critical faculties in France was marked and definite. But there was, one might almost say, little critical theorizing in the French Renaissance. Excepting, of course, Scaliger, there was even nothing of the deification of Aristotle found in Italian criticism. To take notice of a minute but significant detail, there was no attempt to explain Aristotle's doctrine of *katharsis*, the source of infinite controversy in Italy. There was no detailed and consistent discussion of the theory of the epic poem. All these things may be found in seventeenth-century France; but their home was sixteenth-century Italy.[1]

[1] The statement on page 180 in regard to Du Bellay's indebtedness to Dante must be modified in the light of the more recent researches of P. Villey (*Les Sources italiennes de la Deffence et Illustration de la Langue françoyse*, Paris, 1908), who has shown that much of the *Défense* is literally translated from a dialogue of Sperone Speroni, one of "the long series of Italian discussions on the vulgar tongue" to which I refer on the same page. My instinctive sense of Du Bellay's great indebtedness to the Italians has therefore been justified. Among other works which should be consulted by the student I may mention Pierre de Nolhac's *Ronsard et l'Humanisme*, Jugé's *Jacques Peletier du Mans*, Franchet's *Le Poète et son œuvre d'après Ronsard*, and Chamard's critical edition of the *Défense*

CHAPTER II

IT is in keeping with the practical character of
the literary criticism of this period that the members of the Pléiade did not concern themselves with
the general theory of poetry. Until the very end
of the century there is not to be found any systematic poetic theory in France. It is in dramatic
criticism that this period has most to offer, and
the dramatic criticism is peculiarly interesting because it foreshadows in many ways the doctrines
upon which were based the dramas of Racine and
Corneille.

I. *The Poetic Art*

In Du Bellay's *Défense* there is no attempt to
formulate a consistent body of critical doctrine;
but the book exhibits, in a more or less crude form,
all the tendencies for which the Pléiade stands in
French literature. The fundamental idea of the
Défense is that French poetry can only hope to
reach perfection by imitating the classics. The
imitation of the classics implies, in the first place,
erudition on the part of the poet; and, moreover,

it requires intellectual labor and study. The poet
is born, it is true; but this only refers to the ardor
and joyfulness of spirit which naturally excite him,
but which, without learning and erudition, are absolutely useless. "He who wishes poetic immor-
tality," says Du Bellay, "must spend his time in
the solitude of his own chamber; instead of eating, drinking, and sleeping, he must endure hun-
ger, thirst, and long vigils." [1] Elsewhere he speaks
of silence and solitude as *amy des Muses*. From all
this there arises a natural contempt for the ignorant people, who know nothing of ancient learning :
"Especially do I wish to admonish him who aspires
to a more than vulgar glory, to separate himself
from such inept admirers, to flee from the ignorant
people, — the people who are the enemies of all
rare and antique learning, — and to content himself
with few readers, following the example of him who
did not demand for an audience any one beside Plato
himself." [2]

In the *Art Poétique* of Jacques Pelletier du Mans,
published at Lyons in 1555, the point of view is
that of the Pléiade, but more mellow and moderate
than that of its most advanced and radical members. The treatise begins with an account of the
antiquity and excellence of poetry; and poets are
spoken of as originally the *maîtres et réformateurs
de la vie*. Poetry is then compared with oratory
and with painting, after the usual Renaissance
fashion; and Pelletier agrees with Horace in regarding the combined power of art and nature as

[1] *Défense*, ii. 3.   [2] *Ibid*. ii. 11.

necessary to the fashioning of a poet. His conception of the latter's office is not unlike that of Tasso
and Shelley, " It is the office of the poet to give
novelty to old things, authority to the new, beauty
to the rude, light to the obscure, faith to the doubt-
ful, and to all things their true nature, and to their
true nature all things." Concerning the questions
of language, versification, and the feeling for natural
scenery, he agrees fundamentally with the chief
writers of the Pléiade.

The greatest of these, Ronsard, has given expression to his views on the poetic art in his *Abrégé de l'Art Poétique françois* (1565), and later
in the two prefaces of his epic of the *Franciade*.
The chief interest of the *Abrégé* in the present discussion is that it expounds and emphasizes the high
notion of the poet's office introduced into French
poetry by the Pléiade. Before the advent of the
new school, mere skill in the complicated forms of
verse was regarded as the test of poetry. The
poet was simply a *rimeur;* and the term *"poète,"*
with all that it implies, first came into use with
the Pléiade. The distinction between the versifier
and the poet, as pointed out by Aristotle and insisted upon by the Italians, became with the Pléiade almost vital. Binet, the disciple and biographer
of Ronsard, says of his master that " he was the
mortal enemy of versifiers, whose conceptions are
all debased, and who think they have wrought a
masterpiece when they have transposed something
from prose into verse."[1] Ronsard's own account

[1] Ronsard, vii. 310, 325.

of the dignity and high function of poetry must
needs be cited at length : —

" Above all things you will hold the Muses in reverence,
yea, in singular veneration, and you will never let them
serve in matters that are dishonest, or mere jests, or inju-
dicious libels ; but you will hold them dear and sacred, as
the daughters of Jupiter, that is, God, who by His holy
grace has through them first made known to ignorant people
the excellencies of His majesty. For poetry in early times
was only an allegorical theology, in order to make stupid
men, by pleasant and wondrously colored fables, know
the secrets they could not comprehend, were the truth
too openly made known to them. . . . Now, since the
Muses do not care to lodge in a soul unless it is good,
holy, and virtuous, you should try to be of a good disposition, not wicked, scowling, and cross, but animated
by a gentle spirit ; and you should not let anything enter
your mind that is not superhuman and divine. You should
have, in the first place, conceptions that are high, grand,
beautiful, and not trailing upon the ground ; for the principal part of poetry consists of invention, which comes as
much from a beautiful nature as from the reading of good
and ancient authors. If you undertake any great work,
you will show yourself devout and fearing God, commencing it either with His name or by any other which represents some effects of His majesty, after the manner of the
Greek poets . . . for the Muses, Apollo, Mercury, Pallas,
and other similar deities, merely represent the powers of
God, to which the first men gave several names for the
diverse effects of His incomprehensible majesty." [1]

In this eloquent passage the conception of the
poet as an essentially moral being, — a doctrine
first enunciated by Strabo, and repeated by Minturno and others, — and Boccaccio's notion of

[1] Ronsard, vii. 37 *sq.*

o

poetry as originally an allegorical theology, are
both introduced into French criticism.   Elsewhere
Ronsard repeats the mediæval concept that poets

" d'un voile divers
Par fables ont caché le vray sens de leurs vers." [1]

It will be seen also that for Ronsard, poetry is essentially a matter of inspiration; and in the poem
just quoted, the *Discours à Jacques Grévin*, he follows the Platonic conception of divine inspiration
or madness.   A few years later Montaigne said of
poetry that " it is an easier matter to frame it than
to know it; being base and humble, it may be
judged by the precepts and art of it, but the good
and lofty, the supreme and divine, are beyond rules
and above reason.   It hath no community with our
judgment, but ransacketh and ravisheth the same." [2]

In his various critical works Ronsard shows
considerable indebtedness to the Italian theorists,
especially to Minturno.   He does not attempt any
formal definition of poetry, but its function is described as follows: " As the end of the orator is
to persuade, so that of the poet is to imitate, invent,
and represent the things that are, that can be, or
that the ancients regarded as true." [3]   The concluding clause of this passage is intended to justify
the modern use of the ancient mythology; but the
whole passage seems primarily to follow Scaliger [4]

[1] Ronsard, vi. 311 *sq.*
[2] *Essais*, i. 36, Florio's translation.
[3] Ronsard, vii. 322.   *Cf.* Aristotle, *Poet.* ix. 1-4; xxv. 6, 7.
[4] *Poet.* iii. 24.

and Minturno.[1] It is to be observed that verse is not mentioned in this definition as an essential requirement of poetry. It was indeed a favorite contention of his, and one for which he was indebted to the Italians, that all who write in verse are not poets. Lucan and Silius Italicus have robed history with the raiment of verse; but according to Ronsard they would have done better in many ways to have written in prose. The poet, unlike the historian, deals with the verisimilar and the probable; and while he cannot be responsible for falsehoods which are in opposition to the truth of things, any more than the historian can, he is not interested to know whether or not the details of his poems are actual historical facts. Verisimilitude, and not fact, is therefore the test of poetry.

In Vauquelin de la Fresnaye may be found most of the Aristotelian distinctions in regard to imitation, harmony, rhythm, and poetic theory in general; but these distinctions he derived. as has already been said, not directly from Aristotle, but in all probability from Minturno. Poetry is defined as an art of imitation : —

> " C'est un art d'imiter, un art de contrefaire
> Que toute poësie, ainsi que de pourtraire." [2]

Verse is described as a heaven-sent instrument, the language of the gods; and its value in poetry consists in clarifying and making the design compact.[3] But it is not an essential of poetry; Aris-

---

[1] *De Poeta*, pp. 44, 47.   [2] *Art Poét*. i. 187.
[3] *Ibid*. i. 87 *sq.*

totle permits us to poetize in prose; and the
romances of Heliodorus and Montemayor are examples of this poetic prose.[1] The object of poetry
is that it shall cause delight, and unless it succeeds
in this it is entirely futile: —

> " C'est le but, c'est la fin des vers que resjouir :
>   Les Muses autrement ne les veulent ouir."

As it is the function of the orator to persuade and
the physician to cure, and as they fail in their
offices unless they effect these ends, so the poet fails
unless he succeeds in pleasing.[2] This comparison
is a favorite one with the Italian critics. A similar
passage has already been cited from Daniello; and
the same notion is thus expressed by Lodovico
Dolce: "The aim of the physician is to cure dis-
eases by means of medicine; the orator's to persuade by force of his arguments; and if neither
attains this end, he is not called physician or orator.
So if the poet does not delight, he is not a poet, for
poetry delights all, even the ignorant."[3]

But delight, according to Vauquelin, is merely
the means of directing us to higher things; poetry
is a delightful means of leading us to virtue: —

> " C'est pourquoy des beaus vers la joyeuse alegresse
>   Nous conduit aux vertus d'une plaisante addresse."[4]

Vauquelin, like Scaliger, Tasso, Sidney, compares
the poet with God, the great Workman, who made

---

[1] *Art Poét.* ii. 261.   [3] *Osservationi*, Vinegia, 1560, p. 190.
[2] *Ibid.* i. 697 *sq*.   [4] *Art Poét.* i. 744

everything out of nothing.[1]   The poet is a divinely
inspired person, who, *sans art, sans sçavoir*, creates
works of divine beauty.   Vauquelin's contemporary,
Du Bartas, has in his *Uranie* expressed this idea in
the following manner : —

> "Each art is learned by art ; but Poesie
> Is a mere heavenly gift, and none can taste
> The dews we drop from Pindus plenteously,
> If sacred fire have not his heart embraced.

> "Hence is 't that many great Philosophers,
> Deep-learned clerks, in prose most eloquent,
> Labor in vain to make a graceful verse,
> Which many a novice frames most excellent."[2]

While this is the accepted Renaissance doctrine of
inspiration, Vauquelin, in common with all other
followers of the Pléiade, was fully alive to the necessity of artifice and study in poetry ; and he agrees
with Horace in regarding both art and nature as
equally necessary to the making of a good poet.   It
is usage that makes art, but art perfects and regu-
lates usage : —

> "Et ce bel Art nous sert d'escalier pour monter
> A Dieu."[3]

II. *The Drama*

Dramatic criticism in France begins as a reaction
against the drama of the Middle Ages.   The
mediæval drama was formless and inorganic, with-

---

[1] *Art Poét.* i. 19.   *Cf.* Tasso, cited by Shelley, *Defence*, p. 42,
"No one merits the name of creator except God and the poet."
[2] Sylvester's *Du Bartas*, 1641, p. 242.
[3] *Art Poét.* i. 149.

out art or dignity. The classical drama, on the other hand, possessed both form and dignity; and the new school, perceiving this contrast, looked to the Aristotelian canons, as restated by the Italians, to furnish the dignity and art which the tragedy of Greece and Rome possessed, and which their own moralities and farces fundamentally lacked. In the first reference to dramatic literature in French criticism, the mediæval and classical dramas are compared after this fashion; but as Sibilet (1548), in whose work this passage appears, wrote a year or so before the advent of the Pléiade, the comparison is not so unfavorable to the morality and the farce as it became in later critics. "The French morality," says Sibilet, "represents, in certain distinct traits, Greek and Latin tragedy, especially in that it treats of grave and momentous deeds (*faits graves et principaus*); and if the French had always made the ending of the morality sad and dolorous, the morality would be a tragedy. But in this, as in all things, we have followed our natural taste or inclination, which is to take from foreign things not all we see, but only what we think will be useful to us and of national advantage; for in the morality we treat, as the Greeks and Romans do in their tragedies, the narration of deeds that are illustrious, magnanimous, and virtuous, or true, or at least verisimilar; but we do otherwise in what is useful to the information of our manners and life, without subjecting ourselves to any sorrow or pleasure of the issue." [1] It would seem that Sibilet regards

[1] Sibilet, *Art Poét.* ii. 8.

the morality as lacking nothing but the unhappy ending of classical tragedy. At the same time this passage exhibits perhaps the first trace of Aristotelianism in French critical literature; for Sibilet specifies several characteristic features of Greek and Latin tragedy, which he could have found only in Aristotle or in the Italians. In the first place, tragedy deals only with actions that are grave, illustrious, and for the most part magnanimous or virtuous. In the second place, the actions of tragedy are either really true, that is, historical, or if not true, have all the appearance of truth, that is, they are verisimilar. Thirdly, the end of tragedy is always sad and dolorous. Fourthly, tragedy performs a useful function, which is connected in some way with the reformation of manners and life; and, lastly, the effect of tragedy is connected with the sorrow or pleasure brought about by the catastrophe. These distinctions anticipate many of those found later in Scaliger and in the French critics.

In Du Bellay (1549) we find no traces of dramatic theory beyond the injunction, already noted, that the French should substitute classical tragedy and comedy for the old morality and farce. A few years later, however, in Pelletier (1555), there appears an almost complete system of dramatic criticism. He urges the French to attempt the composition of tragedy and comedy. " This species of poetry," he says, " will bring honor to the French language, if it is attempted," — a remark which illustrates the innate predisposition of the French

for dramatic poetry.[1] He then proceeds to distinguish tragedy from comedy much in the same
manner as Scaliger does six years later. It is to
be remembered that Pelletier's *Art Poétique* was
published at Lyons in 1555, while Scaliger's *Poetics*
was published at the same place in 1561. Pelletier
may have known Scaliger personally; but it is
more probable that Pelletier derived his information from the same classical and traditional sources
as did Scaliger. At all events, Pelletier distinguishes tragedy from comedy in regard to style,
subject, characters, and ending in exact Scaligerian
fashion. Comedy has nothing in common with
tragedy except the fact that neither can have more
or less than five acts. The style and diction of
comedy are popular and colloquial, while those of
tragedy are most dignified and sublime. The comic
characters are men of low condition, while those of
tragedy are kings, princes, and great lords. The
conclusion of comedy is always joyous, that of
tragedy is always sorrowful and heart-rending.
The themes of tragedy are deaths, exiles, and
unhappy changes of fortune; those of comedy are
the loves and passions of young men and young
women, the indulgence of mothers, the wiles of
slaves, and the diligence of nurses.[2]

By this time, then, Aristotle's theory of tragedy,
as restated by the Italians, had become part of
French criticism. The actual practice of the French
drama had been modified by the introduction of
these rules; and they had played so important a

[1] Pelletier, *Art Poét.* ii. 7.   [2] *Ibid.*

part that Grévin, in his *Bref Discours pour l'Intelli-gence de ce Théâtre*, prefixed to his *Mort de César* (1562), could say that French tragedy had already attained perfection, even when regarded from the standpoint of the Aristotelian canons. "Our trage-dies," says Grévin, "have been so well polished that there is nothing left now to be desired, — 1 speak of those which are composed according to the rules of Aristotle and Horace." Grévin's *Dis-cours* was published the year after Scaliger's *Poetics*, but shows no indication of Scaligerian influence. His definition of tragedy is based on a most vague and incomplete recollection of Aristotle, "Tragedy, as Aristotle says in his *Poetics*, is an imitation or representation of some action that is illustrious and great in itself, such as the death of Cæsar." He shows his independence or his ignorance of Scaliger by insisting on the inferiority of Seneca, whom Scaliger had rated above all the Greeks; and he shows his independence of the ancients by substi-tuting a crowd of Cæsar's soldiers for the singers of the older chorus, on the ground that there ought not to be singing in the representation of tragedy any more than there is in actual life itself, for tragedy is a representation of truth or of what has the appearance of truth. There are in Grévin's *Discours* several indications that the national feel-ing had not been entirely destroyed by the imita-tion of the classics; but a discussion of this must be left for a later chapter.

In Jean de la Taille's *Art de Tragédie*, prefixed to his *Saül le Furieux* (1572), a drama in which a

biblical theme is fashioned after the manner of
classical tragedy, there is to be found the most ex
plicit and distinct antagonism to the old, irregular
moralities, which are not modelled according to the
true art and the pattern of the ancients.   They are
but *amères épiceries* — words that recall Du Bellay.
But curiously enough, Jean de la Taille differs
entirely from Grévin, and asserts positively that
France had as yet no real tragedies, except possibly a few translated from the classics.   Waging
war, as he is, against the crude formlessness of the
national drama, perfect construction assumes for
him a very high importance.   "The principal
point in tragedy," he says, "is to know how to
dispose and fashion it well, so that the plot is well
intertwined, mingled, interrupted, and resumed,
. . . and that there is nothing useless, without
purpose, or out of place."   For Jean de la Taille,
as for most Renaissance writers, tragedy is the
least popular and the most elegant and elevated
form of poetry, exclusive of the epic.   It deals
with the pitiful ruin of great lords, with the in-
constancy of fortune, with banishment, war, pestilence, famine, captivity, and the execrable cruelty
of tyrants.[1]   The end of tragedy is in fact to move
and to sting the feelings and the emotions of men.
The characters of tragedy — and this is the Aristotelian conception — should be neither extremely
bad, such men as by their crimes merit punishment,
nor perfectly good and holy, like Socrates, who was
wrongfully put to death.   Invented or allegorical

[1] Robert, app. iii.

characters, such as Death, Avarice, or Truth, are
not to be employed. At the same time, Jean de
la Taille, like Grévin, is not averse to the use of
scriptural subjects in tragedy, although he cautions
the poet against long-winded theological discussions.
The Senecan drama was his model in treating of
tragedy, as it was indeed that of the Renaissance
in general; and tragedy approached more and more
closely to the oratorical and sententious manner of
the Latin poet. Ronsard, for example, asserts that
tragedy and comedy are entirely *didascaliques et en-
seignantes,* and should be enriched by numerous excellent and rare *sentences (sententiæ),* "for in a few
words the drama must teach much, being the mirror of human life."[1] Similarly, Du Bellay advises
poets to embellish their poetry with grave *sentences,* and Pelletier praises Seneca principally because he is *sentencieux.*

Vauquelin, in his *Art Poétique,* gives a metrical
paraphrase of Aristotle's definition of tragedy : —

> " Mais le sujet tragic est un fait imité
> De chose juste et grave, en ses vers limité ;
> Auquel on y doit voir de l'affreux, du terrible,
> Un fait non attendu, qui tienne de l'horrible,
> Du pitoyable aussi, le cœur attendrissant
> D'un tigre furieux, d'un lion rugissant."[2]

The subject of tragedy should be old, and should
be connected with the fall of great tyrants and
princes;[3] and in regard to the number of acts, the
number of interlocutors on the stage, the *deus ex*

---

[1] Ronsard, iii. 18 *sq*.   [2] *Art Poet.* iii. 153.
[3] *Ibid.* ii. 1113, 441.

machina, and the chorus,[1] Vauquelin merely paraphrases Horace. Comedy is defined as the imitation of an action which by common usage is
accounted wicked, but which is not so wicked that
there is no remedy for it; thus, for example, a
man who has seduced a young girl may recompense
her by taking her in marriage.[2] Hence while the
actions of tragedy are "virtuous, magnificent, and
grand, royal, and sumptuous," the incidents of
comedy are actually and ethically of a lower grade.[3]
For tragi-comedy Vauquelin has nothing but contempt. It is, in fact, a bastard form, since the
tragedy with a happy ending serves a similar but
more dignified purpose. Vauquelin, like Boileau
and most other French critics after him, follows
Aristotle at length in the description of dramatic
recognitions and reversals of fortune.[4] Most of the
other Aristotelian distinctions are also to be found
in his work.

In the *Art Poétique françois* of Pierre de Laudun,
Sieur d'Aigaliers, published in 1598, these distinctions reappear in a more or less mutilated form.
In the fifth and last book of this treatise, De Laudun
follows the Italian scholars, especially Scaliger and
Viperano. He does not differ essentially from
Scaliger in the definition of tragedy, in the division
into acts and the place of the chorus, in the discussion of the characters and subjects of tragedy, and
in the distinction between tragedy and comedy.[5]

---

[1] *Art Poét.* ii. 459. [3] *Ibid.* iii. 181.
[2] *Ibid.* iii. 143. [4] *Ibid.* iii. 189 *sq.*
[5] Robert, app. iv.

His conception of tragedy is in keeping with the
usual Senecan ideal; it should be adorned by fre-
quent *sentences*, allegories, similitudes, and other
ornaments of poetry. The more cruel and sangui-
nary the tragic action is, the more excellent it will
be; but at the same time, much that makes the action cruel is to be enacted only behind the stage.
Like Pelletier, he objects to the introduction of all
allegorical and invented characters, or even gods
and goddesses, on the ground that these are not
actual beings, and hence are out of keeping with
the theme of tragedy, which must be real and historical. De Laudun has also something to say concerning the introduction of ghosts in the tragic
action; and his discussion is peculiarly interesting
when we remember that it was almost at this very
time, in England, that the ghost played so important a part in the Shakespearian drama. "If the
ghosts appear before the action begins," says De
Laudun, "they are permissible; but if they appear
during the course of the action, and speak to the
actors themselves, they are entirely faulty and rep-
rehensible." De Laudun borrowed from Scaliger
the scheme of the ideal tragedy: "The first act
contains the complaints; the second, the suspicions;
the third, the counsels; the fourth, the menaces
and preparations; the fifth, the fulfilment and effu-
sion of blood." [1] But despite his subservience to
Scaliger, he is not afraid to express his independence of the ancients. We are not, he says, entirely bound to their laws, especially in the number

[1] *Art Poét.* v. 6.

of actors on the stage, which according to classic
usage never exceeded three ; for nowadays, notwith-
standing the counsels of Aristotle and Horace, an
audience has not the patience to be satisfied with
only two or three persons at one time.

The history of the dramatic unities in France
during the sixteenth century demands some attention.   That they had considerable effect on the
actual practice of dramatic composition from the
very advent of the Pléiade is quite obvious; for in
the first scene of the first French tragedy, the
Cléopâtre of Jodelle (1552), there is an allusion to
the unity of time, which Corneille was afterward
to call the *règle des règles :* —

> " Avant que ce soleil, qui vient ores de naître,
> Ayant tracé son jour chez sa tante se plonge,
> Cléopâtre mourra ! "

In 1553 Mellin de Saint-Gelais translated Trissino's
Sofonisba into French, and the influence of the Italian
drama became fixed in France.   But the first distinct
formulation of the unities is to be found in Jean de la
Taille's *Art de Tragédie* (1572).   His statement of
the unities is explicit, " Il faut toujours représenter
l'histoire ou le jeu en un même jour, en un même
temps, et en un même lieu." [1]   Jean de la Taille
was indebted for this to Castelvetro, who two years
before had stated it thus, " La mutatione tragica non può tirar con esso seco se non una giornata
e un luogo." [2]   The unity of time was adopted by
Ronsard about this same time in the following
words : —

[1] Robert, app. iii.   [2] *Poetica*, p. 534.

"Tragedy and comedy are circumscribed and limited to a short space of time, that is, to one whole day. The most excellent masters of this craft commence their works from one midnight to another, and not from sunrise to sunset, in order to have greater compass and length of time. On the other hand, the heroic poem, which is entirely of a martial character (*tout guerrier*), comprehends only the actions of one whole year."[1]

This passage is without doubt borrowed from Minturno (1564):—

"Whoever regards well the works of the most admired ancient authors will find that the materials of scenic poetry terminate in one day, or do not pass beyond the space of two days; just as the action of the epic poem, however great and however long it may be, does not occupy more than one year."[2]

Minturno, it will be remembered, was the first to limit the action of the heroic poem to one year. In another passage he deduces the rule from the practice of Virgil and Homer;[3] but Ronsard seems to think that Virgil himself has not obeyed this law. We have already alluded to the influence of Minturno on the Pléiade. Vauquelin de la Fresnaye, who explicitly acknowledges his indebtedness to Minturno, also follows him in limiting the action of the drama to one day and that of the epic to one year:—

"Or comme eux l'heroic suivant le droit sentier,
  Doit son œuvre comprendre au cours d'un an entier;
  Le tragic, le comic, dedans une journee
  Comprend ce que fait l'autre au cours de son annee.
  Le theatre jamais ne doit estre rempli
  D'un argument plus long que d'un jour accompli."[4]

[1] Ronsard, iii. 19.   [3] *Ibid.* p. 12; *De Poeta*, p. 149.
[2] *Arte Poetica*, p. 71.   [4] *Art Poét.* ii. 253.

The two last lines of this passage bear considerable resemblance to Boileau's famous statement of the unities three-quarters of a century later.[1]

Toward the end of the sixteenth century, then, the unity of time, and in a less degree the unity of place, had become almost inviolable laws of the drama. But at this very period strong notes of revolt against the tyranny of the unities begin to be heard. Up to this time the classical Italian drama had been the pattern for French playwrights; but the irregular Spanish drama was now commencing to exert considerable influence in France, and with this Spanish influence came the Spanish opposition to the unities. In 1582 Jean de Beaubreuil, in the preface of his tragedy of *Régulus*, had spoken with contempt of the rule of twenty-four hours as *trop superstitieux*. But De Laudun was probably the first European critic to argue formally against it. The concluding chapter of his *Art Poétique* (1598) gives five different reasons why the unity of time should not be observed in the drama. The chapter is entitled, " Concerning those who say that the action of tragedy must conclude in a single day ; " and De Laudun begins by asserting that this opinion had never been sustained by any good author. This is fairly conclusive evidence that De Laudun had never directly consulted Aristotle's *Poetics*, but was indebted for his knowledge of Aristotle to the Italians, and especially to Scaliger. The five arguments which he formulates against the unity of time are as follows : —

[1] Boileau, *Art Poét*. iii. 45.

" In the first place, this law, if it is observed by any of the ancients, need not force us to restrict our tragedies in any way, since we are not bound by their manner of writing or by the measure of feet and syllables with which they compose their verses.   In the second place, if we were forced to observe this rigorous law, we should fall into one of the greatest of absurdities, by being obliged to introduce impossible and incredible things in order to enhance the beauty of our tragedies, or else they would lack all grace ; for besides being deprived of matter, we could not embellish our poems with long discourses and various interesting events.   In the third place, the action of the *Troades*, an excellent tragedy by Seneca, could not have occurred in one day, nor could even some of the plays of Euripides or Sophocles.   In the fourth place, according to the definition already given [on the authority of Aristotle], tragedy is the recital of the lives of heroes, the fortune and grandeur of kings, princes, and others ; and all this could not be accomplished in one day. Besides, a tragedy must contain five acts, of which the first is joyous, and the succeeding ones exhibit a gradual change, as I have already indicated above; and this change a single day would not suffice to bring about.   In the fifth and last place, the tragedies in which this rule is observed are not any better than the tragedies in which it is not observed ; and the tragic poets, Greek and Latin, or even French, do not and need not and cannot observe it, since very often in a tragedy the whole life of a prince, king, emperor, noble, or other person is represented ; — besides a thousand other reasons which I could advance if time permitted, but which must be left for a second edition. " [1]

The history of the unity of time during the next century does not strictly concern us here; but it may be well to point out that it was through the offices of Chapelain, seconded by the authority of Cardinal Richelieu, that it became fixed in the

[1] Arnaud, app. iii.

P

dramatic theory of France. In a long letter, dating
from November, 1630, and recently published for
the first time, Chapelain sets out to answer all the
objections made against the rule of twenty-four
hours. It is sustained, he says, by the practice of
the ancients and the universal consensus of the
Italians; but his own proof is based on reason
alone. It is the old argument of *vraisemblance*, as
found in Maggi, Scaliger, and especially Castelvetro,
whom Chapelain seems in part to follow. By 1635
he had formulated the whole theory of the three
unities and converted Cardinal Richelieu to his
views. In the previous year Mairet's *Sophonisbe*, the
first "regular" French tragedy, had been produced.
In 1636 the famous *Cid* controversy had begun.
By 1640 the battle was gained, and the unities became a part of the classic theory of the drama
throughout Europe. A few years later their practical application was most thoroughly indicated by
the Abbé d'Aubignac, in his *Pratique du Théâtre;*
and they were definitely formulated for all time by
Boileau in the celebrated couplet : —

> " Qu'en un lieu, qu'en un jour, un seul fait accompli
> Tienne jusqu'à la fin le théâtre rempli." [1]

III. *Heroic Poetry*

It was the supreme ambition of the Pléiade to
produce a great French epic. In the very first
manifesto of the new school, Du Bellay urges every
French poet to attempt another *Iliad* or *Æneid* for

[1] *Art Poét.* iii. 45.

the honor and glory of France. For Pelletier (1555) the heroic poem is the one that really gives the true title of poet; it may be compared to the ocean, and all other forms to rivers.[1] He seems to be following Giraldi Cintio's discourse on the *romanzi*, published the year before his own work, when he says that the French poet should write a *Heracleid*, the deeds of Hercules furnishing the mightiest and most heroic material he can think of.[2] At the same time Virgil is for him the model of an epic poet; and his parallel between Homer and Virgil bears striking resemblance to the similar parallel in Capriano's *Della Vera Poetica*, published in the very same year as his own treatise.[3] Like Capriano, Pelletier censures the superfluous exuberance, the loquaciousness, the occasional indecorum, and the inferiority in eloquence and dignity of Homer when compared with the Latin poet.

It was Ronsard's personal ambition to be the French Virgil, as in lyric poetry he had been proclaimed the French Pindar. For twenty years he labored on the *Franciade*, but never finished it. In the two prefaces which he wrote for it, the first in 1572, and the second (published posthumously) about 1584, he attempts to give expression to his ideal of the heroic poet. In neither of them does he succeed in formulating any very definite or consistent body of epic theory. They are chiefly interesting in that they indicate the general tendencies of the Pléiade, and show Ronsard's own rhetorical prin-

---

[1] *Art Poét.* ii. 8.   [2] *Ibid.* i. 3.
[3] *Ibid.* i. 5. *Cf.* Capriano, cap. v.

ciples, and his feeling for nature and natural beauty.
The passage has already been cited in which he
speaks of the heroic poem as entirely of a martial
character, and limits its action to the space of one
year. It has also been seen that for him, as for the
Italians, verisimilitude, and not fact, is the test of
poetry. At the same time, the epic poet is to avoid
anachronisms and misstatements of fact. Such
faults do not disturb the reader so much when the
story is remote in point of time; and the poet
should therefore always use an argument, the events
of which are at least three or four hundred years
old. The basis of the work should rest upon some
old story of past times and of long-established re-
nown, which has gained the credit of men.[1] This
notion of the antiquity of the epic fable had been
accepted long ago by the Italians. It is stated, for
example, in Tasso's *Discorsi dell' Arte Poetica*,
written about 1564, though not published until
1587, fifteen years after Tasso had visited Ronsard
in Paris.

Vauquelin de la Fresnaye has the Pléiade veneration for heroic poetry; but he cannot be said to
exhibit any more definite conception of its form
and function. For him the epic is a vast and
magnificent narration, a world in itself, wherein
men, things, and thoughts are wondrously mir-
rored : —

"C'est un tableau du monde, un miroir qui raporte
Les gestes des mortels en differente sorte. . . .

[1] Ronsard, iii. 23, 29.

> Car toute poësie il contient en soyméme,
> Soit tragique ou comique, ou soit autre poëme." [1]

With this we may compare what Muzio had said in 1551 : —

> " Il poema sovrano è una pittura
> De l'universo, e però in sè comprende
> Ogni stilo, ogni forma, ogni ritratto."

But despite this very vague conception of the epic in the French Renaissance, there was, as has been said, a high veneration for it as a form, and for its masters, Homer and especially Virgil.   This accounts for the large number of attempts at epic composition in France during the next century. But beyond the earlier and indefinite notion of heroic poetry the French did not get for a long time to come.   Even for Boileau the epic poem was merely the *vaste récit d'une longue action*. [2]

---

[1] Vauquelin, *Art Poét.* i. 471, 503.
[2] Boileau, *Art Poét.* iii. 161.

CHAPTER III

THE principle for which the Pléiade stood was,
like that of humanism, the imitation of the classics;
and the Pléiade was the first to introduce this as
a literary principle into France. This means, as
regards French literature, in the first place, the
substitution of the classical instead of its own
national tradition; and, secondly, the substitution
of the imitation of the classics for the imitation
of nature itself. In making these vital substitutions,
Du Bellay and his school have been accused of
creating once and for all the gulf that separates
French poetry from the national life.[1] This accusa-
tion is perhaps unfair to the Pléiade, which insisted
on the poet's going directly to nature, which emphasized most strongly the sentiment for natural scenery and beauty, and which first declared the
importance of the artisan and the peasant as subjects for poetry. But there can be but little doubt
that the separation of poetry from the national life
was the logical outcome of the doctrines of the
Pléiade. In disregarding the older French poets
and the evolution of indigenous poetry, in formu-

[1] Brunetière, i. 45.

214

lating an ideal of the poet as an unsociable and ascetic character, it separated itself from the natural tendencies of French life and letters, and helped to effect the final separation between poetry and the national development.

I. *Classical Elements*

It was to Du Bellay (1549) that France owes the introduction of classical ideas into French literature. He was the first to regard the imitation of the classics as a literary principle, and to advise the poet, after the manner of Vida, to purloin all the treasures of Greek and Latin literature for the benefit of French poetry. Moreover, he first formulated the aristocratic conception of the poet held by the Pléiade. The poet was advised to flee from the ignorant people, to bury himself in the solitude of his own chamber, to dream and to ponder, and to content himself with few readers. "Beyond everything," says Du Bellay, "the poet should have one or more learned friends to whom he can show all his verses; he should converse not only with learned men, but with all sorts of workmen, mechanics, artists, and others, in order to learn the technical terms of their arts, for use in beautiful descriptions."[1] This was a favorite theory of the Pléiade, which like some of our own contemporary writers regarded the technical arts as important subjects of inspiration. But the essential point at the bottom of all these discussions is a high

[1] *Défense*, ii. 11.

contempt for the opinion of the vulgar in matters
of art.

The *Quintil Horatian* (1550) represents, as has
already been seen, a natural reaction against the
foreign and classical innovations of the Pléiade.
Du Bellay's advice, " Prens garde que ce poëme soit
eslogné du vulgaire," — advice insisted upon by
many of the rhetoricians of the Italian Renaissance, — receives considerable censure ; on the contrary, says the author of the *Quintil*, the poet must
be understood and appreciated by all, unlearned as
well as learned, just as Marot was. The *Quintil*
was, in fact, the first work to insist on definite-
ness and clearness in poetry, as these were afterward insisted on by Malherbe and Boileau.   Like
Malherbe, and his disciple Deimier, the author
of the *Académie de l'Art Poétique* (1610), in which
the influence of the *Quintil* is fully acknowledged,
the author of the *Quintil* objects to all forms of
poetic license, to all useless metaphors that obscure
the sense, to all Latinisms and foreign terms and
locutions.[1] Du Bellay had dwelt on the importance
of a knowledge of the classical and Italian tongues,
and had strongly advised the French poet to nat-
uralize as many Latin, Greek, and even Spanish
and Italian terms as he could.   The *Quintil* is particularly bitter against all such foreign innovations.
The poet need not know foreign tongues at all ;
without this knowledge he can be as good a poet as
any of the *grœcaniseurs, latiniseurs, et italianiseurs
en françoys*. This protest availed little, and Du

[1] *Cf.* Rucktäschel, p. 10 *sq.*

Bellay's advice in regard to the use of Italian terms was so well followed that several years later, in 1578, Henri Estienne vigorously protested against the practice in his *Dialogues du Nouveau Langage françois italianisé*. As Ronsard and Du Bellay represent the foreign elements that went to make up classicism in France, so the author of the *Quintil Horatian* may be said to represent in his humble way certain enduring elements of the *esprit gaulois*. He represents the national traditions, and he prepares the way for the two great bourgeois poets of France, — Boileau, with his "Tout doit tendre au bon sens," and Molière, with his bluff cry, "Je suis pour le bon sens."

According to Pelletier (1555), French poetry is too much like colloquial speech ; in order to equal classical literature, the poets of France must be more daring and less popular.[1] Pelletier's point of view is here that of the Pléiade, which aimed at a distinct poetic language, diverse from ordinary prose speech. But he is thoroughly French, and in complete accord with the author of the *Quintil Horatian*, in his insistence on perfect clearness in poetry. "Clearness," he says, "is the first and worthiest virtue of a poem."[2] Obscurity is the chief fault of poetry, "for there is no difference between not speaking at all and not being understood."[3] For these reasons he is against all unnecessary and bombastic ornament; the true use of metaphors and comparisons of all sorts is "to explain and represent things as they really are."

[1] *Art Poét.* i. 3.   [2] *Ibid.* i. 9.   [3] *Ibid.* i. 10.

Similarly, Ronsard, while recognizing the value of comparisons, rightfully used, as the very nerves and tendons of poetry, declares that if instead of perfecting and clarifying, they obscure or confuse the idea, they are ridiculous.[1] Obscurity was the chief danger, and indeed the chief fault, of the Pléiade; and it is no small merit that both Ronsard and Pelletier perceived this fact.

The Pléiade exhibits the classic temper in its insistence on study and art as essential to poetry; but it was not in keeping with the doctrines of later French classicists in so far as it regarded the poetic labors as of an unsociable and even ascetic character. In this, as has been seen, Ronsard is a true exponent of the doctrines of the new school. But on the whole the classic spirit was strong in him. He declares that the poet's ideas should be high and noble, but not fantastic. "They should be well ordered and disposed; and while they seem to transcend those of the vulgar, they should always appear to be easily conceived and understood by any one."[2] Here Du Bellay's aristocratic conception of poetry is modified so as to become a very typical statement of the principle underlying French classicism. Again, Ronsard points out, as Vida and other Italian critics had done before, that the great classical poets seldom speak of things by their bare and naked names. Virgil does not, for example, say, "It was night," or "It was day," but he uses some such circumlocution as this : —

"Postero Phœbea lustrabat lampade terras."

[1] Ronsard, iii. 26 *sq.*   [2] *Ibid.* vii. 323.

The unfortunate results of the excessive use of such circumlocutions are well exemplified in the later classicists of France. Ronsard perhaps foresaw this danger, and wisely says that circumlocution, if not used judiciously, makes the style inflated and bombastic. In the first preface to the *Franciade*, he expresses a decided preference for the naïve facility of Homer over the artful diligence of Virgil.[1] In the second preface, however, written a dozen years later, and published posthumously as revised by his disciple Binet, there is interesting evidence, in the preëminence given to Virgil, of the rapidity with which the Latinization of culture was being effected at this period. "Our French authors," says Ronsard, "know Virgil far better than they know Homer or any other Greek writer." And again, "Virgil is the most excellent and the most rounded, the most compact and the most perfect of all poets."[2] Of the naïve facility of Homer we hear absolutely nothing.

We are now beginning to enter the era of rules. Ronsard did not undervalue the "rules and secrets" of poetry; and Vauquelin de la Fresnaye calls his own critical poem *cet Art de Règles recherchées*.[3] In regard to the imitation of the classics, Vauquelin agrees heart and soul with the Pléiade that the ancients

"nous ont desja tracé
Un sentier qui de nous ne doit estre laissé."[4]

Nothing, indeed, could be more classical than his

---

[1] Ronsard, iii. 9 *sq.*   [3] *Art Poét.* iii. 1151.
[2] *Ibid.* iii. 23, 26.   [4] *Ibid.* i. 61.

comparison of poetry to a garden symmetrically laid out and trimmed.[1] Moreover, like the classicists of the next century, he affirms, as does Ronsard also, that art must fundamentally imitate and resemble nature.[2]

The imitation of the classics had also a decided effect on the technique of French verse and on the linguistic principles of the Pléiade. Enjambement (the carrying over into another line of words required to complete the sense) and hiatus (the clash of vowels in a line) were both employed in Latin and Greek verse, and were therefore permitted in French poetry by the new school. Ronsard, however, anticipated the reforms of Malherbe and the practice of French classic verse, in forbidding both hiatus and enjambement, though in a later work of his this opinion is reversed. He was also probably the first to insist on the regular alternation of masculine and feminine rhymes in verse. This had never been strictly adhered to in practice, or required by stringent rule, before Ronsard, but has become the invariable usage of French poetry ever since. Ronsard regards this device as a means of making verse keep tune more harmoniously with the music of instruments. It was one of the favorite theories of the Pléiade that poetry is intended, not to be read, but to be recited or sung, and that the words and the notes should be coupled lovingly together. Poetry without an accompaniment of vocal or instrumental music exhibits but a small part of its harmony or perfection; and while

[1] *Art Poét.* i. 22 *sq.*   [2] *Ibid.* i. 813. *Cf.* Ronsard, ii. 12.

composing verses, the poet should always pronounce them aloud, or rather sing them, in order to test their melody.[1] This conception of music "married to immortal verse" doubtless came from Italy, and is connected with the rise of operatic music. De Laudun (1598) differs from the members of the Pléiade in forbidding the use of words newly coined or taken from the dialects of France, and in objecting to the use of enjambement and hiatus. It is evident, therefore, that while the influence of the Pléiade is visible throughout De Laudun's treatise, his disagreement with Ronsard and Du Bellay on a considerable number of essential points shows that by the end of the century the supremacy of the Pléiade had begun to wane.

The new school also attempted to introduce classical metres into French poetry. The similar attempt at using the ancient versification in Italy has already been incidentally referred to.[2] According to Vasari, Leon Battista Alberti, in his epistle,

"Questa per estrema miserabile pistola mando,"

was the first to attempt to reduce the vernacular versification to the measure of the Latins.[3] In October, 1441, the *Scena dell' Amicizia* of Leonardo Dati was composed and recited before the Accademia Coronaria at Florence.[4] The first two parts of this piece

[1] Ronsard, vii. 320, 332.
[2] The early Italian poetry written in classical metres has been collected by Carducci, *La Poesia Barbara nei Secoli XV e XVI*, Bologna, 1881.
[3] Carducci, p. 2.
[4] *Ibid.* p. 6 *sq.*

are written in hexameters, the third in Sapphics, the fourth in sonnet form and rhymed. The prologues of Ariosto's comedies, the *Negromante* and the *Cassaria*, are also in classical metres. But the remarkable collection of Claudio Tolomei, *Versi e Regole de la Nuova Poesia Toscana*, published at Rome in 1539, marked an epoch in sixteenth-century letters. In this work the employment of classical metres in the vulgar tongue is defended, and rules for their use given; then follows a collection of Italian verse written after this fashion by a large number of scholars and poets, among them Annibal Caro and Tolomei himself. This group of scholars had formed itself into an esoteric circle, the Accademia della Nuova Poesia; and from the tone of the verses addressed to Tolomei by the members of this circle, it would seem that he regarded himself, and was regarded by them, as the founder and expositor of this poetic innovation.[1] Luigi Alamanni, whose life was chiefly spent at the Court of France, published in 1556 a comedy, *La Flora*, written in classical metres; and two years later Francesco Patrizzi published an heroic poem, the *Eridano*, written in hexameters, with a defence of the form of versification employed.[2]

This learned innovation spread throughout western Europe.[3] In France, toward the close of the

---

[1] Carducci, pp. 55, 87, etc.

[2] *Ibid.* pp. 327, 443. *Cf.* Du Bellay, *Défense*, ii. 7.

[3] For the history of classical metres in France, *cf.* Egger, *Hellénisme en France*, p. 290 *sq.*, and Darmesteter and Hatzfeld, *Seizième Siècle en France*, p. 113 *sq.*

fifteenth century, according to Agrippa d'Aubigné, a certain Mousset had translated the *Iliad* and the *Odyssey* into French hexameters; but nothing else is known either of Mousset or of his translations. As early as 1500 one Michel de Bouteauville, the author of an *Art de métrifier françois*, wrote a poem in classical distichs on the English war. Sibilet (1548) accepted the use of classical metres, though with some distrust, for to him rhyme seemed as essential to French poetry as long and short syllables to Greek and Latin. In 1562 Ramus, in his *Grammar*, recommended the ancient versification, and expressed his regret that it had not been accepted with favor by the public. In the same year Jacques de la Taille wrote his treatise, *La Manière de faire des Vers en françois comme en grec et en latin*, but it was not published until 1573, eleven years after his death. His main object in writing the book was to show that it is not as difficult to employ quantity in French verse as some people think, nor even any more difficult than in Greek and Latin.[1] In answer to the objection that the vulgar tongues are by their nature incapable of quantity, he argues, after the manner of Du Bellay, that such things do not proceed from the nature of a language, but from the labor and diligence of those who employ it. He is tired of vulgar rhymes, and is anxious to find a more ingenious and more

[1] Estienne Pasquier, in his *Recherches de la France*, vii. 11, attempts to prove that the French language is capable of employing quantity in its verse, but does not decide whether quantity or rhymed verse is to be preferred.

difficult path to Parnassus. He then proceeds to
treat of quantity and measure in French, of feet
and verse, and of figures and poetic license.[1]

The name most inseparably connected with the
introduction of classical metres into France in the
sixteenth century is that of Jean Antoine de Baïf.
This young member of the Pléiade, after publishing
several unsuccessful volumes of verse, visited Italy,
and was present at the Council of Trent in 1563.
In Italy he doubtless learnt of the metrical innovations then being employed; and upon his return,
without any apparent knowledge of Jacques de la
Taille's as yet unpublished treatise, he set about to
make a systematic reform in French versification.
His purpose was to bring about a more perfect uni-
son between poetry and music; and in order to
accomplish this, he adopted classical metres, based
as they were on a musical prosody, and accepted
the phonetic reforms of Ramus. He also established, no doubt in imitation of the Accademia della
Nuova Poesia, the Académie de Poésie et de Musique, authorized by letters patent from Charles IX.
in November, 1570.[2] The purpose of this academy
was to encourage and establish the metrical and
musical innovations advocated by Baïf and his
friends. On the death of Charles IX. the society's
existence was menaced; but it was restored, with a

---

[1] *Cf.* Rucktäschel, p. 24 *sq.*, and Carducci, p. 413 *sq.*

[2] This academy has been made the subject of an excellent
monograph by É. Fremy, *L'Académie des Derniers Valois*,
Paris, n. d. The statutes of the academy will be found on page 39
of this work, and the letters-patent granted to it by Charles IX.
on page 48.

broader purpose and function, as the Académie du
Palais, by Guy du Faur de Pibrac in 1576, under
the protection of Henry III., and it continued to
flourish until dispersed by the turmoils of the
League about 1585. But Baïf's innovations were
not entirely without fruit. A similar movement,
and a not dissimilar society, will be found somewhat later in Elizabethan England.

II. *Romantic Elements*

Some of the romantic elements in the critical
theory of the Pléiade have already been indicated.
The new movement started, in Du Bellay's *Défense*,
with a high conception of the poet's office. It emphasized the necessity, on the part of the poet, of
profound and solitary study, of a refined and
ascetic life, and of entire separation from vulgar
people and pleasures. Du Bellay himself is romantic in that he decides against the *traditions de règles*,[1]
deeming the good judgment of the poet sufficient
in matters of taste; but the reason of this was that
there were no rules which he would have been willing to accept. It took more than a century for the
French mind to arrive at the conclusion that reason
and rules, in matters of art, proceed from one and
the same cause.

The feeling for nature and for natural beauty is
very marked in all the members of the Pléiade.
Pelletier speaks of war, love, agriculture, and pastoral life as the chief themes of poetry.[2] He warns

[1] *Défense*, ii. 11.   [2] *Art Poét*. i. 3

2

the poet to observe nature and life itself, and not
depend on books alone ; and he dwells on the value
of descriptions of landscapes, tempests, and sunrises,
and similar natural scenes.[1] The feeling for nature
is even more intense in Ronsard ; and like Pelletier,
he urges the poet to describe in verse the rivers,
forests, mountains, winds, the sea, gods and goddesses, sunrise, night, and noon.[2]   In another place
the poet is advised to embellish his work with accounts of trees, flowers, and herbs, especially those
dignified by some medicinal or magical virtues, and
with descriptions of rivers, towns, forests, mountains, caverns, rocks, harbors, and forts.   Here the
appreciation of natural beauty as introduced into
modern Europe by the Italian Renaissance — the
feeling for nature in its wider aspects, the broad
landscape, the distant prospect — first becomes
visible in France.   " In the painting or rather imitation of nature," says Ronsard, " consists the very
soul of heroic poetry."

Ronsard also gives warning that ordinary speech
is not to be banished from poetry, or too much
evaded, for by doing so the poet is dealing a death-
blow to " naïve and natural poetry." [3]   This sympa-
thy for the simple and popular forms of poetry as
models for the poetic artist is characteristic of the
Pléiade.   There is a very interesting passage in
Montaigne, in which the popular ballads of the
peasantry are praised in a manner that recalls the
famous words of Sir Philip Sidney concerning

[1] *Art Poét.* ii. 10; i. 9.   [2] Ronsard, vii. 321, 324.
[3] *Ibid.* iii. 17 *sq.*

the old song of Percy and Douglas,[1] and which
seems to anticipate the interest in popular poetry
in England two centuries later : —

"Popular and purely natural and indigenous poetry has
a certain native simplicity and grace by which it may be
favorably compared with the principal beauty of perfect
poetry composed according to the rules of art ; as may be
seen in the villanelles of Gascony, and in songs coming from
nations that have no knowledge of any science, not even of
writing. But mediocre poetry, which is neither perfect nor
popular, is held in disdain by every one, and receives neither
honor nor reward."[2]

The Pléiade, as has already been intimated,
accepted without reserve the Platonic doctrine of
inspiration. By 1560 a considerable number of the
Platonic dialogues had already been translated into
French. Dolet had translated two of the spurious
dialogues ; Duval, the *Lysis* in 1547 ; and Le Roy,
the *Phædo* in 1553 and the *Symposium* in 1559.
The thesis of Ramus in 1536 had started an anti-
Aristotelian tendency in France, and the literature
of the French Renaissance became impregnated
with Platonism.[3] It received the royal favor of
Marguerite de Navarre, and its influence became
fixed in 1551, by the appointment of Ramus to a
professorship in the Collège de France. Ronsard,
Vauquelin, Du Bartas, all give expression to the
Platonic theory of poetic inspiration. The poet
must feel what he writes, as Horace says, or his
reader will never be moved by his verses ; and for

[1] Sidney, *Defence*, p. 29.
[2] *Essais*, i. 54.
[3] *Cf.* the *Revue d'Hist. litt. de la France*, 1896, iii. 1 *sq.*

the Pléiade, the excitement of high emotions in the reader or hearer was the test or touchstone of poetry.[1]

The national and Christian points of view never found expression in France during the sixteenth century in so marked a manner as in Italy.   There are, indeed, traces of both a national and a Christian criticism, but they are hardly more than sporadic. Thus, it has been seen that Sibilet, as early as 1548, had clearly perceived the distinguishing character- istic of the French genius.   He had noted that the French have only taken from foreign literature what they have deemed useful and of national advantage ; and only the other day a distinguished French critic asserted in like manner that the high importance of French literature consists in the fact that it has taken from the other literatures of Europe the things of universal interest and disre- garded the accidental picturesque details.   Distinct traces of a national point of view may be found in the dramatic criticism of this period.   Thus Grévin, in his *Bref Discours* (1562), attempts to justify the substitution of a crowd of Cæsar's soldiers for the singers of the ancient chorus, in one of his tragedies, on the following grounds : —

" If it be alleged that this practice was observed through- out antiquity by the Greeks and Latins, I reply that it is permitted to us to attempt some innovation of our own, es- pecially when there is occasion for it, or when the grace of the poem is not diminished thereby.   I know well that it will be answered that the ancients employed the chorus of

[1] Ronsard, iii. 28; Du Bellay, *Défense*, ii. 11.

singers to divert the audience, made gloomy perhaps by the
cruelties represented in the play. To this I reply that
diverse nations require diverse manners of doing things, and
that among the French there are other means of doing this
without interrupting the continuity of a story." [1]

The Christian point of view, on the other hand,
is found in Vauquelin de la Fresnaye, who differs
from Ronsard and Du Bellay in his preference for
scriptural themes in poetry.   The Pléiade was essentially pagan, Vauquelin essentially Christian.
The employment of the pagan divinities in modern
poetry seemed to him often odious, for the times
had changed, and the Muses were governed by different laws.   The poet should attempt Christian
themes; and indeed the Greeks themselves, had
they been Christians, would have sung the life and
death of Christ.   In this passage Vauquelin is evi-
dently following Minturno, as the latter was afterward followed by Corneille : —

" Si les Grecs, comme vous, Chrestiens eussent escrit,
   Ils eussent les hauts faits chanté de Iesus Christ. . . .
   Hé ! quel plaisir seroit-ce à cette heure de voir
   Nos poëtes Chrestiens, les façons recevoir
   Du tragique ancien ?   Et voir à nos misteres
   Les Payens asservis sous les loix sulutaires
   De nos Saints et Martyrs ? et du vieux testament
   Voir une tragedie extraite proprement ? " [2]

Vauquelin's opinion here is out of keeping with
the general theory of the Pléiade, especially in
that his suggestions imply a return to the medi-

[1] Arnaud, app. ii.
[2] Vauquelin, *Art Poét.* iii. 845; *cf.* iii. 33; i. 901.

æval mystery and morality plays. The *Uranie* of Du Bartas is another and more fervid expression of this same ideal of Christian poetry. In the *Semaines,* Du Bartas himself composed the typical biblical poem; and tragedies on Christian or scriptural subjects were composed during the French Renaissance from the time of Buchanan and Beza to that of Garnier and Montchrestien. But Vauquelin's ideal was not that of the later classicism; and Boileau, as has been seen, distinctly rejects Christian themes from modern poetry.

Although the linguistic and prosodic theories of the Pléiade partly anticipate both the theory and the practice of later classicism, the members of the school exhibit numerous deviations from what was afterward accepted as inviolable law in French poetry. The most important of these deviations concerns the use of words from the various French dialects, from foreign tongues, and from the technical and mechanical arts. A partial expression of this theory of poetic language has already been seen in Du Bellay's *Défense et Illustration,* in which the poet is urged to use the more elegant technical dialectic terms. Ronsard gives very much the same advice. The best words in all the French dialects are to be employed by the poet; for it is doubtless to the number of the dialects of Greece that we may ascribe the supreme beauty of its language and literature. The poet is not to affect too much the language of the court, since it is often very bad, being the language of ladies and of young gentlemen who make a profession of fighting well rather than of

speaking well.[1] Unlike Malherbe and his school,
Ronsard allows a certain amount of poetic license,
but only rarely and judiciously. It is to poetic
license, he says, that we owe nearly all the beautiful figures with which poets, in their divine rapture,
enfranchising the laws of grammar, have enriched
their works. "This is that birthright," said Dryden, a century later, in the preface of his *State of
Innocence and the Fall of Man*, "which is derived
to us from our great forefathers, even from Homer
down to Ben; and they who would deny it to us
have, in plain terms, the fox's quarrel to the grapes
— they cannot reach it." Vauquelin de la Fresnaye follows Ronsard and Du Bellay in urging the
use of new and dialect words, the employment of
terms and comparisons from the mechanic arts,
and the various other doctrines by which the
Pléiade is distinguished from the school of Malherbe. How these useless linguistic innovations
were checked and banished from the French language forever will be briefly alluded to in the
next chapter.

[1] Ronsard, vii. 322.

CHAPTER IV

I. *The Romantic Revolt*

IT is a well-known fact that between 1600 and
1630 there was a break in the national evolution
of French literature. This was especially so in
the drama, and in France the drama is the connecting link between century and century. The
dramatic works of the sixteenth century had been
fashioned after the regular models borrowed by
the Italians from Seneca. The change that came
was a change from Italian classical to Spanish
romantic models. The note of revolt was beginning to be heard in Grévin, De Laudun, and others.
The seventeenth century opened with the production
of Hardy's irregular drama, *Les Amours de Théa-
gène et Cariclée* (1601), and the influence of the
Spanish romantic drama and the Italian pastoral,
dominant for over a quarter of a century, was inaugurated in France.

The logic of this innovation was best expounded
in Spain, and it was there that arguments in favor
of the romantic and irregular drama were first
formulated. The two most interesting defences of
the Spanish national drama are doubtless the

Egemplar Poético of Juan de la Cueva (1606) and Lope de Vega's *Arte Nuevo de Hacer Comedias* (1609). Their inspiration is at bottom the same. Their authors were both classicists at heart, or rather classicists in theory, yet with differences. Juan de la Cueva's conception of poetry is entirely based on the precepts of the Italians, except in what regards the national drama, for here he is a partisan and a patriot. He insists that the difference of time and circumstance frees the Spanish playwright from all necessity of imitating the ancients or obeying their rules. "This change in the drama," he says, "was effected by wise men, who applied to new conditions the new things they found most suitable and expedient; for we must consider the various opinions, the times, and the manners, which make it necessary for us to change and vary our operations." [1] His theory of the drama was entirely opposed to his conception of the other forms of poetry. According to this standpoint, as a recent writer has put it, "the theatre was to imitate nature, and to please; poetry was to imitate the Italians, and satisfy the orthodox but minute critic." [2] Lope de Vega, writing three years later, does not deny the universal applicability of the Aristotelian canons, and even acknowledges that they are the only true rules. But the people demand romantic plays, and the people, rather than the poet's literary conscience, must be satisfied by the playwright. "I myself," he says,

[1] Sedano, *Parnaso Español*, viii. 61.
[2] Hannay, *Later Renaissance*, 1898, p. 39.

" write comedies according to the art invented by
those whose sole object it is to obtain the applause
of the crowd. After all, since it is the public who
pays for these stupidities, why should we not serve
what it wants ? "[1]

Perhaps the most interesting of all the exposi-
tions of the theory of the Spanish national drama
is a defence of Lope de Vega's plays by one Alfonso
Sanchez, published in 1618 in France, or possibly
in Spain with a false French imprint. The apology
of Sanchez is comprehended in six distinct proposi-
tions. First, the arts have their foundation in
nature. Secondly, a wise and learned man may
alter many things in the existing arts. Thirdly,
nature does not obey laws, but gives them.
Fourthly, Lope de Vega has done well in creating
a new art. Fifthly, in his writings everything is
adjusted to art, and that a real and living art.
Lastly, Lope de Vega has surpassed all the ancient
poets.[2] The following passage may be extracted
from this treatise, if only to show how little there
was of novelty in the tenets of the French romanticists two centuries later : —

" Is it said that we have no infallible art by which to
adjust our precepts ? But who can doubt it ? We have art,
we have precepts and rules which bind us, and the principal
precept is to imitate nature, for the works of poets express
the nature, the manners, and the genius of the age in which
they write. . . . Lope de Vega writes in conformity with
art, because he follows nature. If, on the contrary, the
Spanish drama adjusted itself to the rules and laws of the

[1] Menéndez y Pelayo, iii. 434.   [2] *Ibid*. iii. 447 *sq*.

ancients, it would proceed against the requirements of nature, and against the foundations of poetry. . . . The great Lope has done things over and above the laws of the ancients, but never against these laws."

Another Spanish writer defines art as "an attentive observation of examples graded by experience, and reduced to method and the majesty of laws."[1]

It was this naturalistic conception of the poetic art, and especially of the drama, that obtained in France during the first thirty years of the seventeenth century. The French playwrights imitated the Spanish drama in practice, and from the Spanish theorists seemed to have derived the critical justification of their plays. Hardy himself, like Lope de Vega, argues that "everything which is approved by usage and the public taste is legitimate and more than legitimate." Another writer of this time, François Ogier, in the preface of the second edition of Jean de Schelandre's remarkable drama of *Tyr et Sidon* (1628), argues for intellectual independence of the ancients much in the same way as Giraldi Cintio, Pigna, and the other partisans of the *romanzi* had done three-quarters of a century before. The taste of every nation, he says, is quite different from any other. "The Greeks wrote for the Greeks, and in the judgment of the best men of their time they succeeded. But we should imitate them very much better by giving heed to the tastes of our own country, and the genius of our own language, than by forcing ourselves to follow step by step both their intention and their expression." This would

[1] Menéndez y Pelayo, iii. 464.

seem to be at bottom Goethe's famous statement
that we can best imitate the Greeks by trying to
be as great men as they were. It is interesting to
note, in all of these early critics, traces of that historical criticism which is usually regarded as the
discovery of our own century. But after all, the
French like the Spanish playwrights were merely
beginning to practise what the Italian dramatists
in their prefaces, and some of the Italian critics
in their treatises, had been preaching for nearly a
century.

The Abbé d'Aubignac speaks of Hardy as
"arresting the progress of the French theatre";
and whatever practical improvements the French
theatre owes to him, there can be little doubt that
for a certain number of years the evolution of the
classical drama was partly arrested by his efforts
and the efforts of his school. But during this
very period the foundations of the great literature
that was to come were being built on classical
lines; and the continuance of the classical tradition after 1630 was due to three distinct causes,
each of which will be discussed by itself as briefly
as possible. These three causes were the reaction
against the Pléiade, the second influx of the critical
ideas of the Italian Renaissance, and the influence
of the rationalistic philosophy of the period.

II. *The Reaction against the Pléiade*

The reaction against the Pléiade was effected, or
at least begun, by Malherbe. Malherbe's power or

message as a poet is of no concern here; in his rôle of
grammarian and critic he accomplished certain important and widespread reforms in French poetry.
These reforms were connected chiefly, if not entirely, with the external or formal side of poetry.
His work was that of a grammarian, of a prosodist
— in a word, that of a purist.   He did not, indeed,
during his lifetime, publish any critical work, or
formulate any critical system.   But the reforms he
executed were on this account no less influential or
enduring.   His critical attitude is to be looked for
in the memoirs of his life written by his disciple
Racan, and in his own *Commentaire sur Desportes,*
which was not published in its entirety until very
recently.[1]   This commentary consists of a series of
manuscript notes written by Malherbe about the
year 1606 in the margins of a copy of Desportes.
These notes are of a most fragmentary kind; they
seldom go beyond a word or two of disapproval,
such as *faible, mal conçu, superflu, sans jugement,*
sottise, or *mal imaginé ;* and yet, together with a
few detached utterances recorded in his letters and
in the memoirs by Racan, they indicate quite clearly
the critical attitude of Malherbe and the reforms
he was bent on bringing about.

These reforms were, in the first place, largely
linguistic.   The Pléiade had attempted to widen
the sphere of poetic expression in French litera-

---

[1] The *Commentaire* is printed entire in Lalanne's edition of
Malherbe, Paris, 1862, vol. iv.   The critical doctrine of Malherbe has been formulated by Brunot, *Doctrine de Malherbe,*
pp. 105–236.

ture by the introduction of words from the classics,
from the Italian and even the Spanish, from the
provincial dialects, from the old romances, and from
the terminology of the mechanic arts. All these
archaisms, neologisms, Latinisms, compound words,
and dialectic and technical expressions, Malherbe
set about to eradicate from the French language.
His object was to purify French, and, as it were, to
centralize it. The test he set up was actual usage,
and even this was narrowed down to the usage of
the court. Ronsard had censured the exclusive use
of courtly speech in poetry, on the ground that the
courtier cares more about fighting well than about
speaking or writing well. But Malherbe's ideal
was the ideal of French classicism — the ideal of
Boileau, Racine, and Bossuet. French was to be
no longer a hodgepodge or a patois, but the pure
and perfect speech of the king and his court.
Malherbe, while thus reacting against the Pléiade,
made no pretensions of returning to the linguistic
usages of Marot; his test was present usage, his
model the living language.[1] At the same time his
reforms in language, as in other things, represent a
reaction against foreign innovations and a return
to the pure French idiom. They were in the interest of the national traditions; and it is this
national element which is his share in the body
of neo-classical theory and practice. His reforms
were all in the direction of that verbal and mechanical perfection, the love of which is innate in
the French nature, and which forms the indigenous

[1] *Cf.* Horace, *Ars Poet.* 71, 72.

or racial element in French classicism. He elimi-
nated from French verse hiatus, enjambement, in-
versions, false and imperfect rhymes, and licenses
or cacophonies of all kinds. He gave it, as has
been said, mechanical perfection, —

> " Et réduisit la Muse aux règles du devoir."

For such a man — *tyran des mots et des syllabes*,
as Balzac called him — the higher qualities of poetry
could have little or no meaning. His ideals were
propriety, clearness, regularity, and force. These,
as Chapelain perceived at the time, are oratorical
rather than purely poetic qualities; yet for these,
all the true qualities that go to make up a great
poet were to be sacrificed. Of imagination and
poetic sensibility he takes no account whatsoever.
After the verbal perfection of the verse, the logical
unity of the poem was his chief interest. Logic
and reason are without doubt important things, but
they cannot exist in poetry to the exclusion of
imagination. By eliminating inspiration, as it
were, Malherbe excluded the possibility of lyrical
production in France throughout the period of
classicism. He hated poetic fictions, since for him,
as for Boileau, only actual reality is beautiful. If he
permitted the employment of mythological figures,
it was because they are reasonable and universally
intelligible symbols. The French mind is essentially rational and logical, and Malherbe reintro-
duced this native rationality into French poetry.
He set up common sense as a poetic ideal, and
made poetry intelligible to the average mind. The

Pléiade had written for a learned literary coterie ;
Malherbe wrote for learned and unlearned alike.
For the Pléiade, poetry had been a divine office, a
matter of prophetic inspiration; for Malherbe, it
was a trade, a craft, to be learnt like any other.
Du Bellay had said that " it is a well-accepted fact,
according to the most learned men, that natural
talents without learning can accomplish more in
poetry than learning without natural talents."
Malherbe, it has been neatly said, would have
upheld the contrary doctrine that " learning without natural talents can accomplish more than
natural talents without learning." [1]   After all,
eloquence was Malherbe's ideal; and as the French
are by nature an eloquent rather than a poetic people, he deserves the honor of having first shown
them how to regain their true inheritance.   In a
word, he accomplished for classical poetry in France
all that the national instinct, the *esprit gaulois*,
could accomplish by itself.   Consistent structural
laws for the larger poetic forms he could not give ;
these France owes to Italy.   Nor could he appreciate the high notion of abstract perfection, or the
classical conception of an absolute standard of
taste — that of several expressions or several ways
of doing something, one way and only one is the
right one ; this France owes to rationalistic philosophy.   Malherbe seems almost to be echoing Montaigne when he says in a letter to Balzac : —

" Do you not know that the diversity of opinions is as
natural as the difference of men's faces, and that to wish

[1] Brunot, p. 149.

that what pleases or displeases us should please or displease everybody is to pass the limits where it seems that God in His omnipotence has commanded us to stop ? " [1]

With this individualistic expression of the questions of opinion and taste, we have but to compare the following passage from La Bruyère to indicate how far Malherbe is still from the classic ideal: —

"There is a point of perfection in art, as of excellence or maturity in nature.   He who is sensible of it and loves it has perfect taste ; he who is not sensible of it and loves this or that else on either side of it has a faulty taste.   There is then a good and a bad taste, and men dispute of tastes not without reason." [2]

III. *The Second Influx of Italian Ideas*

The second influx of Italian critical ideas into France came through two channels. In the first place, the direct literary relations between Italy and France during this period were very marked. The influence of Marino, who lived for a long time at Paris and published a number of his works there, was not inconsiderable, especially upon the French concettists and *précieux.* Two Italian ladies founded and presided over the famous Hotel de Rambouillet, — Julie Savelli, Marquise de Pisani, and Catherine de Vivonne, Marquise de Rambouillet. It was partly to the influence of the Accademia della Crusca that the foundation of the French Academy was due. Chapelain and Ménage were

---

[1] *Œuvres,* Lalanne's edition, iv. 91.
[2] *Caractères,* " Des Ouvrages de l'Esprit."

R

both members of the Italian society, and submitted
to it their different opinions on a verse of Petrarch.
Like the Accademia della Crusca, the French Academy purposed the preparation of a great dictionary;
and each began its existence by attacking a great
work of literature, the *Gerusalemme Liberata* in
the case of the Italian society, Corneille's *Cid* in
the case of the French.   The regency of Marie de
Medici, the supremacy of Mazarin, and other political events, all conspired to bring Italy and France
into the closest social and literary relationship.

But the two individuals who first brought into
French literature and naturalized the primal critical concepts of Italy were Chapelain and Balzac.
Chapelain's private correspondence indicates how
thorough was his acquaintance with the critical
literature of Italy.   "I have a particular affection
for the Italian language," he wrote in 1639 to Balzac.[1] Of the *Cid*, he says that "in Italy it would
be considered barbarous, and there is not an academy which would not banish it beyond the confines
of its jurisdiction."[2]   Speaking of the greatness of
Ronsard, he says that his own opinion was in
accord with that of "two great savants beyond the
Alps, Speroni and Castelvetro";[3] and he had considerable correspondence with Balzac on the subject
of the controversy between Caro and Castelvetro in
the previous century.   In a word, he knew and

[1] *Lettres*, i. 413.   The references are to the edition by Tami-
zey de Larroque, Paris, 1880–1883.
[2] *Ibid*. i. 156.
[3] *Ibid*. i. 631 *sq*.

studied the critics and scholars of Italy, and was interested in discussing them. Balzac's interest, on the other hand, was rather toward Spanish literature; but he was the agent of the Cardinal de la Valette at Rome, and it was on his return to France that he published the first collection of his letters. The influence of both Chapelain and Balzac on French classicism was considerable. During the sixteenth century, literary criticism had been entirely in the hands of learned men. Chapelain and Balzac vulgarized the critical ideas of the Italian Renaissance, and made them popular, human, but inviolable. Balzac introduced into France the fine critical sense of the Italians; Chapelain introduced their formal rules, and imposed the three unities on French tragedy. Together they effected a humanizing of the classical ideal, even while subjecting it to rules.

It was to the same Italian influences that France owed the large number of artificial epics that appeared during this period. About ten epics were published in the fifteen years between 1650 and 1665.[1] The Italians of the sixteenth century had formulated a fixed theory of the artificial epic; and the nations of western Europe rivalled one another in attempting to make practical use of this theory. It is to this that the large number of Spanish epics in the sixteenth century and of French epics in the seventeenth may be ascribed. Among the latter

[1] These epics have been treated at length by Duchesne *Histoire des Poèmes Épiques français du XVII Siècle*, Paris, 1870.

we may mention Scudéry's *Alaric*, Lemoyne's *Saint Louis*, Saint-Amant's *Moyse Sauvé*, and Chapelain's own epic, *La Pucelle*, awaited by the public for many years, and published only to be damned for-ever by Boileau.

The prefaces of all these epics indicate clearly enough their indebtedness to the Italians. They were indeed scarcely more than attempts to put the rules and precepts of the Italian Renaissance into practice. "I then consulted the masters of this art," says Scudéry, in the preface of *Alaric*, "that is to say, Aristotle and Horace, and after them Macrobius, Scaliger, Tasso, Castelvetro, Piccolom-ini, Vida, Vossius, Robortelli, Riccoboni, Paolo Beni, Mambrun, and several others; and passing from theory to practice I reread very carefully the *Iliad* and the *Odyssey*, the *Æneid*, the *Pharsalia*, the *Thebaid*, the *Orlando Furioso*, and the *Gerusa-lemme Liberata*, and many other epic poems in diverse languages." Similarly, Saint-Amant, in the preface of his *Moyse Sauvé*, says that he had rigorously observed "the unities of action and place, which are the principal requirements of the epic; and besides, by an entirely new method, I have restricted my subject not only within twenty-four hours, the limit of the dramatic poem, but almost within half of that time. This is more than even Aristotle, Horace, Scaliger, Castelvetro, Pic-colomini, and all the other moderns have ever required." It is obvious that for these epic-makers the rules and precepts of the Italians were the final tests of heroic poetry. Similarly, the Abbé d'Aubignac, at the beginning of his *Pratique du Théâtre*, advises the dramatic poet to study, among other writers, "Aristotle, Horace, Castelvetro, Vida, Heinsius, Vossius, and Scaliger, of whom not a word should be lost." From the Italians also came the theory of poetry in general as held throughout the period of classicism, and expounded by the Abbé d'Aubignac, La Mesnardière, Corneille, Boileau, and numerous others; and it is hardly necessary to repeat that Rapin, tracing the history of criticism at the beginning of his *Réflexions sur la Poétique*, deals with scarcely any critics but the Italians.

Besides the direct influence of the Italian critics, another influence contributed its share to the sum of critical ideas which French classicism owes to the Italian Renaissance. This was the tradition of Scaliger, carried on by the Dutch scholars Heinsius and Vossius. Daniel Heinsius was the pupil of Joseph Scaliger, the illustrious son of the author of the *Poetics ;* and through Heinsius the dramatic theories of the elder Scaliger influenced classical tragedy in France. The treatise of Heinsius, *De Tragœdiœ Constitutione*, published at Leyden in 1611, was called by Chapelain "the quintessence of Aristotle's *Poetics* " ; and Chapelain called Heinsius himself "a prophet or sibyl in matters of criticism."[1] Annoted by Racine, cited as an infallible authority by Corneille, Heinsius's work exercised

[1] *Lettres*, i. 269, 424. On the theories of Heinsius, see Zerbst, *Ein Vorläufer Lessings in der Aristotelesinterpretation*, Jena, 1887.

a marked influence on French tragedy by fixing
upon it the laws of Scaliger; and later the works
of Vossius coöperated with those of Heinsius in
widening the sphere of the Italian influence. It is
evident, therefore, that while French literature had
already during the sixteenth century taken from the
Italian Renaissance its respect for antiquity and its
admiration for classical mythology, the seventeenth
century owed to Italy its definitive conception of the
theory of poetry, and especially certain rigid structural laws for tragedy and epic. It may be said
without exaggeration that there is not an essential
idea or precept in the works of Corneille and
D'Aubignac on dramatic poetry, or of Le Bossu and
Mambrun on epic poetry, that cannot be found in
the critical writings of the Italian Renaissance.

IV. *The Influence of Rationalistic Philosophy*

The influence of rationalistic philosophy on the
general attitude of classicism manifested itself in
what may be called the gradual rationalization of all
that the Renaissance gave to France. The process
thus effected is most definitely exhibited in the evolution of the rules which France owed to Italy. It
has already been shown how the rules and precepts
of the Italians had originally been based on authority alone, but had gradually obtained a general significance of their own, regardless of their ancient
authority. Somewhat later, in England, the Aristotelian canons were defended by Ben Jonson on the
ground that Aristotle understood the causes of

things, and that what others had done by chance
or custom, Aristotle did by reason alone.[1] By this
time, then, the reasonableness of the Aristotelian
canons was distinctly felt, although they were still
regarded as having authoritativeness in themselves;
and it was first in the French classicists of the
seventeenth century that reason and the ancient
rules were regarded as one and inseparable.

Rationalism, indeed, is to be found at the very outset of the critical activity of the Renaissance; and
Vida's words, already cited, "Semper nutu rationis
eant res," represent in part the attitude of the Renaissance mind toward literature. But the "reason" of the earlier theorists was merely empirical
and individualistic; it did not differ essentially
from Horace's ideal of "good sense." In fact, rationalism and humanism, while existing together
throughout the Renaissance, were never to any extent harmonized; and extreme rationalism generally
took the form of an avowed antagonism to Aristotle.
The complete rationalization of the laws of literature is first evident toward the middle of the seventeenth century. "The rules of the theatre," says
the Abbé d'Aubignac, at the beginning of his
Pratique du Théâtre, "are founded, not on authority, but on reason," and if they are called the rules
of the ancients, it is simply "because the ancients
have admirably practised them." Similarly, Corneille, in his discourse Des Trois Unités, says that
the unity of time would be arbitrary and tyrannical
if it were merely required by Aristotle's Poetics,

[1] Discoveries, p. 80.

but that its real prop is the natural reason; and
Boileau sums up the final attitude of classicism in
these words : —

"Aimez donc la *raison ;* que toujours vos écrits
Empruntent *d'elle seule* et leur lustre et leur prix." [1]

Here the rationalizing process is complete, and the
actual requirements of authority become identical
with the dictates of the reason.

The rules expounded by Boileau, while for the
most part the same as those enunciated by the Italians, are no longer mere rules. They are laws dic-
tated by abstract and universal reason, and hence
inevitable and infallible; they are not tyrannical
or arbitrary, but imposed upon us by the very nature of the human mind. This is not merely, as
we have said, the good nature and the good sense,
in a word, the sweet reasonableness, of such a critic
as Horace.[2] There is more than this in the classicists of the seventeenth century. Good sense becomes universalized, becomes, in fact, as has been
said, not merely an empirical notion of good sense,
but the abstract and universal reason itself. From
this follows the absolute standard of taste at the
bottom of classicism, as exemplified in the passage
already cited from La Bruyère, and in such a line
as this from Boileau : —

"La raison pour marcher n'a souvent qu'une voie." [3]

This rationalization of the Renaissance rules of

[1] *Art Poét.* i. 37.
[2] *Cf.* Brunetière, *Études Critiques*, iv. 136; and **Krantz, p. 93**
sq.
[3] *Art Poét.* i. 48.

poetry was effected by contemporary philosophy; if not by the works and doctrines of Descartes himself, at least by the general tendency of the human mind at this period, of which these works and doctrines are the most perfect expressions. Boileau's *Art Poétique* has been aptly called the *Discours de la Méthode* of French poetry. So that while the contribution of Malherbe and his school to classicism lay in the insistence on clearness, propriety, and verbal and metrical perfection, and the contribution of the Italian Renaissance lay in the infusion of respect for classical antiquity and the imposition of a certain body of fixed rules, the contribution of contemporary philosophy lay in the rationalization or universalization of these rules, and in the imposition of an abstract and absolute standard of taste.

But Cartesianism brought with it certain important limitations and deficiencies. Boileau himself is reported to have said that "the philosophy of Descartes has cut the throat of poetry;"[1] and there can be no doubt that this is the exaggerated expression of a certain inevitable truth. The excessive insistence on the reason brought with it a corresponding undervaluation of the imagination. The rational and rigidly scientific basis of Cartesianism was forced on classicism; and reality became its supreme object and its final test: —

"Rien n'est beau que le vrai."

Reference has already been made to various disadvantages imposed on classicism by the very nature

[1] Reported by J. B. Rousseau, in a letter to Brossette, July 21, 1715.

of its origin and growth; but the most vital of all these disadvantages was the influence of the Cartesian philosophy or philosophic temper. With the scientific basis thus imposed on literature, its only safeguard against extinction was the vast influence of a certain body of fixed rules, which literature dared not deviate from, and which it attempted to justify on the wider grounds of philosophy. These rules, then, the contribution of Italy, saved poetry in France from extinction during the classical period; and of this a remarkable confirmation is to be found in the fact that not until the rationalism of the seventeenth and eighteenth centuries was superseded in France, did French literature rid itself of this body of Renaissance rules. Cartesianism, or at least the rationalistic spirit, humanized these rules, and imposed them on the rest of Europe. But though quintessentialized, they remained artificial, and circumscribed the workings of the French imagination for over a century.

PART THIRD

LITERARY CRITICISM IN ENGLAND

LITERARY CRITICISM IN ENGLAND

CHAPTER I

THE EVOLUTION OF ENGLISH CRITICISM FROM ASCHAM TO MILTON

LITERARY criticism in England during the Elizabethan age was neither so influential nor so rich and varied as the contemporary criticism of Italy and France. This fact might perhaps be thought insufficient to affect the interest or patriotism of English-speaking people, yet the most charming critical monument of this period, Sidney's *Defence of Poesy*, has been slightingly referred to by the latest historian of English poetry. Such interest and importance as Elizabethan criticism possesses must therefore be of an historical nature, and lies in two distinct directions. In the first place, the study of the literature of this period will show, not only that there was a more or less complete body of critical doctrine during the Renaissance, but also that Englishmen shared in this creation, or inheritance, of the Renaissance as truly as did their continental neighbors; and on the other hand this study may be said to possess an interest in itself, in so far as it will make the growth of classicism in England intelligible, and will indicate that the

formation of the classic ideal had begun before the
introduction of the French influence.   In neither
case, however, can early English criticism be considered wholly apart from the general body of
Renaissance doctrine; and its study loses in importance and perspicuity according as it is kept distinct from the consideration of the critical literature
of France, and especially of Italy.

English criticism, during the sixteenth and seventeenth centuries, passed through five more or less
distinct stages of development.   The first stage,
characterized by the purely rhetorical study of
literature, may be said to begin with Leonard
Coxe's *Arte or Crafte of Rhetoryke*, a hand-book for
young students, compiled about 1524, chiefly from
one of the rhetorical treatises of Melanchthon.[1] This
was followed by Wilson's *Arte of Rhetorike* (1553),
which is more extensive and certainly more original than Coxe's manual, and which has been called
by Warton "the first book or system of criticism
in our language."   But the most important figure
of this period is Roger Ascham.   The educational
system expounded in his *Scholemaster*, written
between 1563 and 1568, he owed largely to his
friend, John Sturm, the Strasburg humanist, and
to his teacher, Sir John Cheke, who had been
Greek lecturer at the University of Padua; but
for the critical portions of this work he seems
directly indebted to the rhetorical treatises of the
Italians.[2] Yet his obligations to the Italian human-

[1] *Cf. Mod. Lang. Notes*, 1898, xiii. 293.
[2] *Cf.* Ascham, *Works*, ii. 174–191.

ists did not prevent the expression of his stern and
unyielding antagonism to the romantic Italian spirit
as it influenced the imaginative literature of his
time. In studying early English literature it must
always be kept in mind that the Italian Renaissance influenced the Elizabethan age in two different directions. The Italianization of English poetry
had been effected, or at least begun, by the publication of Tottel's *Miscellany* in 1557; on this, the
creative side of English literature, the Italian
influence was distinctly romantic. The influence
of the Italian humanists, on the other hand, was
directly opposed to this romantic spirit; even in
their own country they had antagonized all that
was not classical in tendency. Ascham, therefore,
as a result of his humanistic training, became not
only the first English man of letters, but also the
first English classicist.

The first stage of English criticism, then, was
entirely given up to rhetorical study. It was at
this time that English writers first attained the
appreciation of form and style as distinguishing
features of literature; and it was to this appreciation that the formation of an English prose
style was due. This period may therefore be compared with the later stages of Italian humanism in
the fifteenth century; and the later humanists were
the masters and models of these early English
rhetoricians. Gabriel Harvey, as a Ciceronian of
the school of Bembo, was perhaps their last representative.

The second stage of English criticism — a period

of classification and especially of metrical studies —
commences with Gascoigne's *Notes of Instruction
concerning the making of Verse*,[1] published in 1575,
and modelled apparently on Ronsard's *Abrégé de
l'Art Poétique françois* (1565). Besides this brief
pamphlet, the first work on English versification,
this stage also includes Puttenham's *Arte of English Poesie*, the first systematic classification of
poetic forms and subjects, and of rhetorical figures;
Bullokar's *Bref Grammar*, the first systematic
treatise on English grammar; and Harvey's *Letters*
and Webbe's *Discourse of English Poetrie*, the first
systematic attempts to introduce classical metres
into English poetry. This period was characterized by the study and classification of the
practical questions of language and versification;
and in this labor it was coöperating with the very
tendencies which Ascham had been attempting to
counteract. The study of the verse-forms introduced into England from Italy helped materially
to perfect the external side of English poetry; and
a similar result was obtained by the crude attempts
at quantitative verse suggested by the school of
Tolomei. The Italian prosodists were thus, directly
or indirectly, the masters of the English students
of this era.

The representative work of the third stage — the
period of philosophical and apologetic criticism — is
Sir Philip Sidney's *Defence of Poesy*, published posthumously in 1595, though probably written about

[1] The *Reulis and Cautelis of Scottis Poesie* by James VI. of
Scotland is wholly based on Gascoigne's treatise.

1583. Harington's *Apologie of Poetrie,* Daniel's
Defence of Ryme, and a few others, are also contemporary treatises. These works, as their titles indicate, are all defences or apologies, and were called
forth by the attacks of the Puritans on poetry,
especially dramatic poetry, and the attacks of the
classicists on English versification and rhyme.
Required by the exigencies of the moment to defend poetry in general, these authors did not
attempt to do so on local or temporary grounds, but
set out to examine the fundamental grounds of
criticism, and to formulate the basic principles of
poetry. In this attempt they consciously or uncon-
sciously sought aid from the critics of Italy, and thus
commenced in England the influence of the Italian
theory of poetry. How great was their indebtedness to the Italians the course of the present study
will make somewhat clear; but it is certainly remarkable that this indebtedness has never been
pointed out before. Speaking of Sidney's *Defence
of Poesy,* one of the most distinguished English
authorities on the Renaissance says: " Much as
the Italians had recently written upon the theory
of poetry, I do not remember any treatise which can
be said to have supplied the material or suggested
the method of this apology."[1] On the contrary,
the doctrines discussed by Sidney had been receiving very similar treatment from the Italians for
over half a century ; and it can be said without exaggeration that there is not an essential principle in

[1] J. A. Symonds, *Sir Philip Sidney*, p. 157. *Cf.* also, Sidney,
Defence, Cook's introduction, p. xxvii.

s

the *Defence of Poesy* which cannot be traced back
to some Italian treatise on the poetic art. The age
of which Sidney is the chief representative is therefore the first period of the influence of Italian critics.

The fourth stage of English criticism, of which
Ben Jonson is, as it were, the presiding genius,
occupies the first half of the seventeenth century.
The period that preceded it was in general romantic
in its tendencies; that of Jonson leaned toward a
strict though never servile classicism. Sidney's
contemporaries had studied the general theory of
poetry, not for the purpose of enunciating rules or
dogmas of criticism, but chiefly in order to defend
the poetic art, and to understand its fundamental
principles. The spirit of the age was the spirit, let
us say, of Fracastoro; that of Jonson was, in a
moderate form, the spirit of Scaliger or Castelvetro.
With Jonson the study of the art of poetry became
an inseparable guide to creation; and it is this
element of self-conscious art, guided by the rules
of criticism, which distinguishes him from his
predecessors. The age which he represents is
therefore the second period of the influence of
Italian criticism; and the same influence also is to
be seen in such critical poems as Suckling's *Session
of the Poets,* and the *Great Assises holden in Parnassus,* ascribed to Wither, both of which may be
traced back to the class of critical poetry of which
Boccalini's *Ragguagli di Parnaso* is the type.[1]

[1] *Cf.* Foffano, p. 173 *sq.* In Spain, Lope de Vega's *Laurel de
Apolo* and Cervantes' *Viage del Parnaso* belong to the same
class of poems.

The fifth period, which covers the second half of the seventeenth century, is characterized by the introduction of French influence, and begins with Davenant's letter to Hobbes, and Hobbes's answer, both prefixed to the epic of *Gondibert* (1651). These letters, written while Davenant and Hobbes were at Paris, display many of the characteristic features of the new influence, — the rationalistic spirit, the stringent classicism, the restriction of art to the imitation of nature, with the further limitation of nature to the life of the city and the court, and the confinement of the imagination to what is called " wit." This specialized sense of the word " wit " is characteristic of the new age, of which Dryden, in part the disciple of Davenant, is the leading figure. The Elizabethans used the term in the general sense of the understanding, — wit, the mental faculty, as opposed to will, the faculty of volition. With the neo-classicists it was used sometimes to represent, in a limited sense, the imagination,[1] more often, however, to designate what we should call fancy,[2] or even mere propriety of poetic expression ;[3] but whatever its particular use, it was always regarded as of the essence of poetic art.

With the fifth stage of English criticism this essay is not concerned. The history of literary criticism in England will be traced no farther than 1650, when the influence of France was substituted

---

[1] *Cf*. Dryden, ded. epist. to the *Annus Mirabilis*.

[2] Addison, *Spectator*, no. 62.

[3] Dryden, preface to the *State of Innocence*.

for that of Italy. This section deals especially with the two great periods of Italian influence, — that of Sidney and that of Ben Jonson. These two men are the central figures, and their names, like those of Dryden, Pope, and Samuel Johnson, represent distinct and important epochs in the history of literary criticism.

CHAPTER II

THOSE who have some acquaintance, however superficial, with the literary criticism of the Italian Renaissance will find an account of the Elizabethan theory of poetry a twice-told tale. In England, as in France, criticism during this period was of a more practical character than in Italy; but even for the technical questions discussed by the Elizabethans, some prototype, or at least some equivalent, may be found among the Italians. The first four stages of English criticism have therefore little novelty or original value; and their study is chiefly important as evidence of the gradual application of the ideas of the Renaissance to English literature.

The writers of the first stage, as might be expected, concerned themselves but little with the theory of poetry, beyond repeating here and there the commonplaces they found in the Italian rhetoricians. Yet it is interesting to note that as early as 1553, Wilson, in the third book of his *Rhetoric*, gives expression to the allegorical conception of poetry which in Italy had held sway from the time of Petrarch and Boccaccio, and which, more than anything else, colored critical theory in Elizabethan

England. The ancient poets, according to Wilson,
did not spend their time inventing meaningless
fables, but used the story merely as a framework
for contents of ethical, philosophic, scientific, or
historical import; the trials of Ulysses, for example, were intended to furnish a lively picture
of man's misery in this life.   The poets are, in
fact, wise men, spiritual legislators, reformers, who
have at heart the redressing of wrongs; and in
accomplishing this end, — either because they fear
to rebuke these wrongs openly, or because they
doubt the expediency or efficacy of such frankness
with ignorant people, — they hide their true meaning under the veil of pleasant fables.   This theory
of poetic art, one of the commonplaces of the age,
may be described as the great legacy of the Middle
Ages to Renaissance criticism.

The writers of the second stage were, in many
cases, too busy with questions of versification and
other practical matters to find time for abstract
theorizing on the art of poetry.   A long period of
rhetorical and metrical study had helped to formulate a rhetorical and technical conception of the
poet's function, aptly exemplified in the sonnet
describing the perfect poet prefixed to King
James's brief treatise on Scotch poetry.[1]   The
marks of a perfect poet are there given as skilful-
ness in the rhetorical figures, quick wit, as shown
in the use of apt and pithy words, and a good memory; — a merely external view of the poet's gifts,
which takes no account of such essentials as imag

[1] Haslewood, ii. 103.

ination, sensibility, and knowledge of nature and human life.

Webbe's *Discourse of English Poetrie* (1586) gives expression to a conception of the object of poetry which is the logical consequence of the allegorical theory, and which was therefore almost universally accepted by Renaissance writers. The poet teaches by means of the allegorical truth hidden under the pleasing fables he invents; but his first object must be to make these fables really pleasing, or the reader is deterred at the outset from any acquaintance with the poet's works. Poetry is therefore a delightful form of instruction; it pleases and profits together; but first of all it must delight, " for the very sum and chiefest essence of poetry did always for the most part consist in delighting the readers or hearers." [1] The poet has the highest welfare of man at heart; and by his sweet allurements to virtue and effective caveats against vice, he gains his end, not roughly or tyrannically, but, as it were, with a loving authority.[2] From the very beginnings of human society poetry has been the means of civilizing men, of drawing them from barbarity to civility and virtue. If it be objected that this art — or rather, from the divine origin of its inspiration, this more than art — has ever been made the excuse for the enticing expression of obscenity and blasphemy, Webbe has three answers. In the first place, poetry is to be moralized, that is, to be read allegorically. The *Metamorphoses* of Ovid, for example, will become, when so understood,

[1] Haslewood, ii. 28.   [2] *Ibid*. ii. 42.

a fount of ethical teaching; and Harington, a few
years later, actually explains in detail the allegorical
significance of the fourth book of that poem.[1]   This
was a well-established tradition, and indeed a favorite occupation, of the Middle Ages; and the *Ovide
Moralisé*, a long poem by Chrétien Le Gouais,
written about the beginning of the fourteenth century, and the equally long Ovidian commentary of
Pierre Berçuire, are typical examples of this practice.[2]   In the second place, the picture of vices to
be found in poetry is intended, not to entice the
reader to imitate them, but rather to deter sensible
men from doing likewise by showing the misfortune that inevitably results from evil.   Moreover,
obscenity is in no way essentially connected with
poetic art; it is to the abuse of poetry, and not to
poetry itself, that we must lay all blame for this
fault.

A still higher conception of the poet's function is
to be found in Puttenham's *Arte of English Poesie*
(1589).   The author of this treatise informs us
that he had lived at the courts of France, Italy, and
Spain, and knew the languages of these and other
lands; and the results of his travels and studies
are sufficiently shown in his general theory of
poetry.   His conception of the poet is directly
based on that of Scaliger.   Poetry, in its highest
form, is an art of " making," or creation; and in
this sense the poet is a creator like God, and forms
a world out of nothing.   In another sense, poetry

[1] Haslewood, ii. 128.
[2] *Hist. Litt. de la France*, xxix. 502–525.

is an art of imitation, in that it presents a true and lively picture of everything set before it. In either case, it can attain perfection only by a divine instinct, or by a great excellence of nature, or by vast observation and experience of the world, or indeed by all these together; but whatever the source of its inspiration, it is ever worthy of study and praise, and its creators deserve preëminence and dignity above all other artificers, scientific or mechanical.[1] The poets were the first priests, prophets, and legislators of the world, the first philosophers, scientists, orators, historians, and musicians. They have been held in the highest esteem by the greatest men from the very first; and the nobility, antiquity, and universality of their art prove its preëminence and worth. With such a history and such a nature, it is sacrilege to debase poetry, or to employ it upon any unworthy subject or for ignoble purpose. Its chief themes should therefore be such as these: the honor and glory of the gods, the worthy deeds of noble princes and great warriors, the praise of virtue and the reproof of vice, instruction in moral doctrine or scientific knowledge, and finally, " the common solace of mankind in all the travails and cares of this transitory life," or even for mere recreation alone.[2]

This is the sum of poetic theorizing during the second stage of English criticism. Yet it was at this very time that the third, or apologetic, period was prepared for by the attacks which the Puritans directed against poetry, and especially the drama.

[1] Puttenham, p. 19 *sq.*   [2] *Ibid.* p. 39.

Of these attacks, Gosson's, as the most celebrated, may be taken as the type. Underlying the rant and exaggerated vituperation of his *Schoole of Abuse* (1579), there is a basis of right principles, and some evidence at least of a spirit not wholly vulgar. He was a moral reformer, an idealist, who looked back with regret toward "the old discipline of England," and contrasted it with the spirit of his own day, when Englishmen seemed to have "robbed Greece of gluttony, Italy of wantonness, Spain of pride, France of deceit, and Dutchland of quaffing."[1] The typical evidences of this moral degradation and effeminacy he found in poetry and the drama; and it is to this motive that his bitter assault on both must be ascribed. He specifically insists that his intention was not to banish poetry, or to condemn music, or to forbid harmless recreation to mankind, but merely to chastise the abuse of all these.[2] He praises plays which possess real moral purpose and effect, and points out the true use and the worthy subjects of poetry much in the same manner as Puttenham does a few years later.[3] But he affirms, as Plato had done hundreds of years before, and as a distinguished French critic has done only the other day, that art contains within itself the germ of its own disintegration; and he shows that in the English poetry of his own time this disintegration had already taken place. The delights and ornaments of verse, intended really to make moral doctrine more pleasing and less abstruse

---

[1] Gosson, p. 34. [2] *Ibid.* p. 65.
[3] *Ibid.* pp. 25, 40.

and thorny, had become, with his contemporaries mere alluring disguises for obscenity and blasphemy.

In the first of the replies to Gosson, Lodge's *Defence of Poetry, Musick, and Stage Plays*, written before either of the treatises of Webbe and Puttenham, are found the old principles of allegorical and moral interpretation, — principles which to us may seem well worn, but which to the English criticism of that time were novel enough. Lodge points out the efficacy of poetry as a civilizing factor in primitive times, and as a moral agency ever since. If the poets have on occasion erred, so have the philosophers, even Plato himself, and grievously.[1] Poetry is a heavenly gift, and is to be contemned only when abused and debased. Lodge did not perceive that his point of view was substantially the same as his opponent's; and indeed, throughout the Elizabethan age, there was this similarity in the point of view of those who attacked and those who defended poetry. Both sides admitted that not poetry, but its abuse, is to be disparaged; and they differed chiefly in that one side insisted almost entirely on the ideal perfection of the poetic art, while the other laid stress on the debased state into which it had fallen. A dual point of view was attempted in a work, licensed in January, 1600, which professed to be "a commendation of true poetry, and a discommendation of all bawdy, ribald, and paganized poets."[2] This Puritan movement

[1] Lodge, *Defence (Shakespeare Soc. Publ.*), p. 6.
[2] Arber, *Transcript of the Stat. Reg.*, iii. 154.

against the paganization of poetry corresponds to the similar movement started by the Council of Trent in Catholic countries.

The theory of poetry during the second stage of English criticism was in the main Horatian, with such additions and modifications as the early Renaissance had derived from the Middle Ages. The Aristotelian canons had not yet become a part of English criticism. Webbe alludes to Aristotle's dictum that Empedocles, having naught but metre in common with Homer, was in reality a natural philosopher rather than a poet;[1] but all such allusions to Aristotle's *Poetics* were merely incidental and sporadic. The introduction of Aristotelianism into England was the direct result of the influence of the Italian critics; and the agent in bringing this new influence into English letters was Sir Philip Sidney. His *Defence of Poesy* is a veritable epitome of the literary criticism of the Italian Renaissance; and so thoroughly is it imbued with this spirit, that no other work, Italian, French, or English, can be said to give so complete and so noble a conception of the temper and the principles of Renaissance criticism. For the general theory of poetry, its sources were the critical treatises of Minturno[2] and Scaliger.[3] Yet without any decided novelty of ideas, or even of expression, it can lay

[1] Haslewood, ii. 28.

[2] Sidney's acquaintance with Minturno is proved beyond doubt, even were such proof necessary, by the list of poets (*Defence*, pp. 2, 3) which he has copied from Minturno's *De Poeta*, pp. 14, 15.

[3] Scaliger's *Poetics* is specifically mentioned and cited by

claim to distinct originality in its unity of feeling, its ideal and noble temper, and its adaptation to circumstance. Its eloquence and dignity will hardly appear in a mere analysis, which pretends to give only the more important and fundamental of its principles; but such a summary — and this is quite as important — will at least indicate the extent of its indebtedness to Italian criticism.

In all that relates to the antiquity, universality, and preëminence of poetry, Sidney apparently follows Minturno. Poetry, as the first light-giver to ignorance, flourished before any other art or science. The first philosophers and historians were poets; and such supreme works as the *Psalms* of David and the *Dialogues* of Plato are in reality poetical. Among the Greeks and the Romans, the poet was regarded as a sage or prophet; and no nation, however primitive or barbarous, has been without poets, or has failed to receive delight and instruction from poetry.[1]

But before proceeding to defend an art so ancient and universal, it is necessary to define it; and the definition which Sidney gives agrees substantially with what might be designated Renaissance Aristotelianism. "Poetry," says Sidney,[2] "is an art of imitation, for so Aristotle termeth it in his word μίμησις, that is to say, a representing, counterfeiting, or figuring forth; to speak metaphorically, a

Sidney four or five times; but these citations are far from exhausting his indebtedness to Scaliger.

[1] *Defence*, p. 2 *sq.*; *cf.* Minturno, *De Poeta*, pp. 9, 13.
[2] *Defence*, p. 9.

speaking picture,[1] with this end,—to teach and
delight." [2]   Poetry is, accordingly, an art of imitation, and not merely the art of versifying; for
although most poets have seen fit to apparel their
poetic inventions in verse, verse is but the raiment
and ornament of poetry, and not one of its causes
or essentials.[3]   "One may be a poet without vers-
ing," says Sidney, "and a versifier without poetry." [4]
Speech and reason are the distinguishing features
between man and brute; and whatever helps to
perfect and polish speech deserves high commendation.   Besides its mnemonic value, verse is the
most fitting raiment of poetry because it is most
dignified and compact, not colloquial and slipshod.
But with all its merits, it is not an essential of
poetry, of which the true test is this,—feigning
notable images of vices and virtues, and teaching
delightfully.

In regard to the object, or function, of poetry,
Sidney is at one with Scaliger.   The aim of poetry
is accomplished by teaching most delightfully a
notable morality; or, in a word, by delightful instruction.[5]   Not instruction alone, or delight alone,

---

[1] This ancient phrase had become, as has been seen, a commonplace during the Renaissance.   *Cf.*, *e.g.*, Dolce, *Osservationi*,
1560, p. 189; Vauquelin, *Art Poét.* i. 226; Camoens, *Lusiad.* vii. 70.

[2] Sidney's classification of poets, *Defence*, p. 9, is borrowed
from Scaliger, *Poet.* i. 3.

[3] *Defence*, p. 11.   *Cf.* Castelvetro, *Poetica*, pp. 23, 190.

[4] *Defence*, p. 33.   *Cf.* Ronsard, *Œuvres*, iii. 19, vii. 310; and
Shelley, *Defence of Poetry*, p. 9: "The distinction between
poets and prose writers is a vulgar error."

[5] *Defence*, pp. 47, 51.   *Cf.* Scaliger, *Poet.* i. 1, and vii. i. 2:
"Poetæ finem esse, docere cum delectatione."

as Horace had said, but instruction made delightful; and it is this dual function which serves not only as the end but as the very test of poetry. The object of all arts and sciences is to lift human life to the highest altitudes of perfection; and in this respect they are all servants of the sovereign, or architectonic, science, whose end is well-doing and not well-knowing only.[1] Virtuous action is therefore the end of all learning;[2] and Sidney sets out to prove that the poet, more than any one else, conduces to this end.

This is the beginning of the apologetic side of Sidney's argument.   The ancient controversy — ancient even in Plato's days — between poetry and philosophy is once more reopened; and the question is the one so often debated by the Italians, — shall the palm be given to the poet, to the philosopher, or to the historian?   The gist of Sidney's argument is that while the philosopher teaches by precept alone, and the historian by example alone, the poet conduces most to virtue because he employs both precept and example.   The philosopher teaches virtue by showing what virtue is and what vice is, by setting down, in thorny argument, and without clarity or beauty of style, the bare rule.[3]   The historian teaches virtue by showing the experience of past ages; but, being tied down to what actually happened, that is, to the particular truth of things

---

[1] Aristotle, *Ethics*, i. 1; Cicero, *De Offic.* i. 7.

[2] This was the usual attitude of the humanists; *cf.* Woodward, p. 182 *sq.*

[3] *Cf.* Daniello, p. 19; Minturno, *De Poeta*, p. 39.

and not to general reason, the example he depicts draws no necessary consequence. The poet alone accomplishes this dual task. What the philosopher says should be done is by the poet pictured most perfectly in some one by whom it has been done, thus coupling the general notion with the particular instance. The philosopher, moreover, teaches the learned only; the poet teaches all, and is, in Plutarch's phrase, "the right popular philosopher,"[1] for he seems only to promise delight, and moves men to virtue unawares. But even if the philosopher excel the poet in teaching, he cannot move his readers as the poet can, and this is of higher importance than teaching; for what is the use of teaching virtue if the pupil is not moved to act and accomplish what he is taught?[2] On the other hand, the historian deals with particular instances, with vices and virtues so commingled that the reader can find no pattern to imitate. The poet makes history reasonable; he gives perfect examples of vices and virtues for human imitation; he makes virtue succeed and vice fail, as history can but seldom do. Poetry, therefore, conduces to virtue, the end of all learning, better than any other art or science, and so deserves the palm as the highest and the noblest form of human wisdom.[3]

The basis of Sidney's distinction between the

[1] *Defence*, p. 18.

[2] *Ibid.* p. 22. *Cf.* Minturno, *De Poeta*, p. 106; Varchi, *Lezzioni*, p. 576.

[3] That is, the highest form of *human* wisdom, for Sidney, as a Christian philosopher, naturally leaves revealed religion out of the discussion.

poet and the historian is the famous passage in which Aristotle explains why poetry is more philosophic and of more serious value than history.[1] The poet deals, not with the particular, but with the universal, — with what might or should be, not with what is or has been. But Sidney, in the assertion of this principle, follows Minturno[2] and Scaliger,[3] and goes farther than Aristotle would probably have gone. All arts have the works of nature as their principal object, and follow nature as actors follow the lines of their play. Only the poet is not tied to such subjects, but creates another nature better than ever nature itself brought forth. For, going hand in hand with nature, and being enclosed not within her limits, but only by the zodiac of his own imagination, he creates a golden world for nature's brazen; and in this sense he may be compared as a creator with God.[4] Where shall you find in life such a friend as Pylades, such a hero as Orlando, such an excellent man as Æneas ?

Sidney then proceeds to answer the various objections that have been made against poetry. These objections, partly following Gosson and Cornelius Agrippa,[5] and partly his own inclinations, he reduces to four.[6] In the first place, it is objected that a man might spend his time more profitably than by reading the figments of poets. But since teaching virtue is the real aim of all learning, and since poetry has been shown to accomplish this

---

[1] *Poet.* ix. 1–4.
[2] *De Poeta*, p. 87 *sq.*
[3] *Poet.* i. 1.
[4] *Defence*, pp. 7, 8.
[5] *De Van. et Incert. Scient.* **cap. v.**
[6] *Defence*, p. 34 *sq.*

T

better than all other arts or sciences, this objection
is easily answered.   In the second place, poetry has
been called the mother of lies; but Sidney shows
that it is less likely to misstate facts than other
sciences, for the poet does not publish his figments
as facts, and, since he affirms nothing, cannot ever
be said to lie.[1]   Thirdly, poetry has been called the
nurse of abuse, that is to say, poetry misuses and
debases the mind of man by turning it to wantonness and by making it unmartial and effeminate.
But Sidney argues that it is man's wit that abuses
poetry, and not poetry that abuses man's wit; and as
to making men effeminate, this charge applies to all
other sciences more than to poetry, which in its
description of battles and praise of valiant men
notably stirs courage and enthusiasm.   Lastly, it
is pointed out by the enemies of poetry that Plato,
one of the greatest of philosophers, banished poets
from his ideal commonwealth.   But Plato's *Dialogues* are in reality themselves a form of poetry ;
and it argues ingratitude in the most poetical of
philosophers, that he should defile the fountain
which was his source.[2]   Yet though Sidney perceives
how fundamental are Plato's objections to poetry,
he is inclined to believe that it was rather against
the abuse of poetry by the contemporary Greek
poets that Plato was chiefly cavilling; for poets are
praised in the *Ion*, and the greatest men of every
age have been patrons and lovers of poetry.

[1] *Cf*. Boccaccio, *Gen. degli Dei*, p. 257 *sq.*; and Haslewood,
ii. 127.

[2] *Defence*, pp. 3, 41; *cf*. Daniello, p. 22.

In the dozen years or so which elapsed between the composition and the publication of the *Defence of Poesy*, during which time it seems to have circulated in manuscript, a number of critical works appeared, and the indebtedness of several of them to Sidney's book is considerable. This is especially so of the *Apologie of Poetrie* which Sir John Harington prefixed to his translation of the *Orlando Furioso* in 1591. This brief treatise includes an apology for poetry in general, for the *Orlando Furioso* in particular, and also for his own translation. The first section, which alone concerns us here, is almost entirely based on the *Defence of Poesy*. The distinguishing features of poetry are imitation, or fiction, and verse.[1] Harington disclaims all intention of discussing whether writers of fiction and dialogue in prose, such as Plato and Xenophon, are poets or not, or whether Lucan, though writing in verse, is to be regarded as an historiographer rather than as a poet;[2] so that his argument is confined to the element of imitation, or fiction. He treats poetry rather as a propædeutic to theology and moral philosophy than as one of the fine arts. All human learning may be regarded by the orthodox Christian as vain and superfluous; but poetry is one of the most effective aids to the higher learning of God's divinity, and poets themselves are really popular philosophers and popular divines. Harington then takes up, one by one, the four specific charges of Cornelius Agrippa, that poetry is a nurse of lies, a pleaser of fools, a

[1] Haslewood, ii. 129.   [2] *Ibid.* ii. 123.

breeder of dangerous errors, and an enticer to wantonness ; and answers them after the manner of
Sidney. He differs from Sidney, however, in lay-
ing particular stress on the allegorical interpretation
of imaginative literature. This element is mini-
mized in the *Defence of Poesy;* but Harington
accepts, and discusses in detail, the mediæval conception of the three meanings of poetry, the literal,
the moral, and the allegorical.[1] The death-knell of
this mode of interpreting literature was sounded by
Bacon, who, while not asserting that all the fables
of poets are but meaningless fictions, declared without hesitation that the fable had been more often
written first and the exposition devised afterward,
than the moral first conceived and the fable merely
framed to give expression to it.[2]

This passage occurs in the second book of the
Advancement of Learning (1605), where Bacon has
briefly stated his theory of poetry. His point of
view does not differ essentially from that of Sidney,
though the expression is more compact and logical.
The human understanding, according to Bacon, includes the three faculties of memory, imagination,
and reason, and each of these faculties finds typical expression in one of the three great branches of
learning, memory in history, reason in philosophy,
and imagination in poetry.[3] The imagination, not
being tied to the laws of matter, may join what
nature has severed and sever what nature has joined ;
and poetry, therefore, while restrained in the meas-

---

[1] Haslewood, ii. 127.   [2] Bacon, *Works*, vi. 204–206.
[3] *Cf. Anglia*, 1899, xxi. 273.

ure of words, is in all things else extremely licensed. It may be defined as feigned history, and in so far as its form is concerned, may be either in prose or in verse.   Its source is to be found in the dissatisfaction of the human mind with the actual world; and its purpose is to satisfy man's natural longing for more perfect greatness, goodness, and variety than can be found in the nature of things.   Poetry therefore invents actions and incidents greater and more heroic than those of nature, and hence conduces to magnanimity; it invents actions more agreeable to the merits of virtue and vice, more just in retribution, more in accordance with revealed providence, and hence conduces to morality; it invents actions more varied and unexpected, and hence conduces to delectation.   "And therefore it was ever thought to have some participation of divineness, because it doth raise the mind, by submitting the shows of things to the desires of the mind; whereas reason doth buckle and bow the mind unto the nature of things." [1]   For the expression of affections, passions, corruptions, and customs, the world is more indebted to poets than to the works of philosophers, and for wit and eloquence no less than to orators and their orations.   It is for these reasons that in rude times, when all other learning was excluded, poetry alone found access and admiration.

This is pure idealism of a romantic type; but in his remarks on allegory Bacon was foreshadowing the development of classicism, for from the time of

[1] *Works*, vi. 203.

Ben Jonson the allegorical mode of interpreting poetry ceased to have any effect on literary criticism. The reason for this is obvious. The allegorical critics regarded the plot, or fable, — to use a simile so often found in Renaissance criticism — as a mere sweet and pleasant covering for the wholesome but bitter pill of moral doctrine. The neo-classicists, limiting the sense and application of Aristotle's definition of poetry as an imitation of life, regarded the fable as the medium of this imitation, and the more perfect according as it became more truly and more minutely an image of human life. In criticism, therefore, the growth of classicism is more or less coextensive with the growth of the conception of the fable, or plot, as an end in itself.

This vaguely defines the change which comes over the spirit of criticism about the beginning of the seventeenth century, and which is exemplified in the writings of Ben Jonson. His definition of poetry does not differ substantially from that of Sidney, but seems more directly Aristotelian : —

"A poet, *poeta*, is . . . a maker, or feigner ; his art, an art of imitation or feigning ; expressing the life of men in fit measure, numbers, and harmony ; according to Aristotle from the word ποιεῖν, which signifies to make or feign. Hence he is called a poet, not he which writeth in measure only, but that feigneth and formeth a fable, and writes things like the truth ; for the fable and fiction is, as it were, the form and soul of any poetical work or poem."[1]

[1] *Discoveries*, p. 73. On Jonson's distinction between poet (*poeta*), poem (*poema*), and poesy (*poesis*), see my article in *Modern Philology*, 1905, ii. 459, n.

Poetry and painting agree in that both are arts of imitation, both accommodate all they invent to the use and service of nature, and both have as their common object profit and pleasure; but poetry is a higher form of art than painting, since it appeals to the understanding, while painting appeals primarily to the senses.[1] Jonson's conception of his art is thus essentially noble; of all arts it ranks highest in dignity and ethical importance. It contains all that is best in philosophy, divinity, and the science of politics, and leads and persuades men to virtue with a ravishing delight, while the others but threaten and compel.[2] It therefore offers to mankind a certain rule and pattern of living well and happily in human society. This conception of poetry Jonson finds in Aristotle;[3] but it is to the Italians of the Renaissance, and not to the Stagyrite, that these doctrines really belong.

Jonson ascribes to the poet himself a dignity no less than that of his craft. Mere excellence in style or versification does not make a poet, but rather the exact knowledge of vices and virtues, with ability to make the latter loved and the former hated;[4] and this is so far true, that to be a good poet it is necessary, first of all, to be a really good man.[5] A similar doctrine has already been found in many critical writers of the sixteenth century; but perhaps the noblest expression of this conception of the poet's consecrated character and office occurs in

---

[1] *Discoveries*, p. 49.   [3] *Ibid.* p. 74.
[2] *Ibid.* p. 34.   [4] *Ibid.* p. 34.
[5] *Works*, i. 333.

the original quarto edition of Jonson's *Every Man in his Humour,* in which the " reverend name" of poet is thus exalted : —

> " I can refell opinion, and approve
> The state of poesy, such as it is,
> Blessed, eternal, and most true divine :
> Indeed, if you will look on poesy,
> As she appears in many, poor and lame,
> Patched up in remnants and old worn-out rags,
> Half-starved for want of her peculiar food,
> Sacred invention ; then I must confirm
> Both your conceit and censure of her merit :
> But view her in her glorious ornaments,
> Attired in the majesty of art,
> Set high in spirit with the precious taste
> Of sweet philosophy ; and, which is most,
> Crowned with the rich traditions of a soul,
> That hates to have her dignity prophaned
> With any relish of an earthly thought,
> Oh then how proud a presence doth she bear !
> Then is she like herself, fit to be seen
> Of none but grave and consecrated eyes." [1]

Milton also gives expression to this consecrated conception of the poet. Poetry is a gift granted by God only to a few in every nation; [2] but he who would partake of the gift of eloquence must first of all be virtuous. [3] It is impossible for any one to write well of laudable things without being himself a true poem, without having in himself the experience and practice of all that is praiseworthy. [4] Poets are the champions of liberty and the " strenu-

[1] *Works*, i. 59, *n.*
[2] Milton, *Prose Works*, ii. 479.
[3] *Ibid.* iii. 100.
[4] *Ibid.* iii. 118.

ous enemies of despotism";[1] and they have power to imbreed and cherish in a people the seeds of virtue and public civility, to set the affections in right tune, and to allay the perturbations of the mind.[2] Poetry, which at its best is "simple, sensuous, and passionate," describes everything that passes through the brain of man, — all that is holy and sublime in religion, all that in virtue is amiable and grave. Thus by means of delight and the force of example, those who would otherwise flee from virtue are taught to love her.

[1] *Prose Works*, i. 241.   [2] *Ibid.* ii. **479.**

CHAPTER III

DRAMATIC criticism in England began with Sir Philip Sidney. Casual references to the drama can be found in critical writings anterior to the *Defence of Poesy;* but to Sidney belongs the credit of having first formulated, in a more or less systematic manner, the general principles of dramatic art. These principles, it need hardly be said, are those which, for half a century or more, had been undergoing discussion and modification in Italy and France, and of which the ultimate source was the *Poetics* of Aristotle. Dramatic criticism in England was thus, from its very birth, both Aristotelian and classical, and it remained so for two centuries. The beginnings of the Elizabethan drama were almost contemporary with the composition of the *Defence of Poesy,* and the decay of the drama with Jonson's *Discoveries.* Yet throughout this period the romantic drama never received literary exposition. The great Spanish drama had its critical champions and defenders, the Elizabethan drama had none. It was, perhaps, found to be a simpler task to echo the doctrines of others, than to formulate the principles of a novel dramatic form. But the true explanation has already been suggested.

282

The sources of the dramatic criticism were the writings of the Italian critics, and these were entirely classical. In creative literature, however, the Italian Renaissance influenced the Elizabethans almost entirely on the romantic side. This, perhaps, suffices to explain the lack of fundamental coördination between dramatic theory and dramatic practice during the sixteenth and early seventeenth centuries. Ascham, writing twenty years before Sidney, indicated "Aristotle's precepts and Euripides' example" as the criteria of dramatic art;[1] and in spirit these remained the final tests throughout the Elizabethan age.

I. *Tragedy*

In Webbe's *Discourse of English Poetrie* we find those general distinctions between tragedy and comedy which had been common throughout the Middle Ages from the days of the post-classic grammarians. Tragedies express sorrowful and lamentable histories, dealing with gods and goddesses, kings and queens, and men of high estate, and representing miserable calamities, which become worse and worse until they end in the most woful plight that can be devised. Comedies, on the other hand, begin doubtfully, become troubled for a while, but always, by some lucky chance, end with the joy and appeasement of all concerned.[2] This distinction is said to be derived from imitation of the *Iliad* and the *Odyssey;* and in this, as well in

[1] *Scholemaster*, p. 139.   [2] Haslewood, ii. 40.

his fanciful account of the origins of the drama, Webbe seems to have had a vague recollection of Aristotle. Puttenham's account of dramatic development is scarcely more Aristotelian; [1] yet in its general conclusions it agrees with those in the *Poetics*. His conception of tragedy and comedy is similar to Webbe's. Comedy expresses the common behavior and manner of life of private persons, and such as are of the meaner sort of men. [2] Tragedy deals with the doleful falls of unfortunate and afflicted princes, for the purpose of reminding men of the mutability of fortune, and of God's just punishment of a vicious life. [3]

The Senecan drama and the Aristotelian precepts were the sources of Sidney's theory of tragedy. The oratorical and sententious tragedies of Seneca had influenced dramatic theory and practice throughout Europe from the very outset of the Renaissance. Ascham, indeed, preferred Sophocles and Euripides to Seneca, and cited Pigna, the rival of Giraldi Cintio, in confirmation of his opinion; [4] but this, while an indication of Ascham's own good taste, is an exceptional verdict, and in direct opposition to the usual opinion of contemporary critics. Sidney, in his account of the English drama, could find but one tragedy modelled as it should be on the Senecan drama. [5] The tragedy of *Gorboduc*, however, has one defect that provokes Sidney's censure, — it does not observe the unities of time and place.

[1] Puttenham, p. 47 *sq*.   [3] *Ibid*. p. 49.

[2] *Ibid*. p. 41.   [4] Ascham, *Works*, ii. 189.

[5] *Defence*, p. 47 *sq*.

In all other respects, it is an ideal model for English playwrights to imitate. Its stately speeches and well-sounding phrases approach almost to the height of Seneca's style; and in teaching most delightfully a notable morality, it attains the very end of poetry.

The ideal tragedy — and in this Sidney closely follows the Italians — is an imitation of a noble action, in the representation of which it stirs "admiration and commiseration,"[1] and teaches the uncertainty of the world and the weak foundations upon which golden roofs are built. It makes kings fear to be tyrants, and tyrants manifest their tyrannical humors. Sidney's censure of the contemporary drama is that it outrages the grave and weighty character of tragedy, its elevated style, and the dignity of the personages represented, by mingling kings and clowns, and introducing the most inappropriate buffoonery. There are, indeed, one or two examples of tragi-comedy in ancient literature, such as Plautus's *Amphitryon;*[2] but never do the ancients, like the English, match hornpipes and funerals.[3] The English dramas are neither true comedies nor true tragedies, and disregard both the rules of poetry and honest civility. Tragedy is not tied to the laws of history, and may arrange and modify events as it pleases; but it is certainly bound by the rules of poetry. It is evident, there-

---

[1] *Defence*, p. 28. This is the Elizabethan equivalent for Aristotle's *katharsis* of "pity and terror."

[2] *Cf.* Scaliger, *Poet.* i. 7.

[3] *Defence*, p. 50.

fore, that the *Defence of Poesy*, as a French writer
has observed, "gives us an almost complete theory
of neo-classic tragedy, a hundred years before the
Art Poétique of Boileau : the severe separation of
poetic forms, the sustained dignity of language, the
unities, the *tirade*, the *récit*, nothing is lacking." [1]

Ben Jonson pays more attention to the theory of
comedy than to that of tragedy ; but his conception
of the latter does not differ from Sidney's. The
parts, or divisions, of comedy and tragedy are the
same, and both have on the whole a common end,
to teach and delight; so that comic as well as
tragic poets were called by the Greeks διδάσκαλοι.[2]
The external conditions of the drama require that
it should have the equal division into acts and
scenes, the true number of actors, the chorus, and
the unities.[3] But Jonson does not insist on the
strict observance of these formal requirements, for
the history of the drama shows that each successive poet of importance has gradually and materially altered the dramatic structure, and there is
no reason why the modern poet may not do likewise.   Moreover, while these requirements may
have been regularly observed in the ancient state
and splendor of dramatic poetry, it is impossible to
retain them now and preserve any measure of popular delight.   The outward forms of the ancients,
therefore, may in part be disregarded; but there are
certain essentials which must be observed by the
tragic poet in whatsoever age he may flourish.
These are, "Truth of argument, dignity of persons,

[1] Breitinger, p. 37.   [2] *Discoveries*, p. 81.   [3] *Works*, i. 69.

gravity and height of elocution, fulness and fre-
quency of sentence." [1] In other words, Jonson's
model is the oratorical and sententious tragedy of
Seneca, with its historical plots and its persons of
high estate.

In the address, "Of that Sort of Dramatic Poem
which is called Tragedy," prefixed to *Samson
Agonistes*, Milton has minutely adhered to the Italian theory of tragedy.   After referring to the
ancient dignity and moral effect of tragedy,[2] Milton
acknowledges that, in the modelling of his poem,
he has followed the ancients and the Italians as of
greatest authority in such matters. He has avoided
the introduction of trivial and vulgar persons and
the intermingling of comic and tragic elements;
he has used the chorus, and has observed the laws
of verisimilitude and decorum.   His explanation of
the peculiar effect of tragedy — the purgation of
pity and fear — has already been referred to in the
first section of this essay.[3]

II. *Comedy*

The Elizabethan theory of comedy was based on
the body of rules and observations which the Italian critics, aided by a few hints from Aristotle, had
deduced from the practice of Plautus and Terence.

[1] *Works*, i. 272.

[2] *Cf.* Bacon, *De Augm. Scient.* iii. 13; and Ascham, *Scholemaster*, p. 130.

[3] He seems also to allude to the theory of *katharsis* in the
Reason of Church Government; Prose Works, ii. 479.

It will, therefore, be unnecessary to dwell at any
great length on the doctrines of Sidney and Ben
Jonson, who are the main comic theorists of this
period. Sidney defines comedy as "an imitation
of the common errors of our life," which are represented in the most ridiculous and scornful manner,
so that the spectator is anxious to avoid such errors
himself. Comedy, therefore, shows the "filthiness
of evil," but only in "our private and domestical
matters." [1] It should aim at being wholly delightful, just as tragedy should be maintained by a
well-raised admiration. Delight is thus the first
requirement of comedy; but the English comic
writers err in thinking that delight cannot be obtained without laughter, whereas laughter is neither
an essential cause nor an essential effect of delight.
Sidney then distinguishes delight from laughter
almost exactly after the manner of Trissino. [2] The
great fault of English comedy is that it stirs
laughter concerning things that are sinful, *i.e.*
execrable rather than merely ridiculous — forbidden plainly, according to Sidney, by Aristotle himself — and concerning things that are miserable,
and rather to be pitied than scorned. Comedy
should not only produce delightful laughter, but
mixed with it that delightful teaching which is the
end of all poetry.

Ben Jonson, like Sidney, makes human follies or
errors the themes of comedy, which should be

---

[1] *Defence*, p. 28.
[2] *Ibid.* p. 50 *sq.*   *Cf.* Trissino, *Opere*, ii. 127 *sq.;* and Cicero,
De Orat. ii. 58 *sq.*

> " an image of the times,
> And sport with human follies, not with crimes,
> Except we make them such, by loving still
> Our popular errors, when we know they're ill ;
> I mean such errors as you'll all confess
> By laughing at them, they deserve no less." [1]

In depicting these human follies, it is the office
of the comic poet to imitate justice, to improve the
moral life and purify language, and to stir up gentle
affections.[2] The moving of mere laughter is not
always the end of comedy; in fact, Jonson interprets Aristotle as asserting that the moving of
laughter is a fault in comedy, a kind of turpitude
that depraves a part of man's nature.[3] This conclusion is based on an interpretation of Aristotle
which has persisted almost to the present day. In
the *Poetics*, τὸ γελοῖον, the ludicrous, is said to be
the subject of comedy; [4] and many critics have
thought that Aristotle intended by this to distinguish between the risible and the ridiculous, between mere laughter and laughter mixed with
contempt or disapprobation.[5] The nature and the
source of one of the most important elements in
Jonson's theory of comedy, his doctrine of " humours," have been briefly discussed in the first
section of this essay. It will suffice here to define
a " humour " as an absorbing singularity of character,[6] and to note that it grew out of the concep-

---

[1] *Works*, i. 2.   [3] *Discoveries*, p. 82.

[2] *Ibid.* i. 335.   [4] *Poet.* v. 1.

[5] *Cf.* Twining, i. 320 *sq.*, and Kames, *Elements of Criticism*,
vol. i. chap. 7.

[6] *Cf.* Jonson, *Works*, i. 67 and 31

U

tion of *decorum* which played so important a part
in poetic theory during the Italian Renaissance.

III. *The Dramatic Unities*

Before leaving the theory of the drama, there is one
further point to be discussed, — the doctrine of the
unities.   It has been seen that the unities of time
and place were, in Italy, first formulated together
by Castelvetro in 1570, and in France by Jean de la
Taille in 1572.   The first mention of the unities in
England is to be found, a dozen years later, in the
Defence of Poesy, and it cannot be doubted that Sidney derived them directly from Castelvetro.   Sidney, in discussing the tragedy of *Gorboduc*, finds it
"faulty in time and place, the two necessary com-
panions of all corporal actions; for where the stage
should always represent but one place, and the
uttermost time presupposed in it should be, both
by Aristotle's precept and common reason, but one
day, there [*i.e.* in *Gorboduc*] is both many days and
many places inartificially imagined."[1]   He also objects to the confusions of the English stage, where
on one side Africa and on the other Asia may be
represented, and where in an hour a youth may grow
from boyhood to old age.[2]   How absurd this is,
common sense, art, and ancient examples ought to

[1] *Defence*, p. 48; *cf.* Castelvetro, *Poetica*, pp. 168, 534.

[2] *Cf.* Whetstone, *Promos and Cassandra* (1578), cited in Ward,
Dram. Lit. i. 118; also, Jonson, *Works*, i. 2, 70; Cervantes,
Don Quix. i. 48; Boileau, *Art Poét.* iii. 39.   In the theory of the
drama, Sidney's point of view coincides very closely with that
of Cervantes.

teach the English playwright; and at this day, says Sidney, the ordinary players in Italy will not err in it. If indeed it be objected that one or two of the comedies of Plautus and Terence do not observe the unity of time, let us not follow them when they err but when they are right; it is no excuse for us to do wrong because Plautus on one occasion has done likewise.

The law of the unities does not receive such rigid application in England as is given by Sidney until the introduction of the French influence nearly three quarters of a century later. Ben Jonson is considerably less stringent in this respect than Sidney. He lays particular stress on the unity of action, and in the *Discoveries* explains at length the Aristotelian conception of the unity and magnitude of the fable. "The fable is called the imitation of one entire and perfect action, whose parts are so joined and knit together, as nothing in the structure can be changed, or taken away, without impairing or troubling the whole, of which there is a proportionable magnitude in the members."[1] Simplicity, then, should be one of the chief characteristics of the action, and nothing receives so much of Jonson's censure as "monstrous and forced action."[2] As to the unity of time, Jonson says that the action should be allowed to grow until necessity demands a conclusion; the argument, however, should not exceed the compass of one day, but should be large enough to allow place for digressions and episodes, which are to the fable what furniture is to a house.[3]

[1] *Discoveries*, p. 83.   [2] *Works*, i. 337.   [3] *Discoveries*, p. 85.

Jonson does not formally require the observance of the unity of place, and even acknowledges having disregarded it in his own plays; but he does not favor much change of scene on the stage. In the prologue of *Volpone*, he boasts that he has followed all the laws of refined comedy,

> " As best critics have designed ;
> The laws of time, place, persons he observeth,
> From no needful rule he swerveth."

Milton observes the unity of time in the *Samson Agonistes :* " The circumscription of time, wherein the whole drama begins and ends is, according to ancient rule and best example, within the space of twenty-four hours."

With the introduction of the French influence, the unities became fixed requirements of the English drama, and remained so for over a century. Sir Robert Howard, in the preface of his tragedy, *The Duke of Lerma*, impugned their force and authority; but Dryden, in answering him, pointed out that to attack the unities is really to contend against Aristotle, Horace, Ben Jonson, and Corneille.[1] Farquhar, however, in his *Discourse upon Comedy* (1702), argued with force and wit against the unities of time and place, and scoffed at all the legislators of Parnassus, ancient and modern, — Aristotle, Horace, Scaliger, Vossius, Heinsius, D'Aubignac, and Rapin.

---

[1] *Essay of Dram. Poesy*, p. 118.

IV. *Epic Poetry*

The Elizabethan theory of heroic poetry may be
dismissed briefly. Webbe refers to the epic as
" that princely part of poetry, wherein are dis-
played the noble acts and valiant exploits of puissant
captains, expert soldiers, wise men, with the famous reports of ancient times; " [1] and Puttenham
defines heroic poems as " long histories of the noble
gests of kings and great princes, intermeddling the
dealings of gods, demi-gods, and heroes, and weighty
consequences of peace and war." [2]   The importance
of this form of poetry, according to Puttenham, is
largely historical, in that it sets forth an example
of the valor and virtue of our forefathers.[3]   Sidney
is scarcely more explicit.[4]   He asserts that heroic
poetry is the best and noblest of all forms; he
shows that such characters as Achilles, Æneas, and
Rinaldo are shining examples for all men's imitation; but of the nature or structure of the epic he
says nothing.

The second part of Harington's *Apologie of Poetrie* is given up to a defence of the *Orlando Furioso*,
and here the Aristotelian theory of the epic appears
for the first time in English criticism.   Harington,
taking the *Æneid* as the approved model of all
heroic poetry, first shows that Ariosto has followed
closely in Virgil's footsteps, but is to be preferred
even to Virgil in that the latter pays reverence to
false deities, while Ariosto has the advantage of the

[1] Haslewood, ii. 45.　　[3] *Ibid*. p. 54.
[2] Puttenham, p. 40.　　[4] *Defence*, p. 30.

Christian spirit. But since some critics, "reducing all heroical poems unto the method of Homer and certain precepts of Aristotle," insist that Ariosto is wanting in art, Harington sets out to prove that the *Orlando Furioso* may not only be defended by the example of Homer, but that it has even followed very strictly the rules and precepts of Aristotle.[1] In the first place, Aristotle says that the epic should be based on some historical action, only a short part of which, in point of time, should be treated by the poet; so Ariosto takes the story of Charlemagne, and does not exceed a year or so in the compass of the argument.[2] Secondly, Aristotle holds that nothing that is utterly incredible should be invented by the poet; and nothing in the *Orlando* exceeds the possibility of belief. Thirdly, epics, as well as tragedies, should be full of περιπέτεια, which Harington interprets to mean "an agnition of some unlooked for fortune either good or bad, and a sudden change thereof"; and of this, as well as of apt similitudes and passions well expressed, the *Orlando* is really full.

In conclusion, it may be observed that epic poetry did not receive adequate critical treatment in England until after the introduction of the French influence. The rules and theories of the Italian Renaissance, restated in the writings of Le Bossu, Mambrun, Rapin, and Vossius, were thus brought into English criticism, and found perhaps

[1] Haslewood, ii. 140 *sq.*

[2] *Cf.* Minturno, *Arte Poetica*, p. 71; and Ronsard, *Œuvres*, iii. 19.

their best expression in Addison's essays on *Paradise Lost*. Such epics as Davenant's *Gondibert*, Chamberlayne's *Pharonnida*, Dryden's *Annus Mirabilis*, and Blackmore's *Prince Arthur*, like the French epics of the same period, doubtless owed their inspiration to the desire to put into practice the classical rules of heroic poetry.[1]

1 *Cf.* Dryden, *Discourse on Satire*, in *Works*, xiii. 37.

CHAPTER IV

I. *Introductory: Romantic Elements*

IT were no less than supererogation to adduce evidences of the romantic spirit of the age of Shakespeare. No period in English literature is more distinctly romantic; and although in England criticism is less affected by creative literature, and has had less effect upon it, than in France, it is only natural to suppose that Elizabethan criticism should be as distinctly romantic as the works of imagination of which it is presumably an exposition. As early as Wilson's *Rhetoric* we find evidences of that independence of spirit in questions of art which seems typical of the Elizabethan age; and none of the writers of this period exhibits anything like the predisposition of the French mind to submit instinctively to any rule, or set of rules, which bears the stamp of authority. From the outset the element of nationality colors English criticism, and this is especially noticeable in the linguistic discussions of the age. At the very time when Sidney was writing the *Defence of Poesy*, Spenser's old teacher, Mulcaster, wrote: "I love Rome, but London better; I favor Italy, but **Eng-**

land more; I honor the Latin, but I worship the English." [1] It is this spirit which pervades what may be called the chief expression of the romantic temper in Elizabethan criticism, — Daniel's *Defence of Rhyme* (1603), written in answer to Campion's attack on rhyme in the *Observations in the Art of English Poesy*. The central argument of Daniel's defence is that the use of rhyme is sanctioned both by custom and by nature — "custom that is before all law, nature that is above all art." [2] He rebels against that conception which would limit

> " Within a little plot of Grecian ground
> The sole of mortal things that can avail ; "

and he shows that each age has its own perfections and its own usages. This attempt at historical criticism leads him into a defence of the Middle Ages; and he does not hesitate to assert that even classical verse had its imperfections and deficiencies. In the minutiæ of metrical criticism, also, he is in opposition to the neo-classic tendencies of the next age; and his favorable opinion of *enjambement* and his unfavorable comments on the heroic couplet [3] drew from Ben Jonson an answer, never published, in which the latter attempted to prove that the couplet is the best form of English verse, and that all other forms are forced and detestable. [4]

---

[1] Morley, *English Writers*, ix. 187.

[2] Haslewood, ii. 197.

[3] *Ibid.* ii. 217.

[4] Jonson, *Works*, iii. 470. *Cf.* Gascoigne's comments on *enjambement*, in Haslewood, ii. 11.

II. *Classical Metres*

Daniel's *Defence of Rhyme* may be said to have dealt a death-blow to a movement which for over half a century had been a subject of controversy among English men of letters. In reading the critical works of this period, it is impossible not to notice the remarkable amount of attention paid by the Elizabethans to the question of classical metres in the vernacular. The first organized attempt to introduce the classical versification into a modern language was, as Daniel himself points out,[1] that of Claudio Tolomei in 1539. The movement then passed into France; and classical metres were adopted by Baïf in practice, and defended by Jacques de la Taille in theory. In England the first recorded attempt at the use of quantity in the vernacular was that of Thomas Watson, from whose unpublished translation of the *Odyssey* in the metre of the original Ascham has cited a single distich : —

" All travellers do gladly report great prayse of Ulysses,
   For that he knew many mens maners, and saw many
     cities."[2]

This was probably written between 1540 and 1550; toward the close of the preceding century, we are told, a certain Mousset had already translated the *Iliad* and the *Odyssey* into French hexameters.

Ascham was the first critical champion of the use of quantity in English verse.[3]   Rhyme, he says,

---

[1] Haslewood, ii. 205.　　　　[2] *Scholemaster*, p. 73.
[3] *Ibid.* p. 145 *sq.*

was introduced by the Goths and Huns at a time
when poetry and learning had ceased to exist in
Europe; and Englishmen must choose either to
imitate these barbarians or to follow the perfect
Grecians. He acknowledges that the monosyllabic
character of the English language renders the use
of the dactyl very difficult, for the hexameter "doth
rather trot and hobble than run smoothly in our
English tongue;" but he argues that English will
receive the *carmen iambicum* as naturally as Greek
or Latin. He praises Surrey's blank verse rendering
of the fourth book of the *Æneid*, but regrets that,
in disregarding quantity, it falls short of the "perfect and true versifying." An attempt to put
Ascham's theories into practice was made by
Thomas Blenerhasset in 1577; but the verse of his
Complaynt of Cadwallader, though purporting to be
"a new kind of poetry," is merely an unrhymed
Alexandrine.[1]

In 1580, however, five letters which had passed
between Spenser and Gabriel Harvey appeared in
print as *Three proper, and wittie, familiar Letters* and
Two other very commendable Letters; and from this
correspondence we learn that an organized movement to introduce classical metres into English
had been started. It would seem that for several
years Harvey had been advocating the use of quantitative verse to several of his friends; but the
organized movement to which reference has just

---

[1] *Cf.* Haslewood, ii. p. xxii. The treatises of Gascoigne
(1575) and King James VI. (1584) contain no reference to quantitative verse.

been made seems to have been started independently
by Thomas Drant, who died in 1578. Drant had
devised a set of rules and precepts for English classical verse; and these rules, with certain additions
and modifications, were adopted by a coterie of
scholars and courtiers, among them being Sidney,
Dyer, Greville, and Spenser, who thereupon formed
a society, the Areopagus,[1] independent of Harvey,
but corresponding with him regularly. This society appears to have been modelled on Baïf's
Académie de Poésie et de Musique, which had
been founded in 1570 for a similar purpose, and
which Sidney doubtless became acquainted with
when at Paris in 1572.

From the correspondence published in 1580, it
becomes evident that Harvey's and Drant's systems
of versification were almost antipodal. According
to Drant's system, the quantity of English words
was to be regulated entirely by the laws of Latin
prosody, — by position, diphthong, and the like.
Thus, for example, the penult of the word *carpĕnter*
was regarded as long by Drant because followed by
two consonants. Harvey, who was unacquainted
with Drant's rules before apprised of them by
Spenser in the published letters, follows a more
normal and logical system. To him, accent alone is
the test of quantity, and the law of position cannot
make the penult of *carpĕnter* or *majĕsty* long.
"The Latin is no rule for us," says Harvey;[2] and
often where position and diphthong fall together,

[1] *Cf.* Pulci, *Morgante Maggiore*, xxv. 117.
[2] Haslewood, ii. 280.

as in the penult of *merchaŭndise,* we must pronounce the syllable short. In all such matters, the use, custom, propriety, or majesty of our speech must be accounted the only infallible and sovereign rule of rules.

It was not, then, Harvey's purpose to Latinize our tongue. His intention was apparently two-fold, — to abolish rhyme, and to introduce new metres into English poetry. Only a few years before, Gascoigne had lamented that English verse had only one form of metre, the iambic.[1] Harvey, in observing merely the English accent, can scarcely be said to have introduced quantity into our verse, but was simply adapting new metres, such as dactyls, trochees, and spondees, to the requirements of English poetry.

Drant's and Harvey's rules therefore constitute two opposing systems. According to the former, English verse is to be regulated by Latin prosody regardless of accent; according to the latter, by accent regardless of Latin prosody. By neither system can quantity be successfully attempted in English; and a distinguished classical scholar of our own day has indicated what is perhaps the only method by which this can be accomplished.[2] This method may be described as the harmonious observance of both accent and position; all accented syllables being generally accounted long, and no syllable which violates the Latin law of position

---

[1] Haslewood, ii. 5.

[2] R. Ellis, *Poems and Fragments of Catullus translated in the original metres,* London, 1871, p. xiv. *sq.*

being used when a short syllable is required by the scansion.   These three systems, with more or less variation, have been employed throughout English literature.   Drant's system is followed in the quantitative verse of Sidney and Spenser; Harvey's method is that employed by Longfellow in *Evangeline;* and Tennyson's beautiful classical experiments are practical illustrations of the method of Professor Robinson Ellis.

In 1582, Richard Stanyhurst published at Leyden a translation of the first four books of the *Æneid* into English hexameters.   From Ascham he seems to have derived his inspiration, and from Harvey his metrical system.   Like Harvey he refuses to be bound by the laws of Latin prosody,[1] and follows the English accent as much as possible.   But in one respect his translation is unique.   Harvey, in his correspondence with Spenser, had suggested that the use of quantitative verse in English necessitated the adoption of a certain uniformity in spelling; and the curious orthography of Stanyhurst was apparently intended as a serious attempt at phonetic reform.   Spelling reform had been agitated in France for some time; and in Baïf's *Etrennes de Poésie françoise* (1574), we find French quantitative verse written according to the phonetic system of Ramus.

Webbe's *Discourse of English Poetrie* is really a plea in favor of quantitative verse.   His system is based primarily on Latin prosody, but reconciled with English usage.   The Latin rules are to be fol-

---

[1] Stanyhurst, p. 11 *sq.*

lowed when the English and Latin words agree; but no word is to be used that notoriously impugns the laws of Latin prosody, and the spelling of English words should, when possible, be altered to conform to the ancient rules. The difficulty of observing the law of position in the middle of English words may be obviated by change in spelling, as in the word *mournfŭlly*, which should be spelled *mournfŭly;* but where this is impossible, the law of position is to be observed, despite the English accent, as in *royālty*. Unlike Ascham, Webbe regards the hexameter as the easiest of all classical metres to use in English.[1]

Puttenham is not averse to the use of classical metres, but as a conservative he considers all sudden innovations dangerous.[2] The system he adopts is not unlike Harvey's. Sidney's original enthusiasm for quantitative verse soon abated; and in the *Defence of Poesy* he points out that although the ancient versification is better suited to musical accompaniment than the modern, both systems cause delight, and are therefore equally effective and valuable; and English is more fitted than any other language to use both.[3] Campion, like Ascham, regards English polysyllables as too heavy to be used as dactyls; so that only trochaic and iambic verse can be suitably employed in English poetry.[4] He suggests eight new forms of verse. The English accent is to be diligently observed, and is to yield to nothing save the law of position; hence the

[1] Haslewood, ii. 69.

[2] Puttenham, p. 126 *sq*.

[3] *Defence*, p. 55.

[4] Haslewood, ii. 167.

second syllable of *Trumpington* is to be accounted
long.[1] In observing the law of position, however,
the sound, and not the spelling, is to be the test
of quantity; thus, *love-sick* is pronounced *love-sĭk*,
dangerous is pronounced *dangerŭs*, and the like.[2]

III. *Other Evidences of Classicism*

With Campion's *Observations* (1602) the history
of classical metres in England may be said to
close, until the resuscitation of quantitative verse
in the present century. Daniel's *Defence of Rhyme*
effectually put an end to this innovation; but the
strong hold which the movement seems to have had
during the Elizabethan age is interesting evidence
of the classical tendencies of the period. Ben
Jonson has usually been regarded as the forerun-
ner of neo-classicism in England; but long before
his influence was felt, classical tendencies may
be observed in English criticism. Thus Ascham's
conservatism and aversion to singularity in matters of art are distinctly classical. "He that can
neither like Aristotle in logic and philosophy, nor
Tully in rhetoric and eloquence," says Ascham,
"will from these steps likely enough presume by
like pride to mount higher to the misliking of
graver matters; that is, either in religion to have
a dissentious head, or in the commonwealth to have
a factious heart."[3] His insistence that it is no
slavery to be bound by the laws of art, and the stress
he lays on perfection of style, are no less classical.[4]

---

[1] Haslewood, ii. 186.
[2] *Cf*. Ellis, *op. cit*., p. xvi.
[3] *Scholemaster*, p. 93.
[4] *Ibid*. pp. 118, 121.

Similar tendencies may be observed in the writers that follow Ascham. Harvey's strictures on the *Faerie Queene* were inspired by two influences. As a humanist, he looked back with contempt on mediæval literature in general, its superstitions, its fairy lore, and the like. As a classicist in art, he preferred the regular, or classic, form of the epic to the romantic, or irregular form; and his strictures may be compared in this respect with those of Bembo on the *Orlando* or those of Salviati on the *Gerusalemme*. So Harington attempts to make the *Orlando* chime with the laws of Aristotle, and Sidney attempts to force these laws on the English drama. So also Sidney declares that genius, without "art, imitation, and exercise," is as nothing, and censures his contemporaries for neglecting "artificial rules and imitative patterns."[1] So Webbe attempts to find a fixed standard or criterion by which to judge good and bad poets, and translates Fabricius's summary of the rules of Horace as a guide for English poetry.[2]

English criticism, therefore, may be said to exhibit classical tendencies from its very beginning. But it is none the less true that before Ben Jonson there was no systematic attempt to force, as it were, the classic ideal on English literature. In Spain, as has been seen, Juan de la Cueva declared that poetry should be classical and imitative, while the drama should be romantic and original. Sidney, on the contrary, sought to make the drama classical, while allowing freedom of imagination and

[1] *Defence*, p. 46.   [2] Haslewood, ii. 19, 85 *sq.*

x

originality of form to the non-dramatic poet.   Ben
Jonson was the first complete and consistent English classicist; and his classicism differs from that
of the succeeding age rather in degree than in kind.

Bacon's assertion that poetry is restrained in
the measure of words, but in all other points extremely licensed,[1] is characteristic of the Elizabethan point of view.   The early critics allowed
extreme license in the choice and treatment of
material, while insisting on strict regularity of
expression.   Thus Sidney may advocate the use
of classical metres, but this does not prevent him
from celebrating the freedom of genius and the
soaring heights of the imagination.   There is nothing of these things in Ben Jonson.   He, too, cele-
brates the nobility and power of poetry, and the
dignity of the poet's office; but nowhere does he
speak of the freedom of the imagination or the
force of genius.   Literature for him was not an
expression of personality, not a creation of the
imagination, but an image of life, a picture of the
world.   In other words, he effected what may be
called an objectification of the literary ideal.

In the second place, this image of life can be
created only by conscious effort on the part of the
artist.   For the creation of great poetry, genius,
exercise, imitation, and study are all necessary,
but to these art must be added to make them perfect, for only art can lead to perfection.[2]   It is this
insistence on art as a distinct element, almost as
an end in itself, that distinguishes Jonson from

[1] *Works*, vi. 202.   [2] *Discoveries*, p. 78.

his predecessors; and nowhere is his ideal of art expressed as pithily as in the address to the reader prefixed to the *Alchemist* (1612) : —

"In Poetry, especially in Plays, . . . the concupiscence of dances and of antics so reigneth, as to run away from nature, and be afraid of her, is the only point of art that tickles the spectators. But how out of purpose, and place, do I name art? When the professors are grown so obstinate contemners of it, and presumers on their own naturals, as they are deriders of all diligence that way, and, by simple mocking at the terms, when they understand not the things, think to get off wittily with their ignorance. Nay, they are esteemed the more learned, and sufficient for this, by the many, through their excellent vice of judgment. For they commend writers as they do fencers or wrestlers ; who, if they come in robustiously, and put for it with a great deal of violence, are received for the braver fellows ; when many times their own rudeness is the cause of their disgrace, and a little touch of their adversary gives all that boisterous force the foil. I deny not but that these men, who always seek to do more than enough, may some time happen on some thing that is good and great ; but very seldom ; and when it comes it doth not recompense the rest of their ill. . . . But I give thee warning, that there is a great difference between those that, to gain the opinion of copy [*i.e.* copiousness], utter all they can, however unfitly ; and those that use election and a mean [1] [*i.e.* selection and moderation]. For it is only the disease of the unskilful to think rude things greater than polished ; or scattered more numerous than composed." [2]

Literature, then, aims at presenting an image of life through the medium of art; and the guide

---

[1] *Cf.* Scaliger, *Poet.* v. 3, where the highest virtue of a poet is said to be *electio et sui fastidium ;* and vi. 4, where it is said that the "life of all excellence lies in measure."

[2] *Works,* ii. 3; *cf. Discoveries,* pp. 22–27.

to art, according to Jonson, is to be found in the
rules of criticism.   Thus, for example, success in
comedy is to be attained

> " By observation of those comic laws
>   Which I, your master, first did teach the age ; " [1]

and elsewhere, it will be remembered, Jonson boasts
that he had swerved from no "needful law."   But
though art can find a never-failing guide and moni-
tor in the rules of criticism, he does not believe
in mere servile adherence to the practice or theory
of classical literature.   The ancients are to be regarded as guides, not commanders.[2]   In short, the
English mind was not yet prepared to accept the
neo-classic ideal in all its consequences; and absolute subservience to ancient authority came only
with the introduction of the French influence.

This is, perhaps, best indicated by the history
of Aristotle's influence in English criticism from
Ascham to Milton.   The first reference to the
Poetics in England is to be found in Ascham's
Scholemaster.[3]   There we are told that Ascham,
Cheke, and Watson had many pleasant talks together at Cambridge, comparing the poetic precepts of Aristotle and Horace with the examples
of Euripides, Sophocles, and Seneca.   In Sidney's
Defence of Poesy, Aristotle is cited several times;
and in the drama, his authority is regarded by
Sidney as almost on a par with that of the "com-
mon reason." [4]   Harington was not satisfied until he

---

[1] *Works*, iii. 297.   [3] *Scholemaster*, p. 139.
[2] *Discoveries*, p. 7.   [4] *Defence*, p. 48.

had proved that the *Orlando* agrees substantially
with Aristotle's requirements.   Jonson wrote a
commentary on Horace's *Ars Poetica*, with elucida-
tions from Aristotle, in which

" All the old Venusine [*i.e.* Horace], in poetry,
    And lighted by the Stagyrite [*i.e.* Aristotle], could spy,
    Was there made English ; " [1]

but the manuscript was unfortunately destroyed by
fire in 1623.   Yet Jonson was aware how ridiculous
it is to make any author a dictator.[2]   His admiration for Aristotle was great ; but he acknowledges
that the Aristotelian rules are useless without natural talent, and that a poet's liberty cannot be bound
within the narrow limits prescribed by grammarians and philosophers.[3]   At the same time, he
points out that Aristotle was the first critic, and
the first of all men to teach the poet how to write.
The Aristotelian authority is not to be contemned,
since Aristotle did not invent his rules, but, taking
the best things from nature and the poets, converted them into a complete and consistent code of
art.   Milton, also, had a sincere admiration for " that
sublime art which [is taught] in Aristotle's *Poetics*,
in Horace, and the Italian commentaries of Castelvetro, Tasso, Mazzoni, and others." [4]   But despite all
this, the English independence of spirit never
failed ; and before the French influence we can

1 *Works*, iii. 321; *cf.* i. 335, iii. 487.
2 *Discoveries*, p. 66.
3 *Ibid.* p. 78 *sq.*
4 *Works*, iii. 473.

find no such thing in English criticism as the literary dictatorship of Aristotle.[1]

[1] The chapter on poetry in Peacham's *Compleat Gentleman* (1622) is interesting chiefly because of its indebtedness to Scaliger, who is called by Peacham (p. 91) " the prince of all learning and the judge of judgments, the divine Julius Cæsar Scaliger." This constitutes him a literary arbiter if not dictator. In the *Great Assises holden in Parnassus* (1645), Scaliger is proclaimed one of the lords of Parnassus, in company with Bacon, Sidney, Erasmus, Budæus, Heinsius, Vossius, Casaubon, Mascardi, Pico della Mirandola, Selden, Grotius, and others. The star of scholarship in criticism was passing northward; for the influence of the Dutch critics on Jonson and others, see my *Critical Essays of the Seventeenth Century*, Oxford, 1908, vol. i. pp. xvi-xviii.

CONCLUSION

IT has been established, I think, that by the
middle of the sixteenth century a unified body of
poetic rules and theories had been developed in
Italy, and then passed into France, England, Spain,
Germany, Portugal, and Holland, and through Holland into Scandinavia;[1] so that by the beginning
of the seventeenth century there was a common
body of Renaissance doctrine throughout western
Europe. Each country gave this system a national
cast of its own, but the form which it received in
France ultimately triumphed; and modern classicism therefore represents the supremacy of the
French phase or version of Renaissance Aristotelianism. This critical system was first developed
by the formal treatises on poetics during the Cinquecento, but it is a mistake to consider them as
merely isolated monuments, or as furnishing the
only ways in which poets, critics, and scholars
approached the study of literature. They represent, in fact, but one of several critical heirlooms
which Italy passed on to its foster-child France.

The humanists, as Professor Vossler has shown,[2]
conceived of the nature of poetry in terms, first of

[1] For the influence of Heinsius and other Dutch critics in
Sweden, cf. E. Wrangel, *Sveriges litterära förbindelser med
Holland, särdeles under 1600-talet*, Lund, 1897.

[2] *Poetische Theorien in der italienischen Frührenaissance*,
Berlin, 1900, p. 88.

311

theology, then of oratory, and finally of rhetoric and philology. This development, while apparently in the direction of an æsthetic interest in literature, was really tending toward an exclusive attention to external details, and, as an inevitable result of the growth of erudition, toward a loss of interest in poetry for itself as a creative art. The impassioned defences of poetry by Petrarch, Boccaccio, and Coluccio Salutati, in which its vital impulse was conceived to be at one with that of God himself, were succeeded by calmer studies in which poetry was given a place side by side with the other humanistic disciplines. "When I say letters (*litteras*)," says Ermolao Barbaro, "I mean philosophy which is conjoined with eloquence."[1] "The poet differs in no way from the orator," says Tiphernas, echoing Cicero, "except that he is permitted to roam about more freely, is somewhat more restricted in his numbers, and approaches more closely to music."[2] So that, while Humanism might during its progress emphasize this or that side of humanistic culture, it tended more and more to concern itself with the whole body of classical studies, and to consider them as forming a unity in themselves. The *studia sapientiæ* and the *studia eloquentiæ*, at first carefully distinguished from each other, tended more and more to merge in the single category of *studia litterarum*.[3] "The

[1] *Angeli Politiani Opera*, Lugduni, 1539, p. 457.

[2] K. Müllner, *Reden und Briefe italienischer Humanisten*, Vienna, 1899, p. 187.

[3] *Cf.* V. Rossi, *Il Quattrocento*, Milan, n.d., p. 407 *sq.* (note on pp. 2, 3).

moderns," Vives justly complained, in his *De Causis Corruptarum Artium*, "confound the arts by reason of their resemblance, and of two that are very much opposed to each other make a single art. They call rhetoric grammar, and grammar rhetoric, because both treat of language. The poet they call orator, and the orator poet, because both put eloquence and harmony into their discourses." [1]

To this body of secular learning, — massed under the general head of *litteræ*, or *studia humanitatis*, or *eloquentia*, or *philologia*, according to the predominating interest of the period or the individual taste of the writer, — the chief opposition was represented by the two great mediæval survivals, the tradition of scholastic training and the tradition of chivalry. The defence of letters against the first was undertaken by the pedagogic treatises of the fifteenth and early sixteenth centuries. All the writers on humanistic education — the Italians, Leonardo Bruni, Æneas Sylvius Piccolomini, Maffeo Vegio, Battista Guarino, Jacopo di Porcia, the Frenchman Budæus, the Dutchman Erasmus, the German Sturm, the Spaniard Vives, the Englishmen Elyot and Ascham — not only explain, but also defend, the position of classical literature, and especially classical poetry, in the new scheme of teaching. It is the charges of paganism and immorality which chiefly confront them; and though they advance few, if any, original arguments in answering these

---

[1] *Opera*, ed. Mayans, Valencia, 1785, vi. 64. For the significance of Vives as a critic, see the Italian translation of this book, p. 139, n.

charges, they emphasize the educative and refining influence of literary study, and indicate its value as nourishment for the young mind.

Similarly, the tradition of chivalry — the tradition of the active life *par excellence*, which found little place for culture — raised the question whether or not the study of letters is practically useless to the gentleman, whether it conduces to effeminacy, whether it unfits him for the martial or courtly life. The question was so often debated that Castiglione, in the *Cortegiano* (1528), could say that "as this controversy has already been long waged by very wise men, there is no need to renew it." But few Cinquecento treatises on the courtier, on the gentleman, on honor, on manners and courtesy, fail to discuss the relative merits of letters and arms as accomplishments for perfect manhood; and not a few separate tractates, such as Nifo's *De Armorum Litterarumque Comparatione* and Giacomini Tebalducci Malespini's *Della Nobiltà delle Lettere e delle Armi*, are devoted to the same theme. The controversy between Muzio, who espoused the cause of letters in his *Il Gentilhuomo*, and Mora, who espoused that of arms in his *Il Cavaliere*, is well known. But the consensus of opinion tended wholly in one direction. Castiglione and Guazzo might differ as to whether preëminence should be accorded to letters or arms, but they agreed fundamentally that both are essential to a complete man. The argument centred for the most part on the question of glory: did letters or arms bring the greater fame? So, in early days,

when chivalry had been confronted by the conflict
between arms and love, between the reward of
chivalrous deeds (*ol pretz d'armas e de cavallairia*),
on the one hand, and the delights of gallantry (*lo
joy de dompnas e d'amia*), on the other,[1] it was the
same question of honor, of glory, which was at
stake; it was the same doubt as to the effeminizing
effect of love on valor that agitated the chivalric
mind. But humanism justified culture beyond all
dispute as a gentle accomplishment. Loys le Roy,
in his *Vicissitude*, showed the concurrence of letters
and arms among all civilized nations; and William
Segar, in his *Honor Military and Civil*, summed up
the whole discussion by asserting that "the endeavor of a gentleman ought to be either in arms or
learning, or in them both; and in my own poor
conceit, hardly deserveth he any title of honor that
doth not take pleasure in the one or the other."[2]

The poetics of the Cinquecento thus inherited,
in theoretical form, a defence of classical poetry
against the charges of paganism and immorality,
a defence of the study of letters against the charges
of effeminacy and practical uselessness, a defence
of classical literature as an educative and refining

---

[1] *Cf.* the *tenzone* between Sordello and Bertran d'Alamanon,
in C. de Lollis, *Vita e poesie di Sordello*, Halle, 1896, p. 174.
The formal treatises on love during the Cinquecento are also not
without interest for the history of criticism and poetic theory.
Thus, for example, Equicola, in his *Libro di natura d' amore*,
discusses at some length the treatment of love in classical, Tuscan, French, Provençal, and Spanish poetry — an early example
of comparative criticism.

[2] *Cf.* Einstein, *Italian Renaissance in England*, New York
1902, p. 93.

force, a defence of literary study in general, not as mere humanistic erudition, but as an accomplishment of gentlemen and courtiers, as an element in general culture. Moreover, the defence of the vernacular, tentatively begun in Dante's *De Vulgari Eloquentia*, was carried on to final victory by Bembo and his school, and the discussion was continued by a host of ardent advocates, such as Varchi and Muzio in Italy, Du Bellay and Henri Estienne in France, Juan de Valdés in Spain, and Cheke, Ascham, and Mulcaster in England.

Poetic theory had thus far been chiefly nourished upon the rhetorical and oratorical treatises of Cicero, the moral treatises of Plutarch (especially those upon the reading of poets and the education of youth), the *Institutiones Oratoriæ* of Quintilian, and the *De Legendis Gentilium Libris*[1] of Basil the Great. To these a vast body of classical criticism was added by the sixteenth century. Aldus, in 1503, published the works of the chief Greek rhetoricians. Giulio Cammillo elucidated Hermogenes; Robortelli, Longinus; and commentaries on the *Ars Poetica* of Horace appeared in great number. But the diffusion of Aristotle's *Poetics* was central in developing poetic theory and in furnishing a standard of judgment in criticism; and the

[1] This work was very popular among the humanists. It was translated into Latin by Leonardo Bruni about 1405 (*cf.* Coluccio Salutati, *Epistola*, in *Scelta di Curiosità letterarie*, 1867, lxxx, 221), and is cited, *e.g.*, by Toscanella (Müllner, *op. cit.*, p. 194) and Æneas Sylvius (*Opera*, Basileæ, 1571, p. 983). Vives, as late as 1531, seems to rate it higher than Aristotle's *Poetics* (*Opera*, vi. 342).

outgrowth of the older humanistic heritage and of these new Aristotelian studies was that unified body of doctrine which may be summed up in the phrase "Renaissance poetics." The outworn criteria of *doctrina* and *eloquentia*, by which the humanists had tested all literary endeavor, were superseded by a thousand new ones, — probability, verisimilitude, unity, the fixed norm for each literary *genre*, and the like. Viewed from the standpoint of European criticism as a whole — for the same transformation was effected, not only in Italy, but in all the transalpine countries as well — the development may be summed up by saying that the ideal of classical imitation was merged into that of neo-classical rules. Imitation had been followed by theory, and theory by law.

The immediate problem of criticism was the application of this body of poetic theory to the body of creative literature, past and present. This was largely assisted by the literary controversies of the sixteenth century, such as those concerned with the *Orlando Furioso*, the *Gerusalemme Liberata*, the *Orbecche*, the *Divina Commedia*, the *Pastor Fido*. Even the personal polemics of the time — such as those of Caro and Castelvetro, Sigonio and Robortelli, Giraldi Cintio and Pigna, Aretino and Franco, Dolce and Ruscelli, Domenichi and Doni — were not wholly unfruitful in this respect. Poetic theory even entered the field of linguistic controversy, and so, for example, Varchi's distinction between the versifier and the poet in the *Ercolano*[1] is combated

[1] B. Varchi, *Opere*, Trieste, 1859, ii. 150.

by Castelvetro in his answer to Varchi's dialogue.[1]
No field of intellectual interest was untouched by
it; it enriched the philosophic systems of Telesio,
Campanella, and Bacon, among many others, and
these show the century's advance in comparison
with the paucity or confusion of ideas in regard
to poetry in the earlier work of a Savonarola or
a Vives.

The Italian academies swarmed with lecturers who
elucidated verses of Petrarch, Bembo, Dante, Ariosto,
Tasso, and the like; and though these academic discourses were for the most part trivial and futile,
and chiefly concerned with the interpretation of
external details, yet they could not fail to assist, in
some measure, the assimilation of poetic theory,
and, more important still, to foster (let us hope)
that criticism which has its eyes directly on the
poet's page.   Of these the most characteristic are
the *lezioni* (delivered before the Florentine and
Paduan academies) and the minor treatises of Benedetto Varchi, who is in some respects the representative critic of the mid-Cinquecento.   A master
of poetic theory, he has also ideas of his own on
the method and scope of criticism itself.   In writing
of critical prolegomena, "not only for works of
philosophers, but of all other writers, both in prose
and in verse," he discusses seventeen points, some
absolutely necessary, others merely useful, which
should be considered in the preliminary interpretation of any book: the name and the life of the
author, the title of the book, whether it is legiti·

[1] Varchi, *Opere*, 1859, ii. 217.

mate or not, its aim, its subject, its instrument, its office, its utility, its divisions, the order of the parts, under what form of philosophy it falls, its method of teaching, its proportion, its mode of language, and the like.[1] These are all concerned with externals; all, or nearly all, avoid or ignore the consideration of literature on its purely æsthetic side. Yet these, after all, are mere preliminaries; with what shall we concern ourselves, when we come to the work itself? Varchi tells us, in a brief but important fragment, *Qualità che si ricercano negli scrittori e negli scritti;*[2] and these qualities are four: ethical quality (*bontà*) and philosophic soundness (*dottrina*), with regard to the content of literature; eloquence (*eloquenza*) and art (*arte*), with regard to its treatment. Of these, says Varchi, the two first are nobler than the two last, since they deal with things as the latter do with words; the former give literature its instructive value, the latter its pleasure. But *bontà* and *dottrina* alone do not suffice, for the reason that all things are composed of form, which is the nobler part, and of matter, the less noble; and this form is given to literature by art, which in a sense also includes eloquence, and which alone tests the genius and judgment of a writer. Here, obviously, we are listening once more to the old humanistic catchwords, *doctrina* and *eloquentia*, matter and form, words and things, profit and pleasure, — remnants of classical phrase or mediæval jargon; we still feel the humanistic pedantry and formalism of the

[1] Varchi, *Opere*, ii. 806.   [2] *Ibid*. ii. 813.

Quattrocento, the older scholastic interest in the subtleties of definition.

This may perhaps appear more clearly when we consider how Varchi has put his ideas into practice. It is a favorite practice of his to use a few verses as the text of a philosophic discourse; a sonnet of Della Casa, for example, furnishes the pretext for a lecture on jealousy.[1] But his critical method may best be illustrated by the eight lectures on the *canzoni degli occhi* of Petrarch, read privately at the University of Florence during the spring of 1545.[2] In the first of these he follows in general the method he himself had laid down for all preliminary discussion. He concerns himself with six points: first, the genus to which the three *canzoni* belong, which, as he decides, is that species of rhetoric called "demonstrative or laudative;" secondly, the style of the poems, which is neither high nor low, but in the first *bassamente mezzano*, in the second *mediocremente mezzano*, in the third *altamente mezzano*; thirdly, the species or sort of poetry to which they belong, which is "lyrical," so called because originally intended to be sung to the lyre, "exegetic or narrative," because the poet speaks in his own person, and "mixed," because the versification is in part regulated and in part free; fourthly, their subject and aim, the subject being "natural," or concerned with the things of nature, and the

[1] Varchi, *Opere*, ii. 570. This *lezione* was translated into English in 1615 by Robert Tofte, under the title of *The Blazon of Jealousie*, with interesting marginal illustrations from contemporary English poetry.

[2] *Op. cit.* ii. 439.

poet's aim is to give praise and fame to Madonna Laura; fifthly, their similarities and dissimilarities; and, lastly, their structural dependence on one another.

All this scarcely touches the problem of true criticism, but in the succeeding lectures Varchi treats of the *canzoni* at closer range. His method is to consider one stanza after another, and to discuss its parts minutely. Thus, on the opening lines —

> "Perchè la vita è breve,
> E l'ingegno paventa all' alta impresa," etc., —

after pointing out that the poet here states his theme, he proceeds to make such comments as these:

"*La vita*, i.e. the space of human existence; *è breve*, i.e. short; *e l'ingegno*, i.e. my own; *paventa*, fears and trembles; *all' alta impresa*, i.e. considering the height of the subject, and how difficult it is to attempt praise of such beautiful eyes." [1]

Or on the verses —

> " Quel che pensier non pareggia,
> Non che l'agguagli altrui parlar, o mio " —

he comments:

" That is, the beautiful eyes of Madonna Laura ; nor could a diviner circumlocution be used, nor expressed in lovelier words and more suitable terms; for *parlar*, which is a verb, corresponds with *pensier*, which is a noun, the present subjunctive *agguagli* with the present indicative *pareggia*, and *mio* with *altrui*. All this, we must believe, really indicates that things must be placed first, then conceits or thoughts . . . in the third place words or terms . . .

Y   [1] Varchi, *op. cit.* ii. 446.

CONCLUSION

and lastly, writing . . . since things are much truer than thoughts, thoughts than words, words than writing." [1]

It is inconceivable that such puerile interpretation could illuminate the text of Petrarch, or advance the cause of criticism; but beyond these verbal comments and scholastic distinctions Varchi, in these Petrarchan discourses, does not attempt to go. [2]

Yet these lectures, it must be remembered, were delivered three or four years before the outburst of interest in Aristotle's *Poetics* occasioned by the commentaries of Robortelli (1548) and Maggi (1550) and the Italian translation of Segni (1549); they antedate his own lectures on the theory of poetry by eight years. In order to comprehend clearly what the poetics of the Renaissance accomplished for criticism in a brief period of time, these lectures of 1553 have but to be compared with those of 1545. In the treatment of the lyric, the Cinquecento, being without the guidance of those definite theories and fixed laws which had been elaborated for dramatic and epic poetry, lost itself in details and pedantries. The old scholastic subtleties still follow Varchi in his discourse on "Poetics in General" and in the five on "Poetry," to which I have

---

[1] Varchi, *op. cit.* ii. 448.

[2] The following curious comment on these *lezioni*, to be found in one of Alfonso de' Pazzi's sonnets against Varchi (reprinted in the *Terzo libro dell' opere burlesche*, 1760, p. 338), is not without some justification : —

"Le canzoni degli occhi ha letto il Varchi,
 Ed ha cavato al gran Petrarca gli occhi."

Cf. Graf, *Attraverso il Cinquecento*, Turin, 1888, pp. 26, 64.

already given ample attention;[1] but a surer touch, a new attitude toward his material, indicate that a change of some sort had come. In one of these lectures, after stating that the *Giron Cortese* of Alamanni pleases him more than the *Orlando Furioso* (and a judgment so astounding must be taken into consideration when defining his position as a critic), he says:

" To few, and perhaps to none, is it permitted to affirm: This or that man has erred, this or that thing is bad. Every one can say, many should indeed say : It seems to me that this or that man has erred, this or that thing does not seem to me good. It is conceded to every one to say : The figures of this or that sculptor or painter do not please me ; but to very few indeed is it conceded to affirm : These figures are not good." [2]

This, in another form, is the old concept of the diversity *de gustibus,* but it is important as showing that theory had as yet not been crystallized into dogma. The orthodox neo-classic criticism, having transformed into laws the proper pleasure to be derived from each literary *genre,* was shaken by no such doubts. But early in the eighteenth century Marivaux gave expression to a point of view very much akin to that of Varchi. The critics of his day, according to Marivaux, might assert of a work of art, "That is worthless, that is detestable;" but such reasoning is itself worthless and detestable, since a man of taste may say of a book, "It does not please me," but "he will never decide that it is bad until after he has compared his own ideas

[1] *Supra*, pp. 25, 34, 41, 50, etc.
[2] *Opere*, ii. 691.

with those of others."[1] Here the doubt as to
whether the code of poetics can afford the individual
critic a fixed standard of judgment is a sign that
the neo-classic structure is beginning to crumble;
for it is upon the development of this very concept
that criticism expended its chief effort in the century and three-quarters that separate Varchi from
Marivaux.

The development in this respect is indicated in
a lecture by Torquato Tasso on a sonnet of Della
Casa, delivered more than a quarter of a century
later before the Ferrarese Academy.[2] The method
of Varchi's Petrarchan discourses is here followed,
in first considering the style in which the sonnet
is written, and then elucidating its various parts;
though Varchi's jejune formulæ of the high, mediocre, and low styles are superseded by a more
philosophical discussion of poetic style, based on
the theories of Hermogenes, Demetrius Phalereus,
and Cicero, and the puerile verbal exposition of
Varchi gives place to a method that is not exclusively expository, but is based on Tasso's juster
conception of the function of criticism. At the
very outset he defines his position by contrasting
the method of *imitation*, which judges works of art
merely by their similarity or dissimilarity to some
masterpiece in the same kind, and the method of
art, whose higher function it is

" to investigate the reasons why this verse seems sweet, this
one harsh; this one humble and plebeian, this one noble

[1] G. Larroumet, *Marivaux, sa vie et ses œuvres*, Paris, 1894
p. 448.   [2] Tasso, *Opere*, ed. Rosini, xi. 42 *sq*.

and magnificent; this one too careless, this one too highly
colored; this one cold, this one bombastic, this one insipid;
why here the movement and speed of the speech are praised,
here the slowness and delay; here direct speech, here indirect; here the long period, here the short; and, in a word,
why compositions please or displease: and having found the
reasons of all these things, there form in the mind some
that are universal, true, and infallible, gathered from the
experience of many particulars; and it is the knowledge of
these which Art more properly demands for itself."

Why works of art please or displease! the universal and infallible grounds of our pleasure and displeasure! — here are problems beyond the scope of
Varchi's tentative and empirical method; here is a
significant advance over Varchi's assumption of the
individual basis of the pleasure or displeasure which
poetry gives. Yet Tasso's own method is a com-
promise between the two which he defines; the
method of imitation and that of art are alike
necessary to the critic.

Here criticism is beginning to turn eyes upon
itself, leaping from the two questions which had
interested it most in the sixteenth century, "What
is poetry?" and "What is the meaning of this or
that poem?" to a third question, which it but
vaguely apprehended: "What is criticism?" To
say that this question was first neatly put and definitely discussed in the seventeenth century is to
say that not until then did criticism become a self-
conscious and organized art; and it is characteristic
of this change of attitude that, while Horace and
Vida had written "Arts of *Poetry*," it is literally
an "Essay on *Criticism*" upon which Pope expended

a kindred poetic skill. Writing some forty years after Boileau, he substituted a brief sketch of the history of criticism from Aristotle to Roscommon for the rapid survey of French poetry in the *Art Poétique*.

This new organization of critical method and critical theory was developed on the basis of Renaissance poetics. The body of rules and theories was the same, but the attitude toward them was gradually changing; and the history of this attitude gives us the history of criticism in the seventeenth and eighteenth centuries. At the beginning of the seventeenth century the intellectual ferment in Italy and Spain developed new theories of style, based on the rhetorical discussions of classical antiquity and the Renaissance. It was this ferment of thought which produced the ideal of " wit " which was derived through the French *esprit* from the Italian *ingegno*. A new terminology was being created, indicative of a change of interest from the materials of literature to the moods and faculties of the creative mind. Words like " fancy," " judgment," " wit," " humor," " taste," " the sublime," were acquiring new meaning and a higher vogue. But the rationalism of the classic spirit throttled this initial outburst, and it was not till the middle of the eighteenth century that the human mind, rather than literature itself, was systematically studied for the development of principles of criticism. Tasso, as we have seen, propounded the vital problem why poetry is pleasing to the human mind, but he attempts to find the answer in poetry itself.

With the growth of the rationalistic spirit the main interest of criticism was in fixing a reasonable standard of critical judgment. "Criticism, as it was first instituted by Aristotle," says Dryden, "was meant a standard of judging well; the chiefest part of which is to observe those excellences which should delight a reasonable reader."[1] This is no longer Tasso's problem why certain excellences please; there are in poetry excellences which ought to please the reasonable reader. La Bruyère goes still farther in asserting that for every reader there is one absolute standard of taste:

"There is a point of perfection in art, as of excellence or maturity in nature. He who is sensible of it and loves it has perfect taste; he who is not sensible of it and loves this or that else on either side of it has a faulty taste. There is then a good and bad taste, and men dispute of tastes not without reason."[2]

Dryden's standard of judgment and La Bruyère's standard of taste are both the result of the application of reason to æsthetic pleasure. Yet the development of the ideal of taste[3] was dangerous to the rigid spirit of classicism. The recognition of the subjective basis of taste soon led to a contrast

[1] *Works*, ed. Scott-Saintsbury, v. 112.

[2] *Caractères*, "Des ouvrages de l'esprit." *Cf.* Shaftesbury, *Characteristicks*, London, 1711, iii. 154, 156.

[3] On the early history of the term "taste" *cf.* Croce, *Estetica*, p. 194 *sq.*; Borinski, *Poetik der Renaissance*, p. 308 *sq.*; *Baltasar Gracian und die Hoflitteratur*, p. 39 *sq.*; and Farinelli's valuable review of the last in the *Revista crítica de historia y literatura españolas*, vol. ii., 1896. *Cf.*, however, Addison, *Spectator*, No. 409, June 19, 1712, where Gracián's priority in the use of the term is accepted.

with those neo-classic rules which constituted the external element in art. Pope recognized that taste might give a grace beyond the reach of art; the concept of the *je ne sais quoi*[1] was formulated, to comprehend these elements of æsthetic pleasure not explicable by the rules of Renaissance poetics; and finally, Montesquieu, in his *Essai sur le Goût*, says that

"art gives the rules, and taste the exceptions; taste discovers on what occasions art should submit to it, and on what occasions it should submit to art."[2]

It is natural to find, side by side with this evolution, a kindred development of interest in the subjective processes of art.[3] Montesquieu himself

[1] This phrase had been employed as early as the sixteenth century, both in Italy and in France. Tasso uses it, and Mlle. de Gournay, the *fille d'alliance* of Montaigne, speaks of "l'amour, qui est je ne sçai quoy, doit sourdre aussi de je ne sçai quoy" (Doncieux, *Bouhours*, pp. 264, 265). Bouhours established its use in criticism in the seventeenth century, and was followed in the eighteenth by Marivaux, Montesquieu, Feijóo, and a host of others (*cf.* Croce, *Estetica*, p. 205 *sq.*; Larroumet, *Marivaux*, p. 498 *sq.*). From the time of Shaftesbury (*Characteristicks*, i. 147, etc.) it was also naturalized in England.

[2] *Œuvres complètes*, Paris, 1834, p. 596.

[3] John Morley (*Burke*, p. 19) gives to Burke's essay *On the Sublime and Beautiful* the credit of having first established the principle "that critics of art seek its principles in the wrong place, so long as they limit their search to poems, pictures, engravings, statues, and buildings, instead of first arranging the sentiments and faculties in man to which art makes its appeal;" but this contention, it is scarcely necessary to say, ignores a long line of antecedent speculations on the continent and even in England.

complains that the ancients regarded as positive
qualities all the relative qualities of the soul; the
Platonic dialogues are absurd, since they deal with
the good, the beautiful, the agreeable, and the like,
as positive realities:

"The sources of the beautiful, the good, the agreeable, etc.,
are in ourselves, and to seek for their reasons is merely to
seek for the causes of the pleasures of our soul.   Let us examine then our soul, let us study it in its actions and its
passions.   Poetry, painting, sculpture, architecture, music,
the dance, in fine, the works of nature and of art, can give
pleasure to the soul; let us see why, how, and when they
do so." [1]

The new science of æsthetics was to attempt, and in
a sense to solve, this new problem; the romantic
movement was to apply the fruits of those labors to
literature and to literary criticism.

The attitude toward the body of Renaissance
poetics had thus, during the seventeenth and
eighteenth centuries, undergone a complete transformation.   In the Renaissance itself, the humanistic period, with its ideal of classical imitation,
was followed by a period of theorizing along the
lines of the Aristotelian *Poetics*, and the results
were before long hardened into fixed rules and
dogmas of criticism.   The neo-classical period regarded these rules, first from the attitude of "wit,"
then of reason, and finally of taste.   When Hobbes,
in the address prefixed to his translation of the
Iliad (1675), says that "there be many men called
critics, and *wits*, and *virtuosi*, that are accustomed to

[1] *Œuvres complètes*, p. 587, and note.

censure the poets,"[1] he has indicated the three classes of littérateurs who were to carry on these three phases of critical activity.

Imitation, theory, law; wit, reason, taste, — each in its turn became a guiding principle of criticism, until with the romantic movement all were superseded by the concept of the creative imagination. The first three represent, as it were, the stages through which Renaissance poetics passed in the process of complete codification; the last three represent the stages of its decline and death.[2]

[1] Spingarn, *Critical Essays of the Seventeenth Century*, Oxford, 1908, ii. 68; *cf.* i. p. xc *sq.* See also my article on "Jacobean and Caroline Criticism" in vol. vii of the *Cambridge History of English Literature*.

[2] This Conclusion in part reproduces an article on "The Origins of Modern Criticism" which appeared in *Modern Philology* in April, 1904.

APPENDICES

APPENDIX A

CHRONOLOGICAL TABLE OF THE CHIEF CRITICAL WORKS OF THE SIXTEENTH CENTURY

Date	Italy	Date	France	Date	England
1527	Vida: *De Arte Poetica.*			c. 1524	Cox: *Rhetoric.*
1529	Trissino: *Poetica,* pts. i.–iv.				
1535	Dolce: trans. of Horace's *Ars Poetica.*				
1536	Pazzi: transl. of Aristotle's *Poetics.*				
1536	Daniello: *Poetica.*				
1539	Tolomei: *Versi e Regole della Nuova Poesia.*	1545	Pelletier: trans. of Horace's *Ars Poetica.*		
1548	Robortelli: ed. of Aristotle's *Poetics.*	1548	Sibilet: *Art Poétique.*		
1549	Segni: transl. of Aristotle's *Poetics.*	1549	Du Bellay: *Défense et Illustration.*		
1550	Maggi: ed. of Aristotle's *Poetics.*			1553	Wilson: *Rhetorik.*
1551	Muzio: *Arte Poetica.*				

CHRONOLOGICAL TABLE (*Continued*)

Date	Italy	Date	France	Date	England
1554	Giraldi Cintio: *Discorsi.*	1554	Pelletier: *Art Poétique.*	1567	Drant: transl. of Horace's *Ars Poetica.*
1559	Minturno: *De Poeta.*	1555	Morel: ed. of Aristotle's *Poetics.*		
1560	Vettori: ed. of Aristotle's *Poetics.*	1560	Pasquier: *Recherches.*	1570	Ascham: *Scholemaster.*
1561	Scaliger: *Poetics.*	1561	[Scaliger: *Poetics.*]	1575	Gascoigne: *Notes of Instruction.*
1563	Trissino: *Poetica*, pts. v., vi.				
1564	Minturno: *Arte Poetica.*				
1570	Castelvetro: ed. of Aristotle's *Poetics.*	1565	Ronsard: *Abrégé de l'Art Poétique.*	1579	Gosson: *School of Abuse.*
				1579	Lodge: *Reply to Gosson.*
1575	Piccolomini: ed. of Aristotle's *Poetics.*	1572	Jean de la Taille: preface of *Saül.*	1580	Harvey and Spenser: *Letters.*
				c. 1583	Sidney: *Defence of Poesy* (publ. 1595).
1579	Viperano: *De Arte Poetica.*	1572	Ronsard: preface of *Franciade.*		
1586	Patrizzi: *Della Poetica.*			1585	James VI.: *Reulis and Cautelis.*
1587	T. Tasso: *Discorsi dell' Arte Poetica.*	1573	Jacques de la Taille: treatise on French classical metres.	1586	Webbe: *Discourse of English Poetrie.*
1588	Denores: *Poetica.*				
1597	Buonamici: *Discorsi Poetici.*	1598	De Laudun: *Art Poétique françois.*	1589	Puttenham: *Arte of English Poesie.*
1598	Ingegneri: *Poesia Rappresentativa.*	—	Vauquelin: *Art Poétique.*	1591	Harington: *Apologie of Poetrie.*
1600	Summo: *Discorsi Poetici.*				

APPENDIX B

SALVIATI'S ACCOUNT OF THE COMMENTA-
TORS ON ARISTOTLE'S "POETICS."

THE following is Lionardo Salviati's account of the commentators on Aristotle's *Poetics* up to 1586. The passage is cited from an unpublished Ms. at Florence (Cod. Magliabech. ii. ii. II.), beginning at fol. 371. The title of the Ms. is *Parafrasi e Commento della Poetica d'Aristotile;* and at fol. 370 it is dated January 28, 1586.

DELLI INTERPRETI DI QUESTO LIBRO DELLA POETICA

Averroe primo di tutti quelli interpreti della Poetica che a nostri tempi sono pervenuti, fece intorno a esso una breve Parafrasi, nella quale come che pure alcune buone considerationi si ritrovino, tutta via per la diversità e lontananza de costumi, che tra greco havea, e tra gli arabi poca notizia havendone, pochissima ne potè dare altrui. Appresso hebbe voglia Giorgio Valla di tradur questo libro in latino, ma o che la copia del testo greco lo ingannasse, o che verso di sè fusse l'opera malagevole per ogni guisa massimamente in quei tempi, egli di quella impresa picciola lode si guadagnò. Il che considerando poi Alessandro de Pazzi, huomo delle lingue intendente, et ingegnoso molto, alla medesima cura si diede, et ci lasciò la latina traduzzione, che

[margin notes: Averroës. Valla. Pazzi.]

in tutti i latini comenti fuorch' in quello del Vettorio
si leggie. E per ciò che dotto huomo era, et hebbe
copia di ottimi testi scritti a penna, diede non poca luce
a questa opera, e più anche fatto havrebbe se da la morte
stato non fusse sopravenuto. Ma Francesco Rubertello a

Robortelli.   tempi nostri, nelli studj delle lingue esercita-
tissimo, conoscendo che di maggior aviso
li faceva mestieri, non solamente purgò il testo di molte
macchie che accecato il tenevano, ma il primo fu ancora,
che con distese dichiarationi, et con innumerabili esempli

Segni.   di poeti greci e latini, fece opera di illus-
trarlo. Vulgarizzollo appresso Bernardo
Segni in questo nostro Idioma, et con alcune sue brevi
annotationi lo diede in luce. E nella tradutione per
alcune proprie voci che ai greci vocaboli ottimamente cor-
risposero, non se n' uscì anche egli senza commendazione.
Ma con molto maggior grido et applauso, il comento del

Maggi.   Maggio, chiarissimo filosopho, fu dal mondo
ricevuto; perciochè havendo egli con somma
gloria nella continua lettura della Philosophia i suoi anni
trapassati, con l' ordine principalmente giovò a questo
libro, e col mostrarne la continuatione et in non pochi
luoghi soccorse il Rubertello. E se si fusse alquanto
meno ardente contro di lui dimonstrato, nè così vago
stato fusse di contrapporseli, sarebbe alcuna volta per
avventura uscito fuor più libero il parer suo, e più saldo. A
lato a quel del Maggio fu la latina traduzione et comento

Vettori.   di Pier Vettori pubblicato, il quale essendo
oltre ad ogni altro, delle antiche scritture
diligentissimo osservatore, e nella cognitione delle lingue
havendosi sì come io stimo a tempi nostri, il primo luogo
guadagnato, hauta commodità, et in gran numero di
preziosi et antichi esemplarj scritti a mano, in ogni parte,
ma nella correzzione del testo spetialmente e nella traduzione, ha fatto sì che poco più avanti pare che di lume a

questo libro possa desiderarsi. Fu non di manco a
Castelvetro. questi anni di nuovo da un dotto huomo in
questa lingua volgarizzato et esposto, et più
a lungo che alcun altro che ciò habbia fin quì adoprato
ancor mai. Questo sarà da me per tutto ovunque mi con-
venga nominarlo, il comento vulgare appellato, e per più
brevità con quelle due prime lettere C. V. in questa guisa
lo noterò. Nel qual comento hanno senza alcun fallo di
sottilissimi avvedimenti, ma potrebb' essere, sì come io
credo, più sincero. Perciò che io stimo, che dove egli dal
vero si diparte, il faccia per emulazione per lo più per
dimostrarsi di sottil sentimento e per non dire come li
altri. È la costui tradutione, fuorchè in alcune parti
dove egli secondo che io avviso volontariamente erra, tra
le toscane la migliore. E sono le sue parole et in essa e
nell' espositione molto pure, et in puro volgare fiorentino,
quanto comporta la materia l' una e l' altra è dettata.
Ultimamente la traduzzione, e con essa l' annotazione di
Piccolomini. Mgr. Alessandro Piccolomini sono uscite in
stampa, il quale havendosi con molte altre
sue opere d' astrologia e di filosofia e di rettorica parte com-
poste, parte volgarizzate, non picciol nome e molta ripu-
tazione acquistata, creder si può altrettanto doverli della
presente faticha avvenire. Dietro a sì chiari interpreti
non per emulatione, la quale tra me e sì fatti huomini
Salviati. non potrebbe haver luogo, ma per vaghezza
che io pure havrei di dover ancor io, se io
potessi a questa impresa, alcun aiuto arrecare dopo lo
studio di dieci anni che io ci ho spesi, scendo, quantunque
timido, in questo campo, più con accesa volontà, che con
speranza, o vigore desideroso che avanti che venirmi gloria
per false opinioni, sieno i miei difetti discretamente da
savio giudice gastigati.

BIBLIOGRAPHY

THIS bibliography includes a list of the principal books and editions used in the preparation of the essay, and should be consulted for the full titles of works cited in the text and in the foot-notes.

I. SOURCES

Ascham, R. *The Scholemaster*, edited by E. Arber. London, 1870.

—— *The Whole Works*, edited by Rev. Dr. Giles. 3 vols. in 4 parts. London, 1864.

Aubignac, Abbé d'. *La Pratique du Théâtre.* 2 vols. Amsterdam, 1715.

Bacon, F. *Works*, edited by J. Spedding, R. L. Ellis, and D. D. Heath. 15 vols. Boston, 1863.

Batteux, C. *Les Quatres Poétiques d'Aristote, d'Horace, de Vida, de Despréaux.* Paris, 1771.

Berni, F. *Rime, Poesie Latine, e Lettere*, per cura di P. Virgili. Firenze, 1885.

Boccaccio, G. *Geneologia degli Dei*, trad. per G. Betussi. Vinegia, 1547.

—— *Vita di Dante*, per cura di F. Macrì-Leone. Firenze, 1888.

Bruno, G. *Opere*, raccolte da A. Wagner. 2 vols. Lipsia, 1830.

Butcher, S. H. *Aristotle's Theory of Poetry and Fine Art, with a Critical Text and a Translation of the Poetics.* London, 1895.

Carducci, G. *La Poesia Barbara nei Secoli XV e XVI.* Bologna, 1881.

Caro, A. *Apologia degli Academici di Bianchi di Roma contra M. Lodovico Castelvetro.* Parma, 1558.

Castelvetro, L. *Poetica d' Aristotele vulgarizzata et sposta.* Basilea, 1576.

—— *Opere Varie Critiche*, colla vita dell' autore scritta da L. A. Muratori. Milano, 1727.

Cook, A. S. *The Art of Poetry: The Poetical Treatises of Horace, Vida, and Boileau, with the translations by Howes, Pitt, and Soame.* Boston, 1892.

Dacier, A. *La Poétique traduite en François, avec des Rémarques.* Paris, 1692.

Daniello, B. *La Poetica.* Vinegia, 1536.

Dante Alighieri. *Tutte le Opere*, per cura di E. Moore. Oxford, 1894.

Denores, J. *Discorso intorno a que' Principii che la Comedia, la Tragedia, et il Poema Heroico ricevono dalla Philosophia.* Padova, 1587.

—— *In Epistolam Q. Horatij Flacci de Arte Poetica, ex quotidianis Tryphonis Gabrielij Sermonibus Interpretatio.* Venetiis, 1553.

—— *Poetica, nel qual si tratta secondo l' opinion d' Arist. della Tragedia, del Poema Heroico, & della Comedia.* Padova, 1588.

Donatus, A. *Ars Poetica.* Bononiæ, 1659.

Dryden, J. *An Essay of Dramatic Poesy*, edited by T. Arnold. Oxford, 1889.

Du Bellay, J. *Œuvres Choisies*, publiées par L. Becq de Fouquières. Paris, 1876.

Fracastoro, G. *Opera.* 2 vols. Genevæ, 1621.

Giraldi Cintio, G. B. *Scritti Estetici: De' Romanzi, delle Comedie, e delle Tragedie, ecc.* (Daelli's *Biblioteca Rara*, lii., liii.) 2 vols. Milano, 1864.

Gosson, S. *The Schoole of Abuse*, edited by E. Arber. London, 1868.

Haslewood, J. *Ancient Critical Essays upon English Poets and Poesy.* 2 vols. London, 1811–1815.

Ingegneri, A. *Della Poesia Rappresentativa.* Firenze, 1734.

Jonson, B. *Timber, or Discoveries made upon Men and Matter,* edited by F. E. Schelling. Boston, 1892.

—— *Works,* with Notes and Memoir by W. Gifford, edited by F. Cunningham. 3 vols. London, n. d.

Klette, T. *Beiträge zur Geschichte und Litteratur der Italienischen Gelehrtenrenaissance.* 3 parts. Greifswald, 1888–1890.

Le Bossu, R. *Treatise of the Epic Poem,* made English by W. J. Second edition. 2 vols. London, 1719.

Lionardi, A. *Dialogi della Inventione Poetica.* Venetia, 1554.

Luisino, F. *In Librum Q. Horatii Flacci de Arte Poetica Commentarius.* Venetiis, 1554.

Maggi, V., and Lombardi, B. *In Aristotelis Librum de Poetica Explanationes.* Venetijs, 1560.

Milton, J. *Prose Works,* edited by J. A. St. John. (Bohn's Library.) 5 vols. London, 1848.

Minturno, A. S. *L' Arte Poetica.* Venetia, 1564.

—— *De Poeta Libri Sex.* Venetiis, 1559.

Muzio, G. *Rime Diverse: Tre Libri di Arte Poetica, Tre Libri di Lettere in rime sciolti, ecc.* Vinegia, 1551.

Partenio, B. *Della Imitatione Poetica.* Vinegia, 1560.

Patrizzi, F. *Della Poetica: La Deca Istoriale, La Deca Disputata.* Ferrara, 1586.

Petrarca, F. *Opera quæ extant Omnia.* Basileæ, 1554.

Piccolomini, A. *Annotationi nel Libro della Poetica d'Aristotele.* Vinegia, 1575.

Pope, A. *Selecta Poemata Italorum, qui Latine Scripserunt.* 2 vols. Londini, 1740.

Puttenham, G. *The Arte of English Poesie,* edited by E. Arber. London, 1869.

Rapin, R. *Reflections on Aristotle's Treatise of Poesie* (transl.). London, 1674.

Robortelli, F.   *In Librum Aristotelis de Arte Poetica Ex-*
plicationes.   Florentiæ, 1548.

Ronsard, P. de.   *Œuvres Complètes*, publiées par P.
Blanchemain.   8 vols.   Paris, 1857–1867.

Salviati, L.   *Parafrasi e Commento della Poetica di Aris-*
totile, 370 folios, Cod. Magliabechiano, ii. ii. II.   Ms.
—— *Trattato della Poetica, Lettura Terza*, 22 folios, Cod.
Magliabechiano, vii. 7, 715.   Ms.

Scaliger, J. C.   *Poetices Libri Septem*.   Editio Quinta.
In Bibliopolio Commeliano, 1617.

Segni, A.   *Ragionamento sopra le Cose pertinenti alla*
Poetica.   Fiorenza, 1581.

Segni, B.   *Rettorica et Poetica d'Aristotele tradotte in lingua*
vulgare Fiorentina.   Vinegia, 1551.

Sidney, Sir P.   *The Defense of Poesy, otherwise known as*
An Apology for Poetry, edited by A. S. Cook.   Boston,
1890.

Speroni, Sperone.   *Opere*.   5 vols.   Venezia, 1740.

Stanyhurst, R.   *Translation of the First Four Books of the*
Æneid of P. Virgilius Maro, edited by E. Arber.
London, 1880.

Summo, F.   *Discorsi Poetici*.   Padova, 1600.

Tasso, B.   *Delle Lettere: aggiuntovi il Ragionamento della*
Poesia.   2 vols.   Padova, 1733.

Tasso, T.   *Opere, colle Controversie sulla Gerusalemme*,
per cura di G. Rosini.   33 vols.   Pisa, 1821–1832.

Trissino, G. G.   *Tutte le Opere*.   2 vols.   Verona, 1729.

Twining, T.   *Aristotle's Treatise on Poetry, translated with*
Notes and two Dissertations on Poetical and Musical
Imitation.   Second edition.   2 vols.   London, 1812.

Varchi, B.   *Lezzioni, lette nell' Accademia Fiorentina*.   Fiorenza, 1590.

Vauquelin de la Fresnaye, J.   *L'Art Poétique*, publié par
G. Pellissier.   Paris, 1885.

Vettori, P.   *Commentarii in primum Librum Aristotelis de*
Arte Poetarum.   Florentiæ, 1560.

Webbe, W. *A Discourse of English Poetrie*, edited by E. Arber. London, 1871.

Woodward, W. H. *Vittorino da Feltre and other Humanist Educators: Essays and Versions*. Cambridge, 1897.

II. SECONDARY WORKS

Arnaud, C. *Études sur la Vie et les Œuvres de l'Abbé d'Aubignac, et sur les Théories Dramatiques au XVIIe Siècle*. Paris, 1887.

Aronstein, P. "Ben Jonson's Theorie des Lustspiels," in *Anglia* (1895), vol. xvii.

Baillet, A. *Jugemens des Savans sur les Principaux Ouvrages des Auteurs*, revûs par M. de la Monnoye. 8 vols. Amsterdam, 1725.

Borinski, K. *Die Poetik der Renaissance, und die Anfänge der litterarischen Kritik in Deutschland*. Berlin, 1886.

Bourgoin, A. *Les Maîtres de la Critique au XVIIème Siècle*. Paris, 1889.

Breitinger, H. *Les Unités d'Aristote avant le Cid de Corneille*. Deuxième édition. Genève et Bâle, 1895.

Brunetière, F. *L'Évolution des Genres dans l'Histoire de la Littérature*. Deuxième édition. Vol. i. Paris, 1892.

Brunot, F. *La Doctrine de Malherbe d'après son Commentaire sur Desportes*. Paris, 1891.

Canello, U. *Storia della Letteratura Italiana nel Secolo XVI*. Milano, 1880.

Cecchi, P. L. *T. Tasso, il Pensiero e le Belle Lettere Italiane nel Secolo XVI*. Firenze, 1877.

Cloetta, W. *Beiträge zur Litteraturgeschichte des Mittelalters und der Renaissance*. 2 vols. Halle, 1890–1892.

Comparetti, D. *Vergil in the Middle Ages*, translated by E. F. M. Benecke. London, 1895.

Y

Croce, B.   *Estetica come Scienza dell' Espressione e Linguistica generale*.   Palermo, 1902.

De Sanctis, F.   *Storia della Letteratura Italiana*.   Sesta edizione.   2 vols.   Napoli, 1893.

Di Niscia, G.   "La Gerusalemme Conquistata e l' Arte Poetica di Tasso," in *Il Propugnatore* (1889), N.S. vol. ii. parts 1, 2.

Ebert, A.   *Allgemeine Geschichte der Literatur des Mittelalters im Abendlande*.   3 vols.   Leipzig, 1874–1887.

Egger, É.   *Essai sur l'Histoire de la Critique chez les Grecs*.   Deuxième édition.   Paris, 1886.

—— *L'Hellénisme en France*.   2 vols.   Paris, 1869.

Faguet, É.   *La Tragédie française au XVIe Siècle*.   Paris, 1894.

Foffano, F.   *Ricerche Letterarie*.   Livorno, 1897.

Gaspary, A.   *Geschichte der Italienischen Literatur*.   2 vols.   Strassburg, 1885–1888.

Hamelius, P.   *Die Kritik in der Englischen Literatur des 17. und 18. Jahrhunderts*.   Leipzig, 1897.

Jacquinet, P.   *Francisci Baconi de Re Litteraria Judicia*.   Parisiis, 1863.

Koerting, G.   *Geschichte der Litteratur Italiens im Zeitalter der Renaissance*.   3 vols.   Leipzig, 1878–1884.

Krantz, É.   *L'Esthétique de Descartes, étudiée dans les Rapports de la Doctrine cartésienne avec la Littérature classique française au XVIIe Siècle*.   Paris, 1882.

Langlois, E.   *De Artibus Rhetoricæ Rhythmicæ*.   Parisiis, 1890.

Lintilhac, E.   *De J.-C. Scaligeri Poetice*.   Paris, 1887.

—— "Un Coup d'État dans la République des Lettres," in the *Nouvelle Revue* (1890), vol. lxiv.

Menéndez y Pelayo, M.   *Historia de las Ideas Estéticas en España*.   Segunda edición.   9 vols.   Madrid, 1890–1896.

Müller, E.   *Geschichte der Theorie der Kunst bei den Alten*.   2 vols.   Breslau, 1834–1837.

Natali, G. *Torquato Tasso, Filosofo del Bello, dell' Arte, e dell' Amore.* Roma, 1895.

Pellissier, G. *De Sexti Decimi Sæculi in Francia Artibus Poeticis.* Paris, 1882.

Perrens, F. T. *Jérome Savonarole.* 2 vols. Paris, 1853.

Quadrio, F. S. *Della Storia e della Ragione d' ogni Poesia.* 5 vols. Milano, 1739–1752.

Quossek, C. *Sidney's Defense of Poesy und die Poetik des Aristoteles.* Krefeld, 1884.

Robert, P. *La Poétique de Racine.* Paris, 1890.

Rosenbauer, A. *Die Poetischen Theorien der Plejade nach Ronsard und Dubellay.* Erlangen, 1895.

Rucktäschel, T. *Einige Arts Poétiques aus der Zeit Ronsard's und Malherbe's.* Leipzig, 1889.

Schelling, F. E. *Poetic and Verse Criticism of the Reign of Elizabeth.* Philadelphia, University of Pennsylvania Press, 1891.

Solerti, A. *Vita di Torquato Tasso.* 3 vols. Torino, 1895.

Symonds, J. A. *Renaissance in Italy.* 7 vols. New York, 1888.

Teichmüller, G. *Aristotelische Forschungen.* 2 vols. Halle, 1869.

Tiraboschi, G. *Storia della Letteratura Italiana.* 9 vols. Firenze, 1805–1813.

Vossler, K. *Poetische Theorien in der italienischen Frührenaissance.* Berlin, 1900.

—— "Pietro Aretino's künstlerisches Bekenntnis," in *Neue Heidelberger Jahrbücher*, 1900, vol. x.

For further bibliographical information, see the Italian translation of this book (*La Critica letteraria nel Rinascimento, traduzione italiana del Dr. Antonio Fusco, con correzzioni e aggiunte dell' autore e prefazione di B. Croce.* Bari, 1905, pp. 337–347).

INDEX